vtiger CRM v6.5.0: User and Administration Manual

Trade Marks

Many of the designations used by manufacturers and retailers to distinguish their products are claimed as trademarks. Where those designations appear in this book, and crm-now was aware of a trademark claim, the designations have been printed in caps or initial caps. While every precaution has been taken during the preparation of this book, the publisher assumes no responsibility for errors or omissions, or for damage resulting from the use of the information contained herein.

Acknowledgement

The vtiger CRM manual has been in the preparation since the CRM version 4.0.0. Completion of this manual would not have been possible without the help and encouragement of a lot of people. The outstanding vtiger team, its user community, and a number of other people contributed their technical feedback as this book was being written. I would also like to thank the people who contributed to this manual with informal reviews, suggestions, and corrections during the writing process.

More information about vtiger, the team, the CRM project and its community can be found at:

www.vtiger.com

This manual has been sponsored by the crm-now GmbH. For more Information about crm-now you may look up:

www.crm-now.de

Print: Lulu

ISBN: 978-1-365-24752-1

Preface

This manual is a comprehensive, step-by-step guide to using vtiger, the powerful Open Source Customer Relationship Management system. The vtiger CRM system is one of the best and most exciting professional-quality Open Source CRM products around, and it is intended primarily for B2B companies with longer sales cycles and a stable product or service portfolio.

vtiger provides your organization with an easy-to-use, powerful, comprehensive and integrated solution for managing customer relationships. Because it is Open Source and it provides professional features, the vtiger CRM system has been adopted by a large and growing community of users.

This manual is based on the official Open Source v6.5.0 release.

The manual is intended to be a clear and supportive reference work for vtiger users and administrators.

However, this manual is not the official vtiger documentation and does not include documentation intended for in-depth customization, technical systems setups and development purposes. I hope to answer most of the questions you might have about the various features and modules of the vtiger CRM. The following subject areas are covered in particular:

- General approach of vtiger CRM. With all its modules and their relationship to each other, vtiger CRM can be a bit overwhelming at first. I'll get you up to speed quickly on how the pieces fit together.
- How to start using the CRM system. What should you do first?
- Sales force automation. After you have entered data into the system, how does the system support your efforts in an automated fashion?
- Understanding all the relationships. Most data entered into the CRM system is somehow related. These relationships are extensively documented, including their intended purpose. If suitable, examples of proper usage are provided.
- Customizing the CRM system. Each company is different. I explain how you can tailor vtiger CRM to fit your company's needs.
- Security Settings. I explain the principles and the implementation of role-based security.
- Tools. The CRM system comes with a set of tools that supports the organization of sales teams as well as the reporting to management. I show you how these tools can be used.

Table of Contents

1 Introduction

This chapter explains how to utilize this manual and provides an overview of the various considerations and the preparation a user should undertake before starting to work with the CRM system.

1.1 About this Manual

With the help of this manual you will quickly become familiar with the CRM system. The aim of this manual is to bring together the knowledge about the vtiger CRM functions and features with the sales processes, as they are defined by companies using the CRM system. I will explain how to configure the system to fit your needs and how to use it effectively.

Please keep in mind that this CRM system is a tool for your sales, marketing, and/or service organization. It is especially suited for companies:

- which are in the B2B or B2C business
- which have longer sales cycles
- which do not frequently change their product or service offers
- which are operating with sales, services or marketing teams located at multiple locations

I believe that most vtiger CRM system users and administrators will benefit by reading this manual from cover to cover. Yet, I am also more than aware that if you are involved in CRM today, your hectic schedule can force you to first skim through this manual to read the highlights, until you can find a quiet moment to read more thoroughly.

So I have tried to make it easy for you. The document has a progressive structure, starting with the basics and becoming more detailed as you move ahead. References to other useful resources are also provided.

The names of organizations or contacts used in the examples contained in this manual are imaginary. Any resemblances to existing companies or persons are purely coincidental.

The use of the vtiger CRM software and its related user documentation is subject to the terms and conditions of the applicable licenses.

The Manual's Target Group

This manual has been written for vtiger CRM users and administrators. It does not provide any guidance or instructions for developers. I expect most readers will have some familiarity with Customer Relationship Management concepts. Although I provide a description of all features as they are implemented at their release dates, this book cannot be sufficient as your only reference material for vtiger CRM. This depends on your needs and experience, but also on the progress vtiger CRM makes. For a list of some other good resources, consult the Appendix chapters.

The manual is divided into four parts and appendixes:

Chapter 1: Introduction

Describes how the manual should be read.

Chapter 2: Data Entry for the CRM System

Explains how customer contacts are defined and how to use the CRM system to collect customer information. Shows what type of sales activities the CRM system supports and how these activities are being entered. Provides all the information required to understand the sales process supported by the CRM system. A list of all possibilities for entering product and price lists into the system.

Chapter 3: Working with the CRM System

Describes how it all fits together and how the CRM system can be used to coordinate the work of sales, marketing and service staff as well as to increase the productivity of each individual user. Explains all the automated functions available, how sales processes can be defined and which after sales services are offered.

Chapter 4: Administrative Tasks

Describes in detail how to manage users and privileges, and how to customize templates and the CRM system configuration.

Appendix: Administration Examples

Provides some sample configurations and FAQ's for security setups. Explains in detail how to assign access privileges based on a hierarchical organization structure.

You can view the latest version of this book on the manual's web site at

www.vtiger-hilfe.de.

Request for Comments

Please help me to improve future editions of this book by reporting any errors, inaccuracies, bugs, misleading or confusing statements, and any plain old typos that you can find. Email anything you can have found and comments to the author at vtigermanual@crm-now.de.

You can identify the manual version by its ID number located on the second page of this document.

This manual uses the following terms and syntax when explaining procedures and steps:

Menu references

All CRM related menu references are written in **bold**.

Example: as shown in the **Calendar** menu.

Menu-based instructions

Instructions to be entered via the menu are also written **bold** and put in brackets. Multiple instructions are separated by the ">" sign.

Example: Please click on **[Contacts]** > **[New]**.

All screenshots in this manual are based on the actual software release as provided after an installation.

1.2 First Steps

Becoming a User

Before you can start working with the CRM system you must be identified as an authorized user by the CRM system. This is done by means of a login procedure which requires a Username and a Password. Both are provided to you by your CRM system administrator.

PC Setup and other Requirements

For the simple use of the CRM system you do not need to install any software on your computer system. You can operate the CRM system solely by utilizing your preferred web browser.

Please note the following minimum requirements and follow the browser setup instructions.

Hardware requirements:

PC or Thin Client with browser and minimum screen resolution of 1024 * 768 pixels.

Browsers:

Firefox 35.0 or newer, Microsoft Internet Explorer 10.0 or newer, Safari 3.1 or newer; other browsers have not been certified but should nevertheless work well if they have compliant standards.

Your browser configuration must meet the following requirements:

Cookies

You must allow cookies.

Java

You must have JavaScript enabled in the security settings of your browser.

If you want to have your desktop computer software linked to the CRM system, you can install some extensions on your computer at a later time. For this purpose, please refer to the appropriate other manuals listed in Appendix Resources.

Caution: Depending on your browser type and version, there might be a minor bug within page caching that can affect AJAX client performance in some cases. If your CRM system slows down, it is recommended that you empty your browser's cache.

1.3 Login

Your CRM system administrator will provide you with a URL to be used as the access address to the CRM system of your browser. You will also need the username and the password of your CRM account.

Upon starting the CRM software, the login screen will appear as shown in Figure 1-1. The user must type a username and password into the appropriate fields in order to continue. A user can also choose a different theme or language after having logged-in at the **[My Preferences]** menu. Username, password, themes and languages are provided by the system administrator.

After entering the username and password, press **<Enter>**, or the **<Sign in>** button.

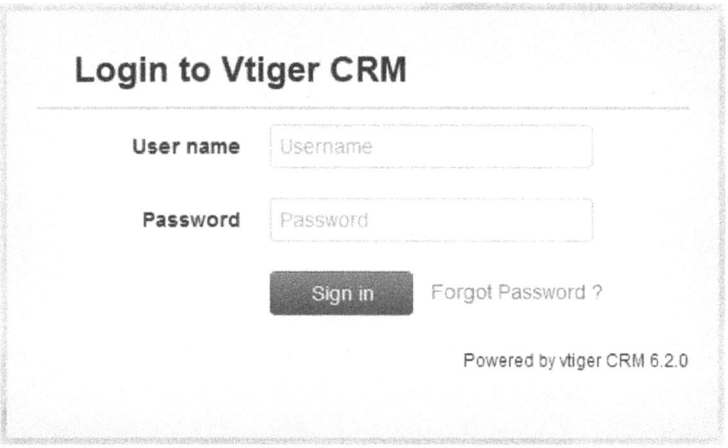

Figure 1-1: Login Screen

Most browsers are able to store your username and password to simplify usage. However, this can be a security risk if you cannot make certain that nobody else has access to your computer. Unauthorized persons can get access to your confidential data. This is especially true if you are using a notebook which could be stolen or misplaced.

Your access privileges to the CRM system are set by the administrator when configuring the CRM system. The following privilege types are available:

- The permission to use certain CRM modules.
- The permission to user certain CRM functions
- The permission to view data in certain CRM modules.
- The permission to edit or to change data in certain CRM modules.
- The permission to delete data in certain CRM modules.
- The permission to export or import data from certain CRM modules.

The CRM system makes sure that you are only allowed to access certain operations if you have the proper privileges. Please contact your system administrator if you want to know more about the privileges set in your system or if you want to have them changed.

1.4 How to Start

For optimal utility, the CRM system needs to be configured in accordance with your company's needs. Every user with administrator privileges is allowed to modify the basic settings. All the possibilities are described in Chapter 5 of this manual.

In addition, there are many functions available which allow users to configure the presentation of data without changing the basic settings and without administrator access privileges. All the options will be explained in the following sections.

Even without a lot of configuration, you will quickly be able to start with the CRM system. Data about customers is the core of each CRM system, so a good way to begin is to start entering data. Since the CRM system is much more than a simple storage system, it is recommended that you make yourself familiar with the sales process as described in Section 4. Start by entering customer data as a **Lead**. Then convert such a lead into a **Sales Opportunity**. Watch how contacts, accounts and opportunities are generated automatically. You can also import lead data from your existing office environment in order to speed up the process.

As the **first step,** it is recommended to start by entering the contact information of your most important active customers. You can add further information at a later time. You will also need to enter your company as an account and an employee's data as contacts. You will need these entries in order to be able to efficiently communicate with other users.

The export and import functions will help you to exchange data between your office environment and the CRM system. CRM data can be used by a large variety of other applications in your office.

After you have entered your contacts, you will have a wide variety of automated CRM functions available.

As the **second step,** it is recommended that you begin by entering your product and/or service offerings. In section 3.5 and 3.6 you will find detailed instructions for entering product and service information as well as price books. Again, start by entering only the most important information. You can append the other data later.

If multiple users start using the CRM system at the same time, please keep in mind that you only have to enter all the different information just once. Make sure that you communicate with the others.

Use your CRM data immediately when you schedule the next customer contact. Familiarize yourself with the activity functions as they are described in the calendar section 3.2 and define your sales process using different sales stages.

Over time you will improve your capability to operate the system on a step-by-step basis. Within a short time, these processes will become second nature.

2 CRM Configuration

The graphical users interface (GUI) consists of the start page and many other menus like accounts, contacts, opportunities or calendar. The amount of available menus depends on the settings provided by your CRM systems administrator. The content of the start menu is configurable by the individual users.

2.1 Navigation

The smart design of the CRM system will allow you to get most information quickly. You can navigate within the CRM as if you were browsing a website. It is **not** recommended to use the back and forward buttons of the browser within the CRM. These buttons can cause problems when browsing through pages with dynamically generated content.

It is recommended to use the icons and links provided by the CRM system for navigation. Advanced users can switch to tabbed browsing to speed up the handling process. You can reach each CRM page within a few clicks.

All CRM pages are in hierarchical order. You can switch between pages at the same hierarchical level or you can access a page directly. At the top of the CRM system, as illustrated in Figure 2-1, you have access to different area types and functions with which to navigate and to work with the CRM.

For the majority of tasks, you can configure the CRM so that you get to the interesting data with a single click. If you have to click multiple times to get to your data, check your individual settings and look for a better configuration.

2.2 Menus

All menus for data collection and presentation in the CRM are similarly constructed and operate similarly. This means that you can quickly learn how to use the CRM if you are familiar with the general structure as explained in the following chapters.

2.2.1 CRM Home Page

After having logged-in, you will see your homepage screen as shown in Figure 2-1. Based on the theme you selected, the system settings installed by your administrator and the data stored in the CRM system, your actual screen can look somewhat different than the one displayed here. Subsequent chapters will explain how you can customize the homepage and how you can use the CRM functions. Please note that each individual CRM user has their own homepage.

The main area of the homepage, as illustrated in the center of Figure 2-1, displays a block summary of the most important CRM information as so-called Widgets. You can change the order of these widgets by dragging and dropping. You can also change the content of your homepage by using the **[Add Widgets]** function or by selecting homepage components in the **My Preferences** menu.

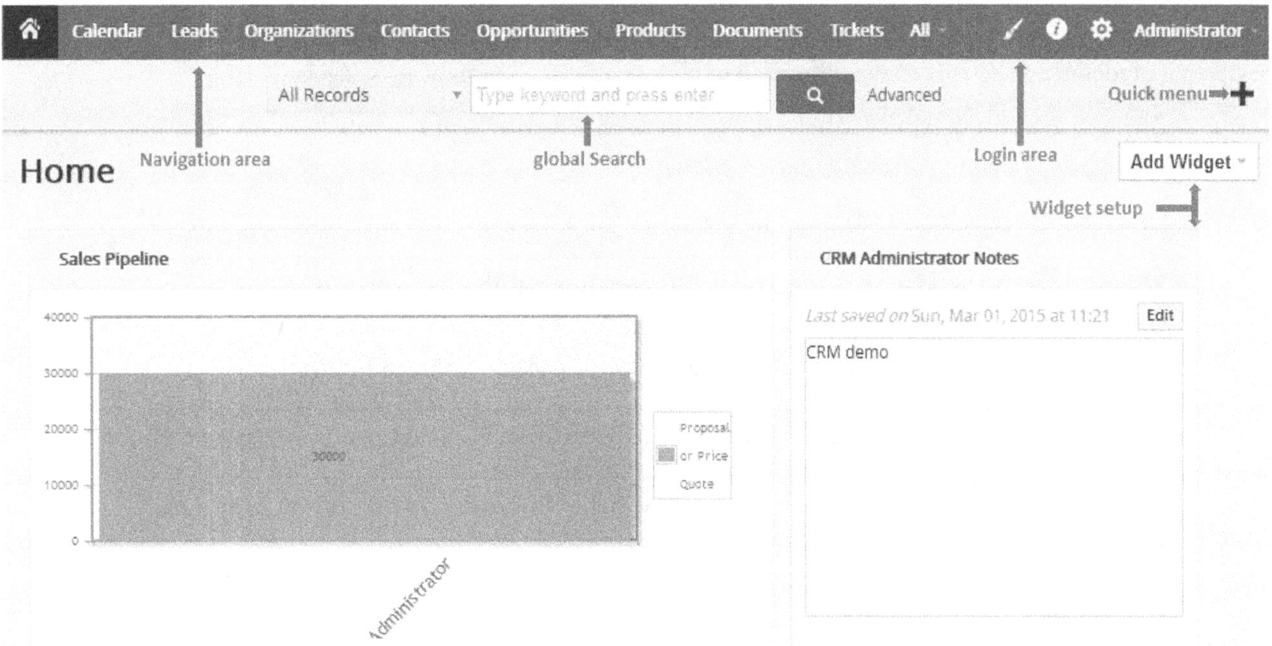

Figure 2-1: CRM Homepage

Please note that all data stored in the CRM system has an owner. The owner is indicated with an **"assigned to":** entry. If you create a new entry, the data will automatically be assigned to you unless you change this intentionally. Only data assigned to you will be shown on the homepage.

Table 2-1: CRM Base Functions

Navigation area	Function
Login area:	In this area you can access your preference data, get help or release information, or leave the CRM system. The ⚙ icon is only available to the CRM administrator.
Navigation area:	In the Navigation Area you can switch between the functions and data lists offered by the CRM system.
Quick Menu:	In the Quick Menu you can quickly reach data entry pages with limited functionality defined by the CRM administrator. However, this is a very comfortable entry point for new records if you do not want to leave your current CRM view.
Global Search:	In the Search Area you can search the entire database. You can use small or capital letters and you can extend your search by clicking on **[Advanced]** and defining certain conditions.

2.2.1.1 Widgets

You shall use the possibility to place your own widgets on the homepage. Click on **[Add Widget]** in order to select an existing predefined widget. It is recommended to choose at least the following widgets:

Table 2-2: Recommended Widgets for Homepage

Widget Name	Function
Key Metrix:	User defined lists are one of the most powerful CRM tools and this is explained in chapter 2.2.3. This widget provides a list of your user defined lists which are marked to be displayed on the homepage.
Upcoming Activities:	This widget lists all activities from your calendar which are planned for today.
Overdue Activities:	This widget lists all activities from your calendar which has are due.
Notepad:	You can use a notepad widget to make your own notes on the homepage.
Mini List:	This widget provides you with functions with which to create your own widget contents. You can consider such a widget after you have created CRM data.

2.2.1.2 Global Search

The global search is a powerful and convenient tool to find certain information in the entire CRM system.

As shown in Figure 2-2, you can use a pick-list to restrict the search to specific modules.

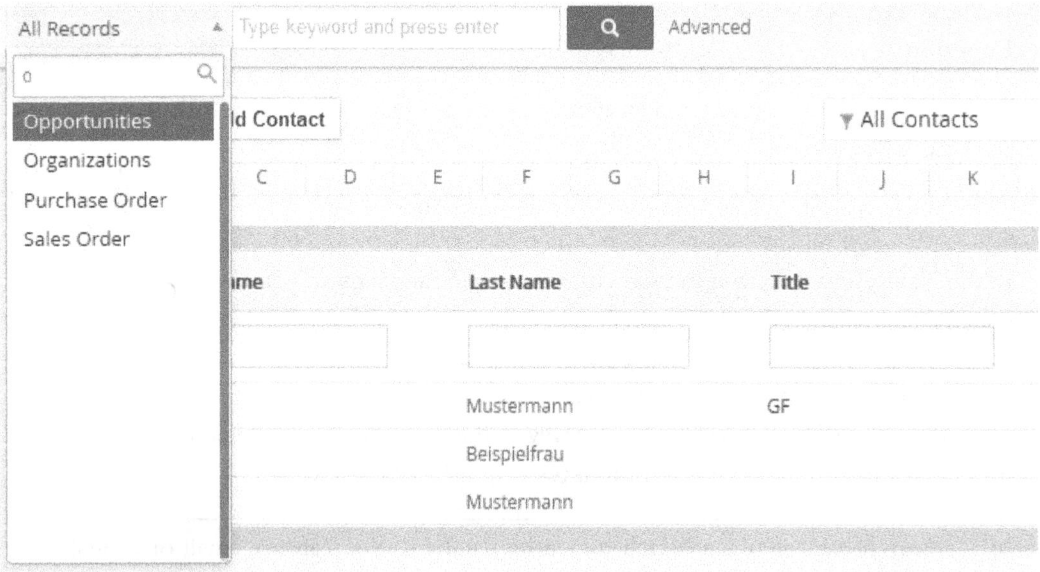

Figure 2-2: Global Search Menu

For a search you can use any word with small or capital letters or even incomplete words. If you search for multiple terms, each single word gets linked with a logical AND.

Note: The Global Search covers the so called Entity Fields only. Therefore, you cannot use this search for instance to find the content of custom fields. In this case use the advanced search or consider to use one of the free or commercial extension menus provided by vtiger's community.

You can expand your search for a particular CRM module by using the **[Advanced]** search option as shown in Figure 2-3. The entering of search criteria becomes somewhat more complicated, but you also have the possibility to save your settings as a custom list view.

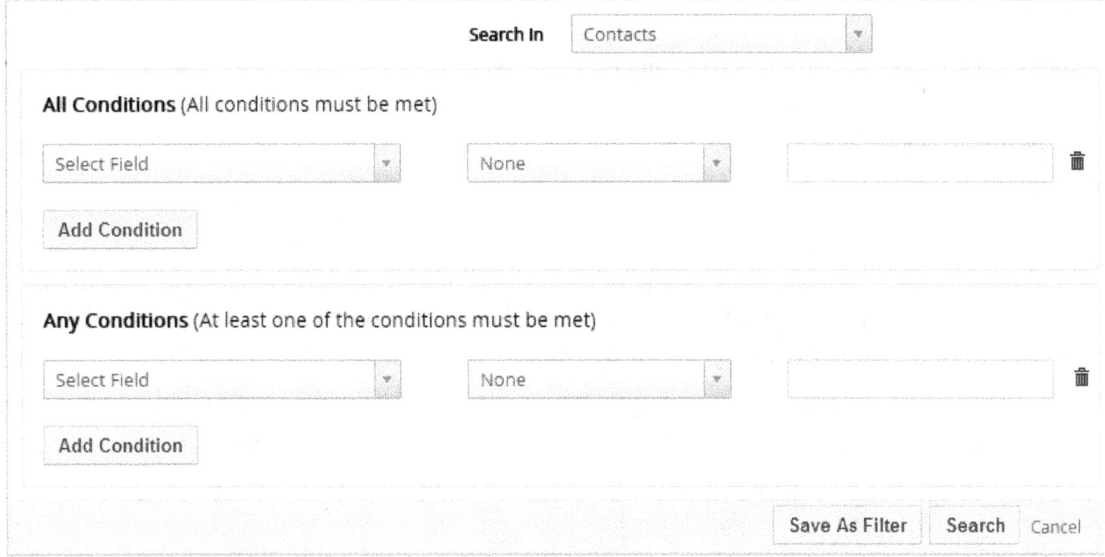

Figure 2-3: Advanced Search Menu

Select the module first and then the filter criteria. Before you start your search by clicking on the **[Search]** button, take a second to consider whether you will perform this search again later. If you do indeed plan to do this, it is suggested that you hit the **[Save as Filter]** button in order to save your search as a custom filter. The advantages and functions of custom filters are explained in chapter 2.2.3.

Limits:

At the current CRM version the global search does not support the following actions. You can use the module related search instead:

- search for Created Time, Modified Time, Assigned to, Checkboxes, Radio Button and Related to fields
- search for document file names
- search for Calendar Send Reminder, Calendar Repeat and Calendar Follow up fields
- search for product and service line items in orders, quotes or invoices
- search for time and date for events
- search for dates in other format as YYYY-MM-DD
- search for am/pm time entries
- search for currency entries other that the base currency

2.2.2 CRM Views

For the data collection and in order to view your data, the CRM uses the following 4 menu types:

- List View
- Create and Edit View
- Detail View
- Related List View

For each of these views, certain rules apply and certain functions are available. The service is so basically always the same, regardless of whether you enter, for instance, new account or contact data. However, in each module special features can exist which are explained in the following chapters for account entries but which are applicable mutatis mutandis to all other modules.

2.2.2.1 List View

When you click on menus in the navigation area, you will see a list of all data stored in the CRM system related to your menu selection. As the view name would expect, your data will be displayed in a list as a table in this view.

In Figure 2-4, you see a list view with 2 entries as an example. It is easy to imagine that such a list with hundreds or thousands of entries can become unmanageable and to look up an entry could be difficult in the extreme.

Therefore, the CRM offers a number of tools which make your lists easier to manage. One of the most important tools is the custom lists as they are explained in chapter 2.2.3.

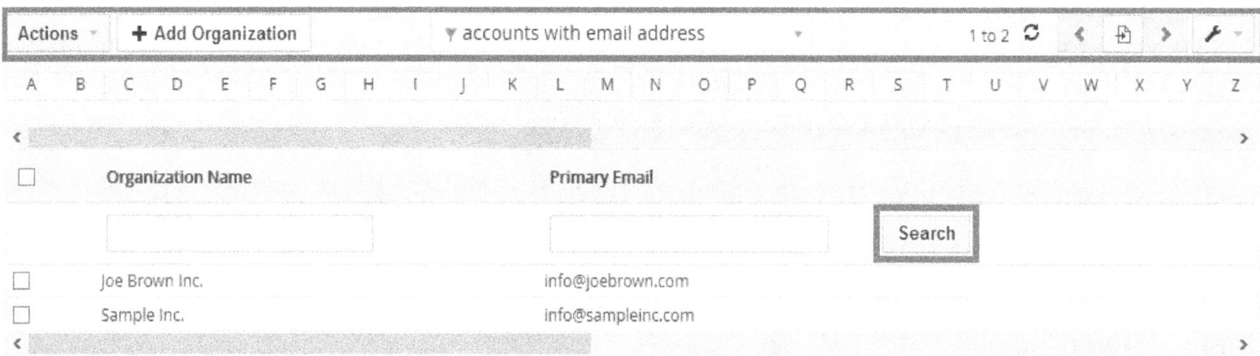

Figure 2-4: List View

On the top of the list view, you can perform the following operations:

Table 2-3: List View Operations

Name	Function
Action:	With this button, you list all the actions that you can perform with selected data from your list at the same time. The possible actions are explained in detail in chapter 2.2.3.1.

Add Organization:	This button retrieves the create view needed for entering master data of a new organization.
Accounts with email address:	At the center you see all available list views. In chapter 2.2.3.2 is explained how you can create customized list views.
1 to 2	Icons for navigation within the list are offered here. You can browse multiple pages or go directly to a specific page.
	This icon is only available to CRM administrators and is used to configure the menus for all CRM users.

Above your list of organizations, there is an alphabetical search. In addition, you can enter search terms for each column field.

With the + icon you get directed to the so called quick create menu. As shown in Figure 2-5, the number of entry fields is limited. (You CRM Administrator can add or remove fields to this menu.) The purpose of this menu is to provide you quick access, without having to leave the current menu.

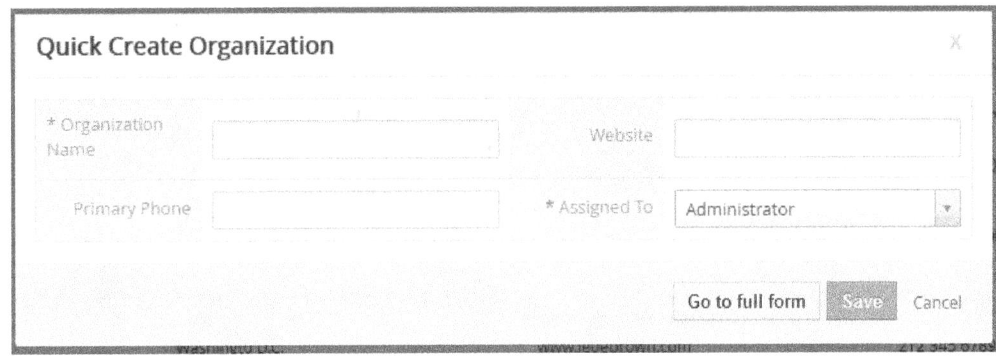

Figure 2-5: Quick Create Menu

Extended Navigation

On the left side of a list view, you will see another foldaway menu with other navigation options as shown in Figure 2-6. You can control the display of this menu at a user's **My Preferences** menu as explained in chapter 2.3.1.

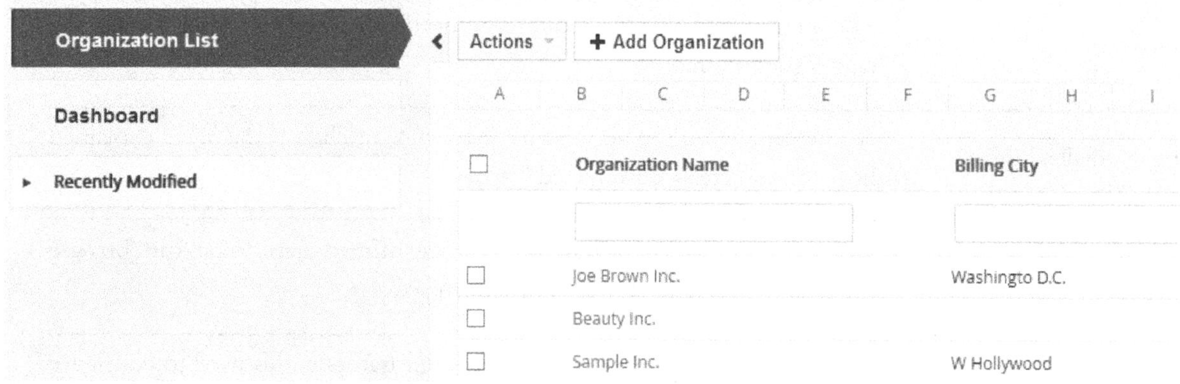

Figure 2-6: Extended Navigation Menu

2.2.2.2 Create View and Edit View

You can create a new CRM record by clicking on **[Add Organization]**. The entry fields of this view are called **master data**. You should enter only the information that is relevant for your company. Non-relevant input fields or fields whose meaning is not clear remain free or should be removed by your administrator. Examples of master data entries for a new organization have been provided in Figure 2-7 already.

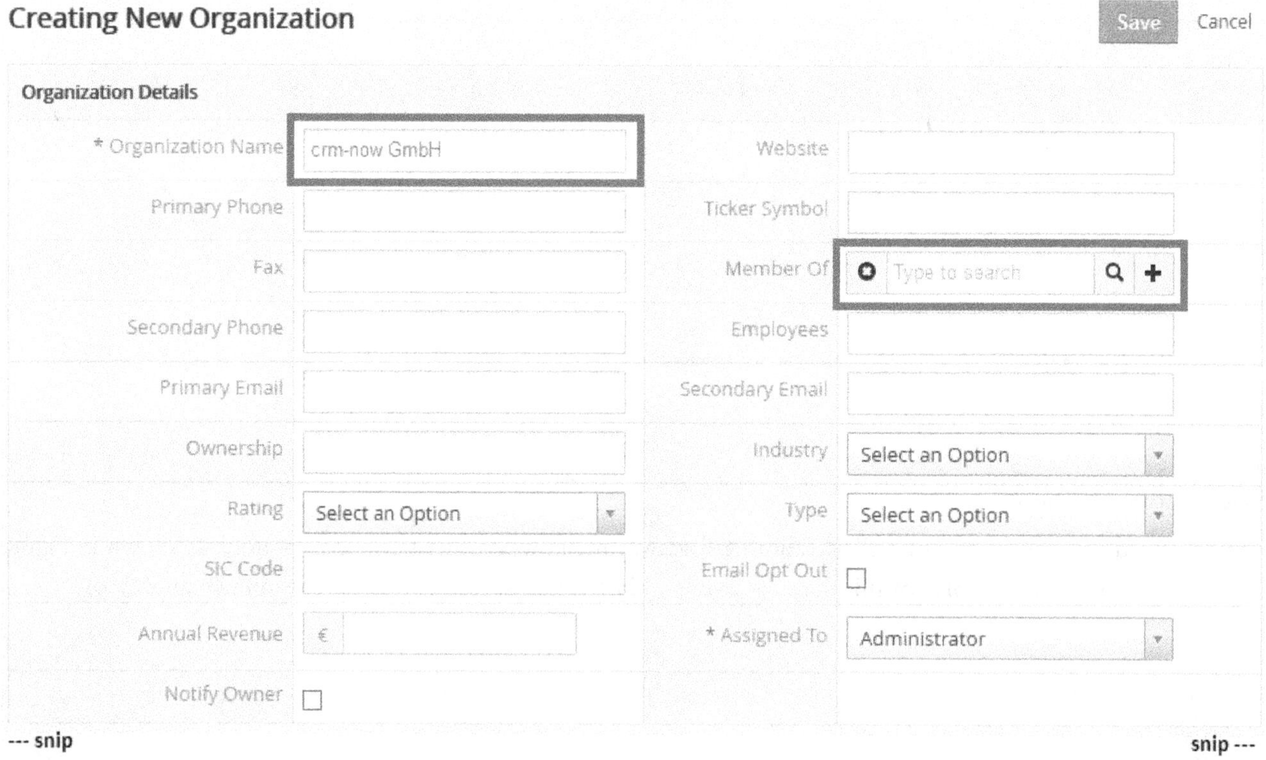

Figure 2-7: Create and Edit View

The following special features are available for this view.

Special Feature **Description**

Special Feature	Description
Record numbers:	Each CRM record gets an automatically assigned number when you create a record. This cannot get specified by individual users. Rather, the CRM administrator determines for each module a numbering scheme, which is then used for saving. You can see this number in the detailed view of a record.
Mandatory fields:	You can identify a mandatory field by the red * icon close to a field name. Records for which the required fields have not been specified cannot be created. Your CRM administrator can specify which fields are to be marked as mandatory.
Automatic Search:	In the case of a number of fields, your CRM will search the existing database while you type characters and it will display the matches it finds, starting after the 3rd character. This is, for instance, the case for the field **Organization Name.** This prevents that unnecessary duplicates are created.
Related Fields:	The field **Member Of** in Figure 2-7 is a so called related field. This means that you cannot make a direct entry into this field. But you can set a reference to a master data entry of another record. As with the automatic search, you can find an existing record by typing in at least 3 characters. Or you can pull-up the search menu by the icon. You can also create a new entry by the + icon.

When finished, click on **[Save]** in order to transfer your data to the CRM.

2.2.2.3 Detail View

Click on an entry in a list view to reach the detail view of a record as shown in Figure 2-8.

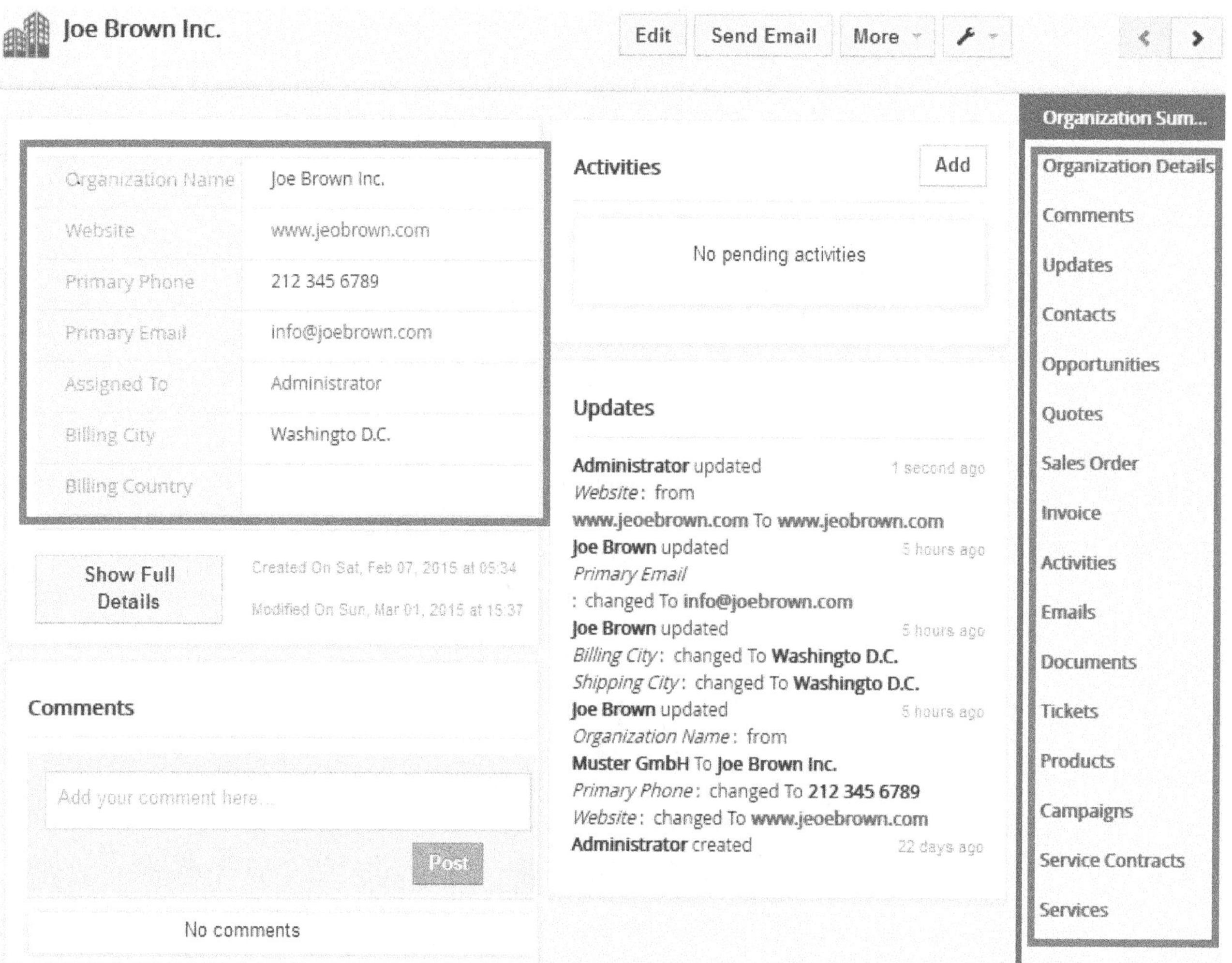

Figure 2-8: Detail View

On the left side you see the data which had been enabled for the so called compact detail view. The content of this view is defined by the CRM administrator.

On the right side you see the so called **related lists** which are explained further in the next chapter 2.2.2.4. These lists include all modules which have a relation to the master data. These are, for instance, the contacts connected with an account, or the offers you have made. The order of the related lists is configurable by the CRM administrator.

2.2.2.4 Related List View

Related lists are lists which display the relation of a record to the master data of other modules at the detail view.

In Figure 2-8, you see on the right-hand side all the modules which have a relationship to an account. You can click on a module name to get its related list. In the following Figure 2-9 the content of the related **contacts** list is shown.

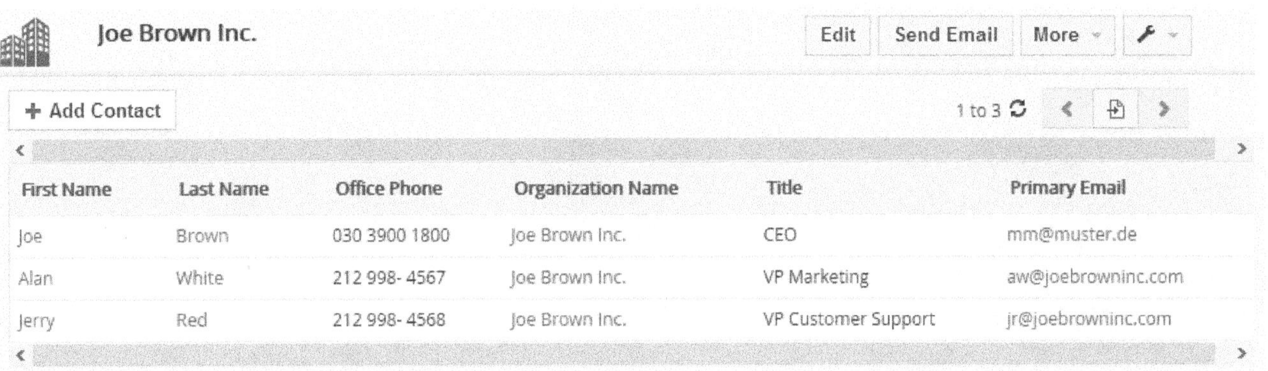

Figure 2-9: Related List Content

Related lists represent the structured data storage in your CRM. You can see at any detail view what data records are connected to each other.

The columns displayed at a related list are set by the CRM system.

2.2.3 List View Operations

Over time, data lists can become very large and difficult to handle. Furthermore, due to limited screen size, only a few columns can be displayed at any one time. Therefore, it is appropriate and in many cases also necessary to adapt the list views to the respective needs of the users.

Generally, each user can create individual lists with a specific content and make these lists available to other users. Thus, you have a very effective tool for managing larger data sets, being informed automatically about changes, or selecting data for further use.

2.2.3.1 List View Actions

The menu shown in Figure 2-10 lists the actions that you can perform in a list view. The content of this list depends on the enabled CRM functions. In the following, typical actions are explained.

There are 2 types of actions:

- actions that you can be performed with the selected records in the list (selected records changing actions)
- Actions which modify your data (CRM record changing actions)

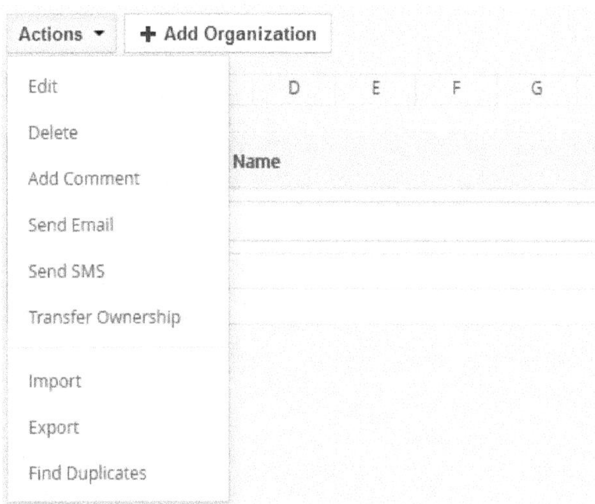

Figure 2-10: List View Actions

Record changing functions always refer to the records, which are shown in a list view and which you have marked by the checkbox at the beginning of each line.

Table 2-4: Selected Records Changing Actions

Action	Function
Edit:	This function opens the mass edit menu for the marked records. That means that you can use this menu to modify the content of multiple records at once.
Delete:	This function deletes the market records. Note that a deletion moves records into the recycling bin.
Add Comment:	This function allows you to add a comment to all marked records.
Send Email:	This function allows you to send an email to all marked records based on the primary email address. The CRM does not check whether an email address is in the records. Therefore, it is recommended to use this function only on custom list views which filter the records by means of existing email information.
Transfer Ownership	Every CRM record has an owner, set by the **assigned** to field. This function allows you not only to transfer the ownership of records to a different CRM user/group, but also allows you to modify the ownership of related records.

CRM record changing actions work independently of your list view. By calling such a function you are leaving the list view.

Table 2-5: CRM record changing actions

Action	Function
Import:	This action calls the import menu. The import procedure is explained in detail in chapter 3.1.
Export:	This action exports your listed data in the CSV format. The character format of the exported file is UTF-8 as it is used by the CRM internally. For further use with other applications you can convert UTF-8 characters to any other character format. The details are displayed in chapter 3.1.4. List view exports include all master data. If you need to select the columns or need an Excel™ export, it is recommended to use the report exports.
Find Duplicates:	This action can help you to find and remove record duplicates and it is explained in Section 4.1.2.

2.2.3.2 Customize Lists

In order to get a list view of data related to your particular interests you can create a custom list view based on the following parameters:

- The content of the columns (what will be displayed),
- Various logical AND and OR operations between data stored in the CRM system.

For instance, in order to create a new list view for accounts, click on the **funnel icon** as shown in Figure 2-11. In the popup window that opens click **[Create New Filter]**.

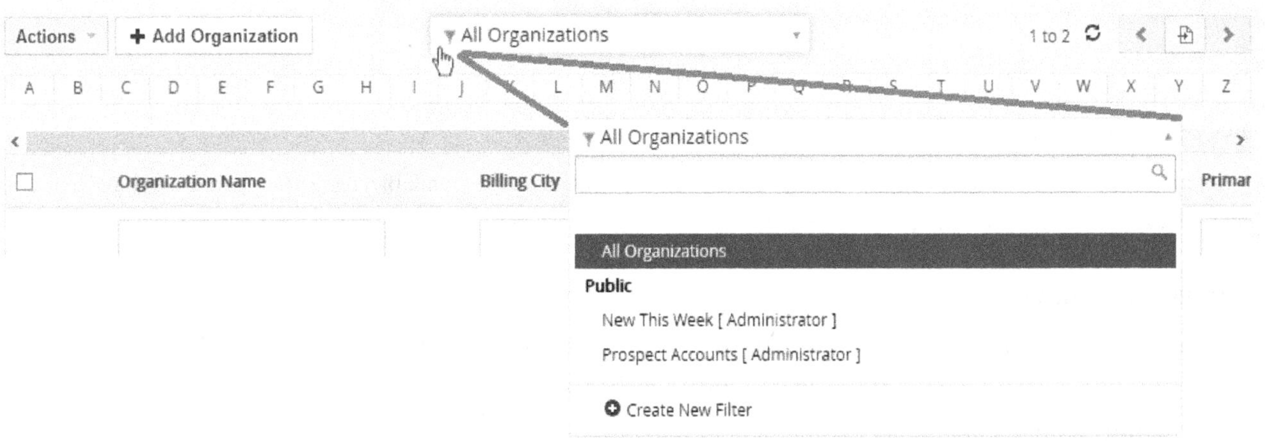

Figure 2-11: Create List View Custom Filter

The filter create view is illustrated in Figure 2-12. For a creation of a new list view, the following approach is recommended:

- Enter a short but unique name for your list.
- Select the content of the columns. Keep in mind that the more columns you select the more space on your screen is required. Up to 12 columns are available.

- Set logical AND or OR operations for further filtering your data with the advanced filter menu.

You can change the default list view by selecting the **[Set as Default]** check box. You can also select the created list view to be present at the key metrics, located at home, by marking the **[List in Metrics]** check box. The function of the key metrics is explained later in this section of the manual.

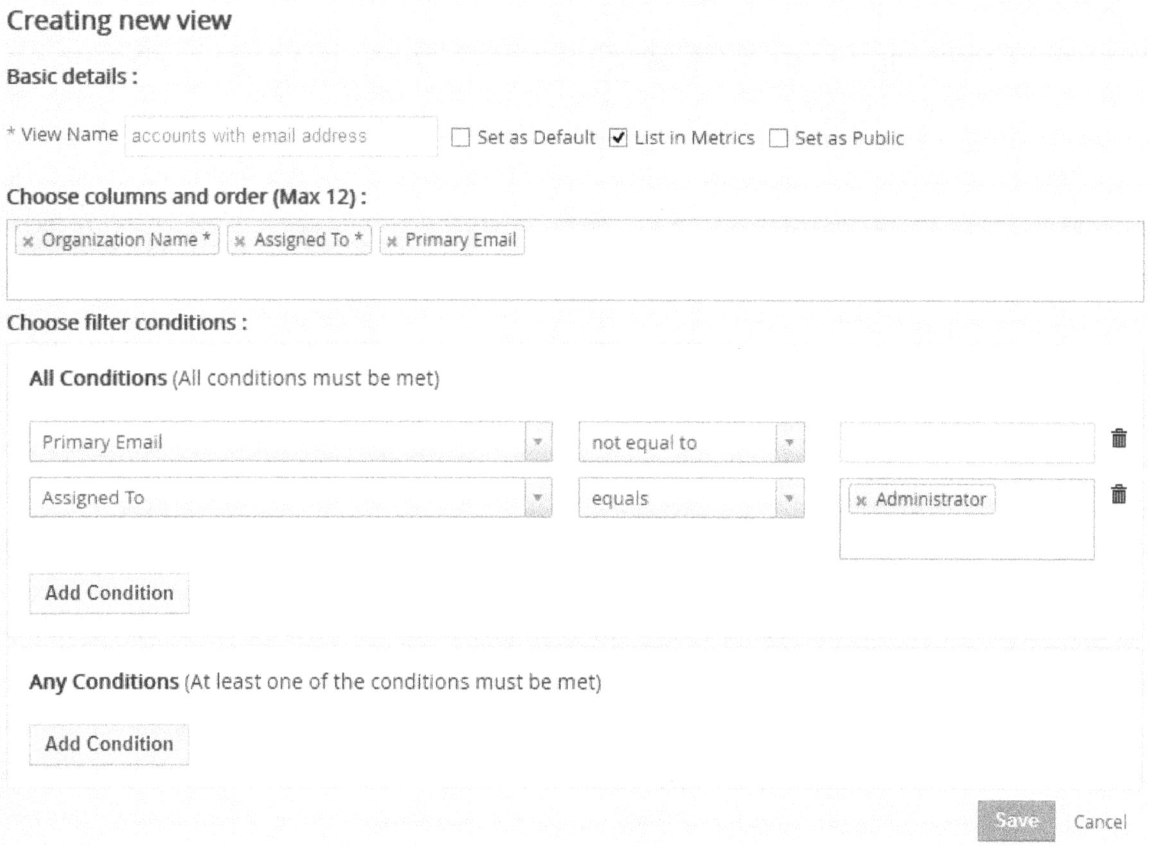

Creating new view

Basic details :

* View Name accounts with email address ☐ Set as Default ☑ List in Metrics ☐ Set as Public

Choose columns and order (Max 12) :

× Organization Name * × Assigned To * × Primary Email

Choose filter conditions :

All Conditions (All conditions must be met)

Primary Email | not equal to

Assigned To | equals | × Administrator

Add Condition

Any Conditions (At least one of the conditions must be met)

Add Condition

Save Cancel

Figure 2-12: Custom Filter Create View

If you mark the check box **[Set as Public]**, your list view will also be available for other users after review and approval by a user with administration privileges.

Approve Customize Lists

The admin user will see your created list view as a pending view as illustrated at Figure 2-13 and will have to approve this view to make it available to all the other CRM users. An admin user is also empowered to reverse the process and deny public access to a custom view. As a user with admin privileges, you will see all the public, pending and private list views of other users.

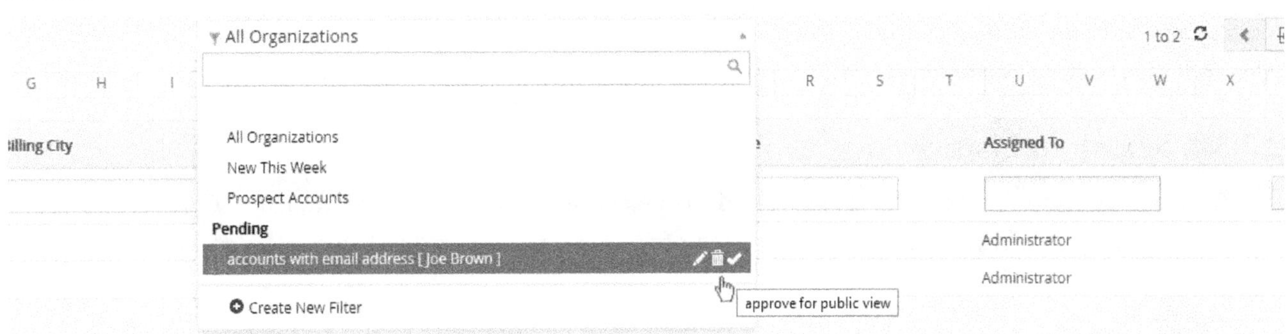

Figure 2-13: Approve Custom View

Individual lists make working with the CRM system much easier. However, mistakes in the list composition, especially by logical AND and OR operations, can lead to unexpected results. Therefore, inexperienced users should begin with simple lists and simple logical filters, and should examine the results carefully.

2.2.3.3 Key Metrics

The key metrics view is located on your homepage. It offers a comprehensive view of the most important data stored within your CRM system. This is done by providing a quantitative summary of the information selected by your criteria.

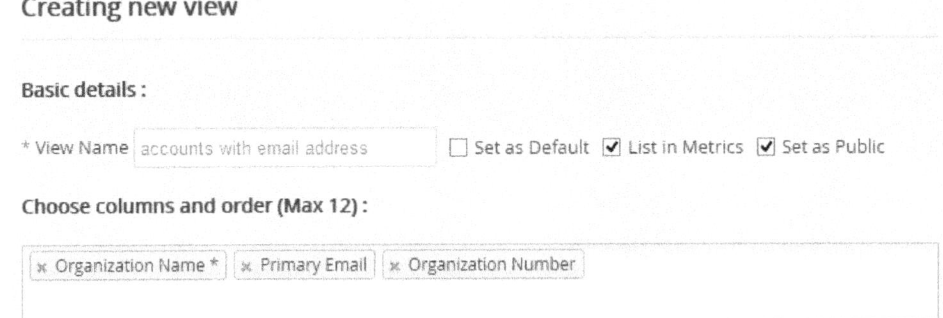

Figure 2-14: Key Metrics Setup

The content of the key metrics is defined by your custom list views. If the check box **[List in Metrics]** is marked as shown in Figure 2-14, the CRM will consider this list as part of the key metrics. As a result, the CRM automatically calculates the data displayed at the key metrics.

You can use the key metrics to answer questions such as:

- How many quotes are sent to prospect customers?
- How many tickets of a special customer are open?
- How many sales opportunities are in the last stage?

You can have other questions or you can find your own criteria. The possibilities for listings in key metrics are limited only by the CRM's capabilities of creating list views. You can use key metrics for critical processes in order to immediately recognize whether something has changed. For instance, a sales person can immediately see if the service team has critical tasks to complete on behalf of a special customer; a manager can watch the progress in a sales cycle; a service colleague can see whether the company has won new customers etc.

2.2.3.4 Search in Lists

If you have many entries in your list views of leads, contacts, accounts etc., a search function helps you to find a specific entry fast. Type in your search criteria on top of your list, as illustrated in Figure 2-15, and hit the **[Search]** button.

Figure 2-15: Search in Lists

This search function searches for entries related to the listed master data. If you need to search for field content which is not part of your list, you can use the module related global search as explained in chapter 2.2.1.2.

2.3 Special Menus

The CRM has some menus with a structure and a functionality that differs to the general rules as explained in the previous chapters.

2.3.1 My Preferences

When you click on **My Preferences** a new window opens and allows you to view and edit user information and to set your own preferences. Most of these fields are self-explanatory. Some fields which serve special purposes are explained in the following.

Click on the **[Edit]** button to make changes. Alternatively you can move your mouse pointer over an entry. An edit function is then offered, which you can use to change one particular entry.

CRM Password

Every user can define and change their own passwords. It is recommended to change the password frequently.

Usernames and passwords have to be a combination of small or capital letters and numbers. It is recommended that you use at least 8 digits. The more digits you have, the more secure CRM access is. The use of special characters such as %, / or characters with accent marks (such as ä, ö, ü or ß), as they are used in some languages, is not allowed. A good password for example looks like Dhe4K39b. User names, once created, cannot be changed. However, you might create a new user and transfer all data to the new user.

In order to change your password, click on the **[Change Password]** button. You have to enter your new password twice. Click on **[Save]** in order to make your new password valid.

For security reasons, your password is never stored. The CRM stores the result of a so called hash function to compare the entered password during a login. This means that if you lose your password, nobody can recover it and you will need a new password. Your CRM administrator can create a new password for you without knowing your old password.

User Login & Role

The field marked in Figure 2-16 displays the role assigned to the user. The role provides the users privileges. This field cannot be edited by a user. Only the CRM administrator can be change user's role.

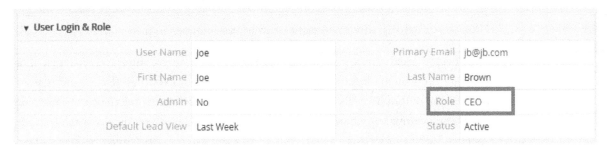

Figure 2-16: User Role

More Information

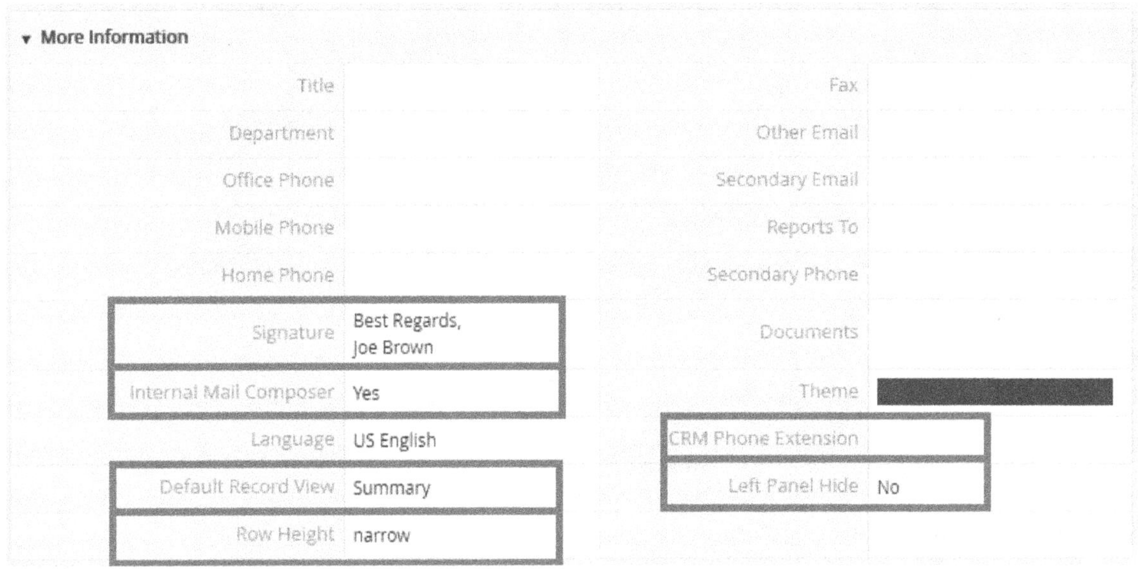

Figure 2-17: More Information Block

Field	Description
Signature:	This field defines the signature which is automatically added to outgoing emails. You can use HTML tags to format your signature. Please note that the space is limited. Your system administrator can increase this space if necessary. At the Appendix FAQ section, you will find more information of how you can format your signature and give it a special look.

Field	Description
Internal Mail Composer:	This field defines whether the internal CRM mail composer is used when clicking on an email address. If switched off, the mail composer installed on your computer is used.
Default Record View:	The settings refer to the detail view of a record. You can decide whether you would like to see all the master data or just a subset.
Row Height:	Here you can change the row height of your presentations in the browser.
CRM Phone Extension:	This field is used for a parameter setup of your Asterisk interface. Asterisk is a software implementation of a telephone private branch exchange (PBX) and is used for placing outbound calls by means of a simple click on a telephone number or displaying information about the caller stored in the CRM if you receive a call by your Asterisk PBX. Before you can use this feature an Asterisk PBX must be installed on your premises.
Left Panel Hide	This field also refers to the Detail View of a record. You can decide whether you would like to see the navigation list on the left side as illustrated in Figure 2-18.

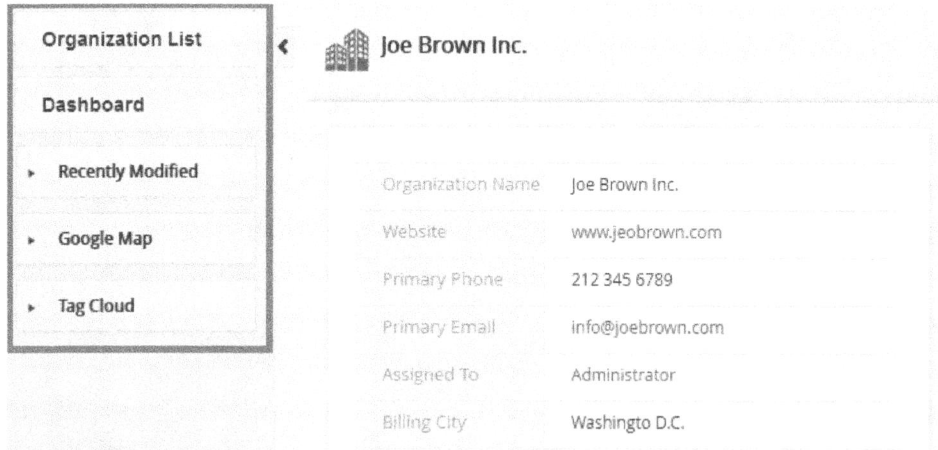

Figure 2-18: Left Panel in Detail View

Calendar Settings

You can use the fields from this block to set your preferences for the calendar display.

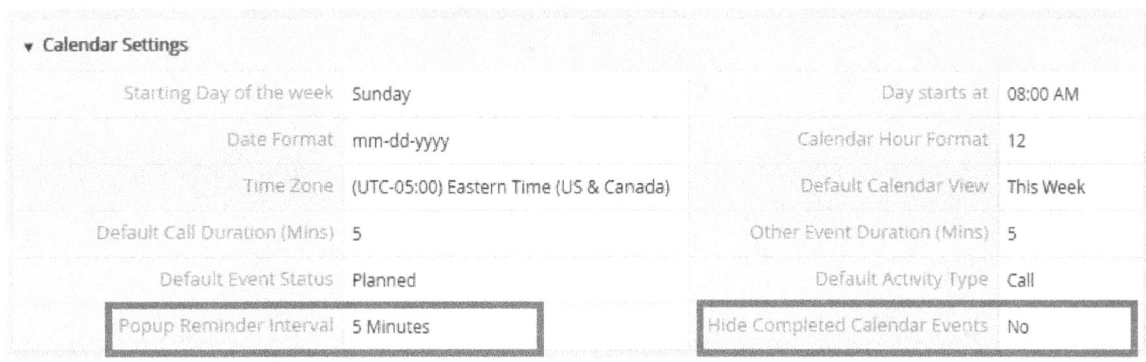

Figure 2-19: Calendar Preferences

The marked fields in Figure 2-19 serve the following purpose:

Field Name	Purpose
Popup Reminder Interval:	Unfinished events or tasks can generate browser popups which reminds the CRM user of this appointment.
Hide completed Calendar Events:	Here you can set whether completed calendar events will still be displayed.

Currency and Number Field Configuration

Individual requests for representing numbers and currencies in CRM are made in this menu. As shown in Figure 2-20, you can also decide whether the digits to be 0 after the decimal point.

Figure 2-20: Currency and Number Format Settings

User Advanced Options

The field **Access Key** displays an identification number to be used with CRM extensions and cannot be changed. You can also enable the display of a tag cloud, as explained in chapter 4.1.1.

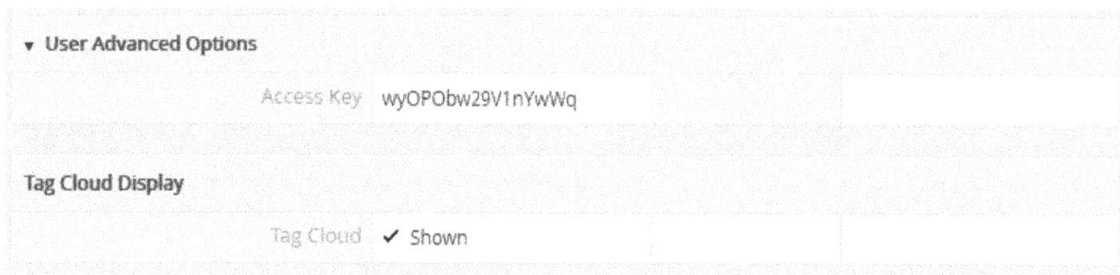

Figure 2-21: User Advanced Options

2.3.2 Quick Create Menu

The quick menu allows you to quickly create a new record. Click on the + icon that you see in any view on the right side below the navigation area. On the opened selection list, you can select the CRM module to which you want to make an entry. Then a window will open for input. The modules and the related fields as they are made available in the quick menu can be set in the module manager as explained in chapter 5.3.4.

2.3.3 RSS

RSS is a web feed format used for web syndication and stands for Really Simple Syndication. Web feeds are widely used by the web community for sharing the latest entries headlines or their full text, and even attach multimedia files. Some providers allow other websites to incorporate their syndicated headline or headline and short summary feeds. RSS is used for many purposes, including marketing, bug-reports, as well as other activities involving periodic updates or publications. Many corporations are turning to RSS in order to deliver their news, replacing email and fax distribution. The news media is also utilizing RSS by bypassing traditional news sources like CRM. Users are able to have news constantly fed to them instead of searching for them.

The CRM system provides an RSS reader which can check a list of feeds on behalf of the users and displays any updated articles that it finds as illustrated in Figure 2-22.

Add Feed Source

Rss Feed Sources

SPIEGEL mobil

Feeds List From : SPIEGEL mobil

Delete | Set As Default

Subject	Sender
Greeks in the Crisis:	SPIEGEL mobil
Postwar Rape:	SPIEGEL mobil
Family Feud:	SPIEGEL mobil
The Warming World:	SPIEGEL mobil
SPIEGEL Interview with Naomi Klein:	SPIEGEL mobil
'Risk Has Gotten Greater':	SPIEGEL mobil
Community Response:	SPIEGEL mobil

Figure 2-22: RSS Feed Display

Click on the **[Add Feed Source]** button in order to enter a new RSS address. You can search the web for RSS feeds you are interested in. Every RSS feed has a unique address similar to web URLs.

2.3.4 Our Sites

You can link the CRM system with other web sites which are of any interest to your business. Users do not need to leave the CRM system in order to access third party web sites or other Intranet or Internet sites. You can use this function, for instance, for monitoring important customers, your own web site, or the websites of your competitors. It is also very useful for tracking shipments, or conducting web-based communication with vendors.

Figure 2-23: Our Sites

Before you can see any website menu, you need to bookmark a site. Click on **[Add Bookmark]** in order to enter a new web site. Click on the **[Bookmark Name]** in order to see the bookmarked web sites.

2.3.5 Documents

Documents are practical to add further information to CRM entries. Any digital data can be considered as a document. You can enter a document by using the **Documents** menu but it is recommended that you add documents directly at the related lists of certain CRM modules.

Documents can have one or many relationships. That means you can add one document to multiple related lists.

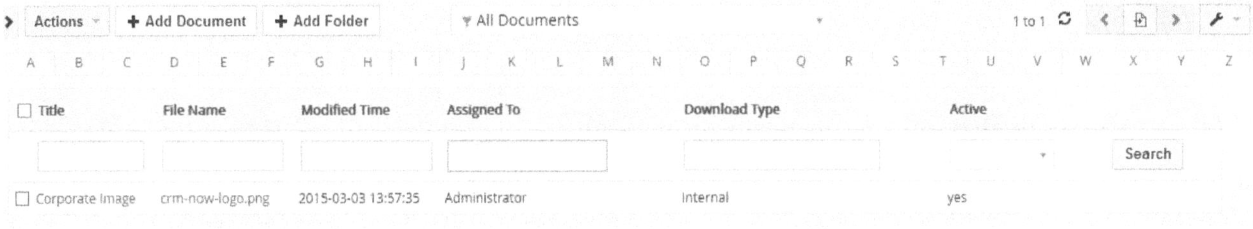

Figure 2-24: Document List View

As displayed in Figure 2-24 the CRM comes with a default document folder setup and you can add additional folders if required by clicking on the **[Add Folder]** button. Note that empty folders are hidden from the view.

Click on the **[Add Document]** button in order to create a new document as shown in Figure 2-25. You need to give the document a unique name and to select the folder in which the document is going to be saved. The create view allows you to enter three different document types:

- **Text:** Use the editor at the **Description** field to enter your information.
- **File:** At the **Download Type** field select **Internal** and browse at your computer or network for the file

you want to upload to the CRM. Such a file will be available for download from the CRM as long the check box for **[Active]** is switched to **Yes**

- **External Source:** At the **Download Type** field select **External** and enter the web or LAN address (URL) of your files.

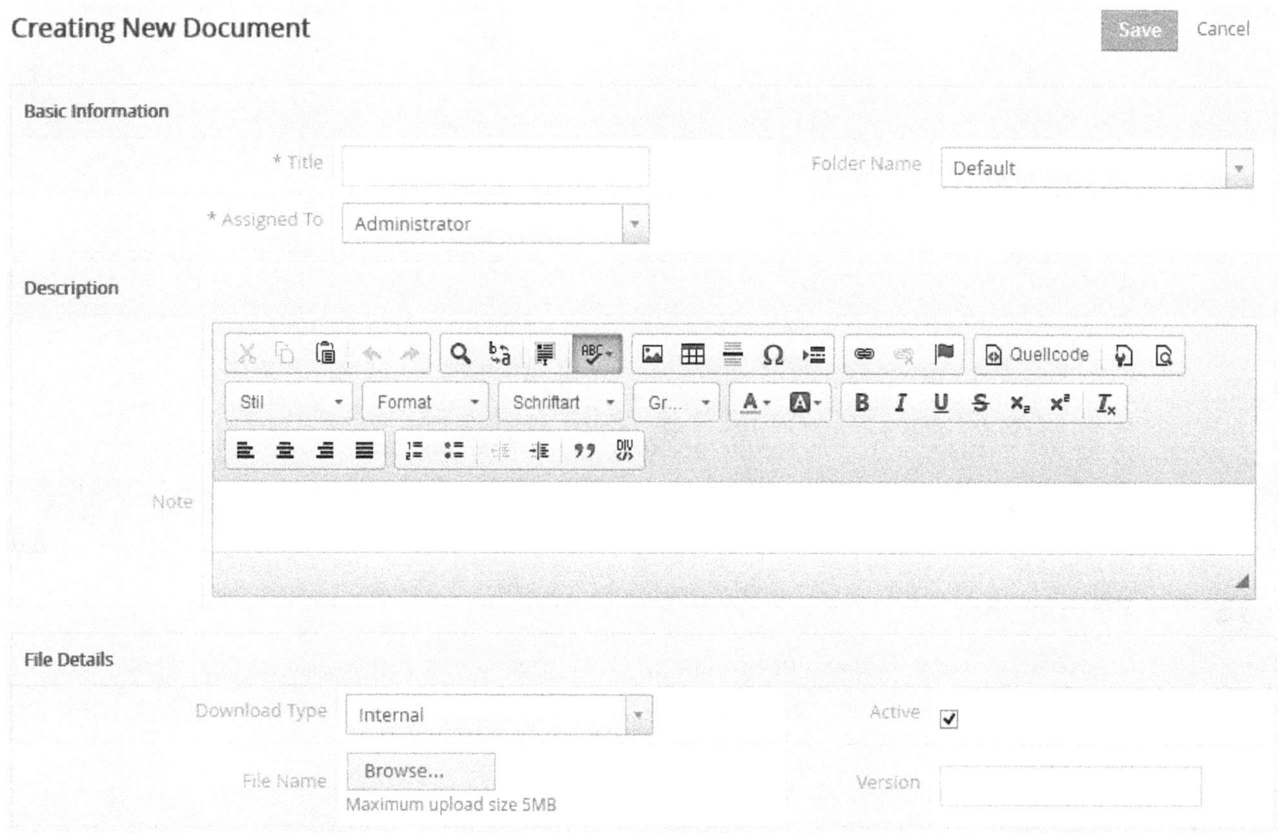

Figure 2-25: Document Create View

2.3.6 Recycle Bin

This menu is only available if you have installed the appropriate optional CRM package. In most cases it is not recommended to delete any data from the CRM. If you do it unintentionally, the deleted data can be restored from the recycle bin.

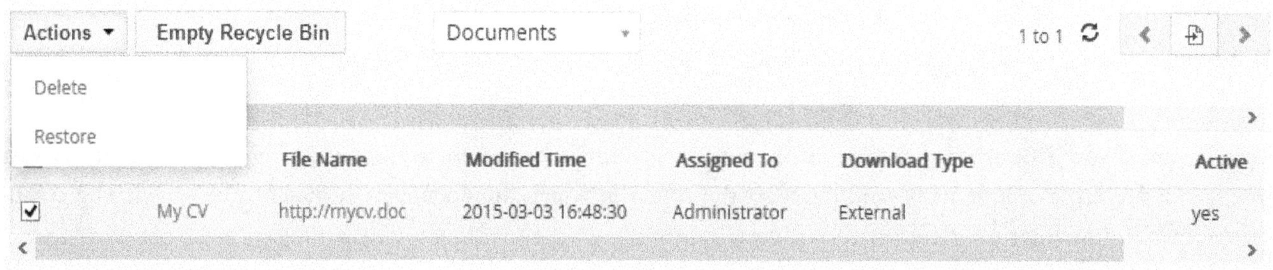

Figure 2-26: Recycle Bin

Open the **Recycle Bin** menu as illustrated in Figure 2-26 and select the CRM module for which would like to restore deleted data. Then all deleted records will be displayed. You are only allowed to restore the data if you have proper permissions to do so. You can restore records either individually or multiple records all at once, but only within the selected module. When a record from particular module gets restored, all the related records from other modules are also restored automatically if possible.

The CRM administrator is empowered to empty the recycle bin and to remove the deleted entries from the CRM system permanently. Please note that removed data can no longer be recovered.

2.3.7 Account Hierarchies

If you are dealing with companies that are distributed across multiple sites or working with branches, it can be useful to map the hierarchies in CRM.

You can use the **Member Of** field to set a reference to another organization.

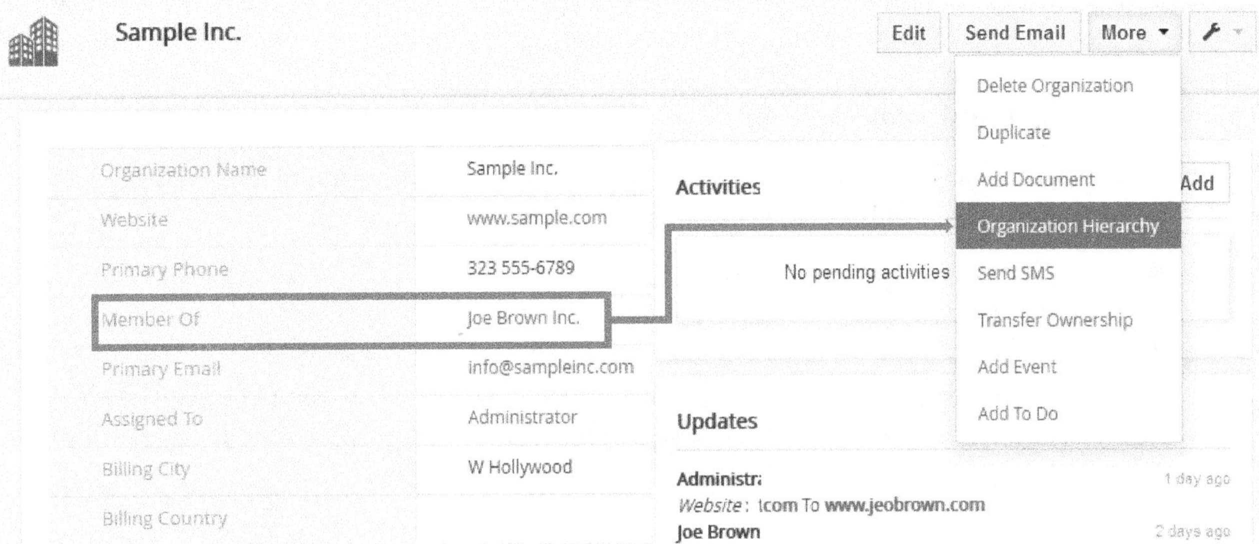

Figure 2-27: Account Hierarchies

Click on **[Organizational Hierarchy]** in order to get an overview over the affiliated companies as shown in Figure 2-28.

Organization Hierarchy

Organization Name	Billing City	Website	Primary Phone	Assigned To
Joe Brown Inc.	Washingto D.C.	www.jeobrown.com	212 345 6789	Administrator
.. .. Sample Inc.	W Hollywood	www.sample.com	323 555-6789	Administrator

Close

Figure 2-28: Organization Hierarchy View

3 Data Entry for the CRM System

The CRM system offers almost endless possibilities to enter, to process or to display your business data. This includes:

- A **workflow for your entire sales process**, from the first contact with a prospective client to post-sale support, and
- A **contact management** for your customers and vendors, related to individual persons, enterprises or groups,
- A time and priority controlled **activity management,**
- A **product and service catalog.**

You must decide what functions are important to you and your business and what you want to use. The following sections will describe in detail how to enter data into the CRM system and how the data is presented and managed.

3.1 Data Import and Export

The export and import functions will help you to exchange data between your office environment and the CRM system. CRM data can be used by a large variety of other applications in your office.

In most cases, already existing inventory data have to be imported into the CRM. A legacy data import requires some preparation and is often underestimated in terms of the time required. It also requires some technical expertise. In the following, some instructions are given and it is explained how you should prepare your data.

For the import and export of contact data, you can also consider the MS Outlook plug-in for Windows operated computers or the Thunderbird extension for Linux, Mac and Windows operating systems, as they are provided with the CRM system.

3.1.1 Data Format for Imports

Before you can import data, you have to format these data in order to meet the CRM's requirements.

The first requirement is that the data must be presented in the ASCII format with comma separated values (CSV) and UTF-8 or ISO-ISO-8859-1 coded character sets or as VCF files.

The CSV file format is often used to exchange data between different database applications. Your file must have the extension csv with lower-case letters.

A VCF (vCard) file is also a text file. You can get such files from other applications like Outlook™. The structure of VCF files is complex and will not be explained here. See Appendix A for further information.

Since a common standard for the CSV format does not exist, your data sets must be formatted according to the following rules:

- All fields are separated by commas or semicolons and must be individually wrapped by double-quote characters. The separator symbol can get defined by the delimiter parameter during the step 1 imports.
- All data sets must include the mandatory fields (e.g. Last Name and Company for leads).

- All data sets must include values for pick lists (use --None-- if you do not have a value).
- Fields that contain embedded line-breaks or fields with leading or trailing spaces are not allowed.
- Number fields have to contain numbers only without "." or "," characters for separating thousands (for instance, use 3800 instead of 3,800).
- Fields containing double quote characters should be avoided. If you have to use them, they must be surrounded by double-quotes, and the embedded double-quotes must each be represented by a pair of consecutive double quotes.
- The first record in your file can be a header record containing column (field) names. It is recommended to use a header but if you don't, you can remove the header check during the imports step 1. Do not use special characters or umlauts in the header.
- Dates must be imported in the following format: year-month-day hour: minute: second, for example: "2015-01-07 00:00:00"
- Entries for Multi-Select Combo Boxes must be separated by a |##| character string, for example: "America |##| Europe"
- Check boxes must be imported in the following format: 1 for yes, 0 for no
- References to other modules can get set by using

There are special requirements for your quote, order or invoice imports. In the case of such an import, please follow these rules:

- The item names must be identical to your entries in your products or service module. You must have created a product or service entry before import.
- It is recommended to specify whether the item name originates from products or services. This is done by means of a prefix like:
  Product::::Your Product Name or Service:::: Your Service Name
- The quantity and selling price fields are mandatory
- The tax values for line items must be in percentage format, as it is calculated on the total amount field.
- Tax type is mandatory. Tax type should be specified either as *group* or as *individual.*
- An import of the items **Total, Pre-Tax Total, Received, Balance** and **Grand Total** are not possible.

Please note that the import of faulty quotes, orders or invoices can create unpredictable results in your CRM system. It is recommended that such an import is only carried out if the data has been previously tested on a test system. You can also consider using a web service for such a purpose.

The second requirement is that you have to include all custom fields with your import if you have created such fields before. In case you do not have any contents for the custom fields, you can leave the field in your data list empty but you must import it. If you do not import these fields, the status of these fields in your CRM's database remains undefined and you can't use such fields for filter functions.

```
"Company", "Street", "City", "ZIP", "Country", "Phone", "Last name"
"Samples Inc.","123 Samplestreet","Scity","12345","USA","(123)123-4567","Miller"
"XYZ Inc.", "Main Street 33","Xcity","55555","Germany","","Brown"
```

If you do not have a full set of data available, you must wrap an empty entry with double-quote characters as it can be seen in the sample above for the missing telephone number in line 3. If you have data sets which do not have all mandatory fields included, these data sets will be ignored during an import.

If your data contains line feed or carriage return characters, it is recommended that you remove these before importing the data into Excel. Such characters might be created by the CRM system if you have entries that use multiple lines. This might for instance be the case if you separate street name and suite number in an address entry with an additional line.

Account and the last name are mandatory fields for leads. As an exception, you can leave the last name field blank in your import data, but you must map this field. If you do not provide a last name, the corresponding lead entry will be filled with '?????'.

3.1.2 Hints for CSV and Excel Formats

The file formats used in Microsoft Excel have become a pseudo standard throughout the industry, even among non-Microsoft platforms. Excel is an application that also produces and uses CSV. Unfortunately, depending on your Excel version the import of CSV data can cause some problems. Some Excel versions do not automatically accept comma separated values. If you experience formatting problems after opening exported CRM data, such as all fields are listed in one column, you can use the following instructions to clean them up:

- Import the CSV file, rather than just opening it. On the data menu, choose import external data, and then import your data. Browse to the CSV file from the CRM, and click open. This brings up the **Text Import Wizard**.
- In step 1, select **Delimited**.
- In step 2, check **Comma**. You will see a preview that shows how the data will be separated.
- In step 3, you can select each column in turn and choose a format. For the CRM date, choose text and you will be presented with a well sorted Excel sheet.

If you want to import contact data from your office application, you need to make sure that this data is well formed. The following list describes how you can use contact data from your Microsoft Outlook:

1. Check the data format

- Unfortunately, in many cases, data to be imported needs to be checked and modified manually before importing. That is a necessary task to make sure that all data is well formed.
- Export your contact data from Outlook in the Excel format.

- Start Excel and open your data file.
- Look for any special characters such as commas (,) semicolons (;) and double-quotes (") and substitute those, e.g. with a space character.
- Look up the column that contains the mandatory fields. Make sure that each individual data set has a mandatory entry. Do not use any special characters.
- Remove all columns which you do not need in the CRM system.
- Check the content of each individual entry. Make sure that it contains the information you intend to have there. Removing wrong entries later in the CRM system will cause a lot of work. It is better to do it now.

2. Create a CSV file

If you are sure that you have valid and good data, you need to create a CSV file that works with the CRM system. There are tools available online, see Annex A, which do the formatting for you and exports a well formed CSV file.

3.1.3 Import Menu

The following section describes the import and export function for accounts. If you want to import or export contacts or other modules, you can refer to this description, keeping in mind that some of the specifics will be different.

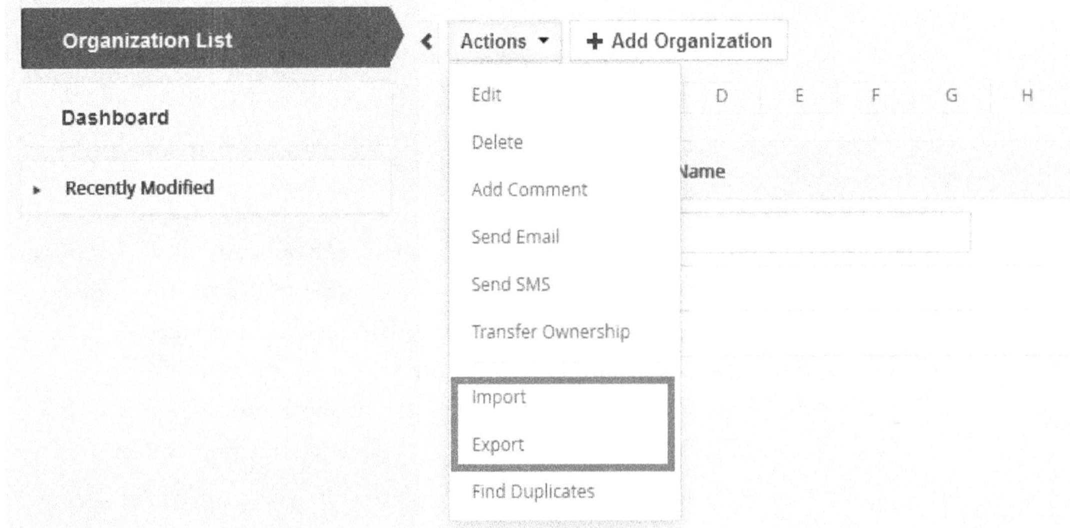

Figure 3-1: Import and Export Menus

In order to export or to import data, click on a module name. You will get to a **List View**. At the top of the list you will find the import and export actions as shown in Figure 3-1. These actions are only active if they have been enabled by the CRM system administrator.

Click on the **[Import]** and new window will open as shown in Figure 3-2. As **Step 1,** you have to select your data source by browsing your computer or network.

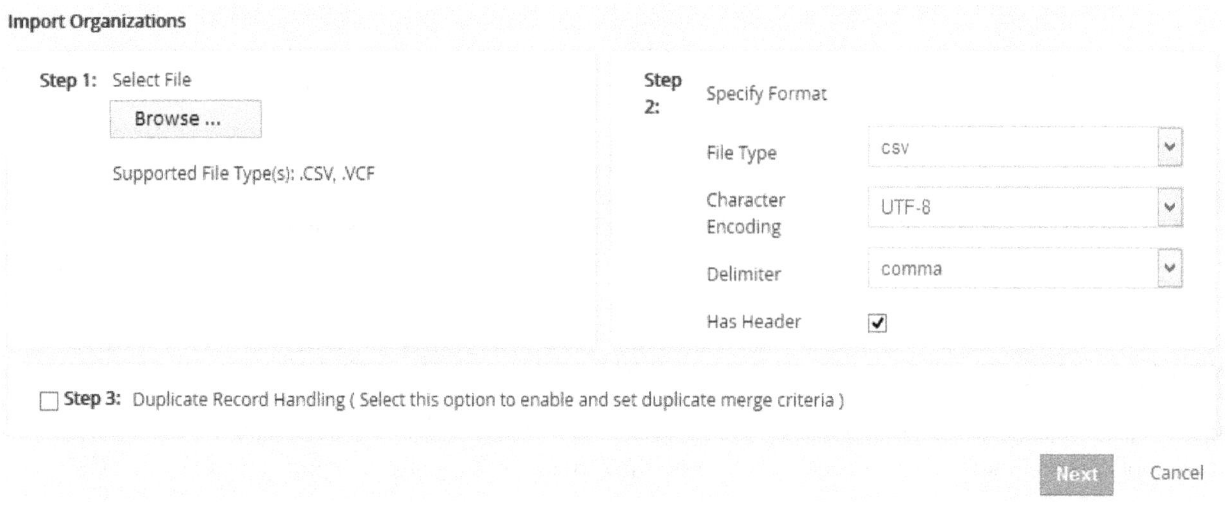

Import Organizations

Step 1: Select File

Browse ...

Supported File Type(s): .CSV, .VCF

Step 2: Specify Format

File Type: csv

Character Encoding: UTF-8

Delimiter: comma

Has Header: ☑

☐ **Step 3:** Duplicate Record Handling (Select this option to enable and set duplicate merge criteria)

Next Cancel

Figure 3-2: Import Menu Steps 1-3

As **Step 2,** you define the data format as it exists for your import file. The CRM system uses a character set internally which is UTF-8 (Unicode compatible) coded. Unicode is an industry standard allowing computers to consistently represent and manipulate text expressed in any of the world's writing systems. Please refer to Appendix A UTF-8 coding for further information. You can import data which is UTF-8 or ISO-8859-1 coded. If you use data which is based on ISO-8859-1 your data will be converted to the required UTF-8 format automatically.

All of the data you intend to import must contain the mandatory fields as they are marked with a red * sign at a master data's edit view and values for all your pick lists. You can find sample import data in chapter 3.1.1. If your data contain more information as the available fields in the CRM system can provide for, you can start to use **Custom Fields** as explained in chapter 5.3.1.2.

Step 3 is optional and controls the duplicate handling. You can select your criteria for duplicate identification and decide within the CRM has to do when a duplicate is identified. Duplicates are only recognized if the contents of records have an identical spelling. This is a limitation which always needs to be considered. Therefore, in many cases it is recommended to check for duplicates with other tools before importing.
With the skip operation the CRM ignores your import data. The overwrite operation substitutes the existing data by the new data. The merge operation keeps the existing data as long there is no new content in the import data.

Click on **[Next]** in order to get to the **Step 4** as illustrated in Figure 3-3. At this menu you have to link your data with the corresponding CRM fields. You see the standard fields as they are offered by the CRM and your custom fields if you have created them beforehand. It is not necessary that you create references for all data types in your file, but you must link the mandatory and all the pick list fields.

Import Organizations

Step 4: Map the Columns to Module Fields --Select Saved Mapping--

Header	Row 1	CRM Fields	Default Value
Company	Samples Inc.	Organization Name (*)	
Street	123 Samplestreet	Billing Address	
City	Scity	Billing City	
ZIP	12345	Billing Postal Code	
Country	USA	Billing Country	
Phone	(123)123-4567	Primary Phone	
Last name	Miller	None	

☑ Save as Custom Mapping import1

Import Cancel

Figure 3-3: Import Menu Step 4

You can also define a default value which gets used if you have not provided content for all fields in your file. You must make this entry for **Pick Lists** or **Multipick Lists** if you are not sure that you provide content in your import file for all data sets.

The allowed import file size is almost unlimited. The limits are set by your server settings and whether the internal program for the import of large files is operating. Files with more than 1000 data sets are imported in the background. If you are not sure how your CRM operates you can consider carrying out multiple imports for up to 1000 data sets for which no background program is required.

If you have to make multiple imports, the CRM offers to store the references you have selected for future use. Mark the check box **[Save as Custom Mapping]** and write a name of this reference into the entry field. Make sure that this name has not been used before. This **Custom Mapping** will be available at step 4 as **Select Saved Mapping** when you carry out the next import.

At the final import step, the CRM shows you the result of the import operation as you can see it in Figure 3-4.

Import Organizations - Result

Records successfully imported	:	2 / 2
Records created	:	2
Records overwritten	:	0
Records skipped	:	0
Records merged	:	0
Records failed importing	:	0 / 2

Import More | Last Imported Records | Undo Last Import | Finish

Figure 3-4: Import Results

You can review your import data, accept it or reject it.

If you import contacts with account information, the import will generate contact and account entries which refer to each other. During an import, the CRM checks whether the contact's account name already exists. If it does, it will link the imported contact to the existing account automatically. Therefore, it is always better to import the accounts data first.

3.1.4 Data Export

Export Data

You can select the following criteria for your export:

- all records of this module
- only the records you have marked at the list view of this module
- all records which meets your search criteria at the list view of this module
- all data of the current page at the list view of this module without search criteria set

You have to make your decision at the list view about the data you would like to export, before you hit the export action as illustrated in Figure 3-1. For instance, if you would like to export all records of contacts where the last name starts with a **B**, carry out a search with **B** as your search criteria. You then subsequently hit the **export icon** on the list view menu, if this function is available to you, and the menu as shown Figure 3-5 will be displayed.

Export Records

Export Selected Records — No record selected.
Export data in current page
Export all data

Export Organizations — Cancel

Figure 3-5: Export Menu

At this menu you can change you selection criteria if desired and click on the **[Export Organization]** button. A new window for uploading data to your computer opens. The upload window you will see depends on your operating system.

If you click on **[OK]**, all data will be exported to your computer. The data is provided as an ASCII file with comma separated values, also called CSV format. Your data is exported in the UTF-8 character format. For further uses, you can have to convert the data to the character set used at your computer or application. Please refer to Annex UTF-8 coding for further information about UTF-8 and convenient conversion tools.

3.2 Calendar and Activities

The CRM system provides a calendar such as you would normally find at your desktop. This calendar distinguishes between events and tasks (ToDos), all together called activities. Events are calls and meetings but your CRM administrator can add other types of activities, such as vacation or road show. Be careful when scheduling your activities. Even if you consider a meeting as a task, the CRM system does not. The operational differences between **Events** and **Tasks** will be explained in the following sections.

The CRM system offers several possibilities to enter or to schedule calendar related activities. You might use the calendar directly, the quick menu, or you might create activities during the sales process in leads or opportunities, or during services at the **Trouble Ticket** menu. Calendar entries can and should be linked to other data stored in CRM system, such as contacts, leads or accounts. Figure 3-6 illustrates a possible calendar menu.

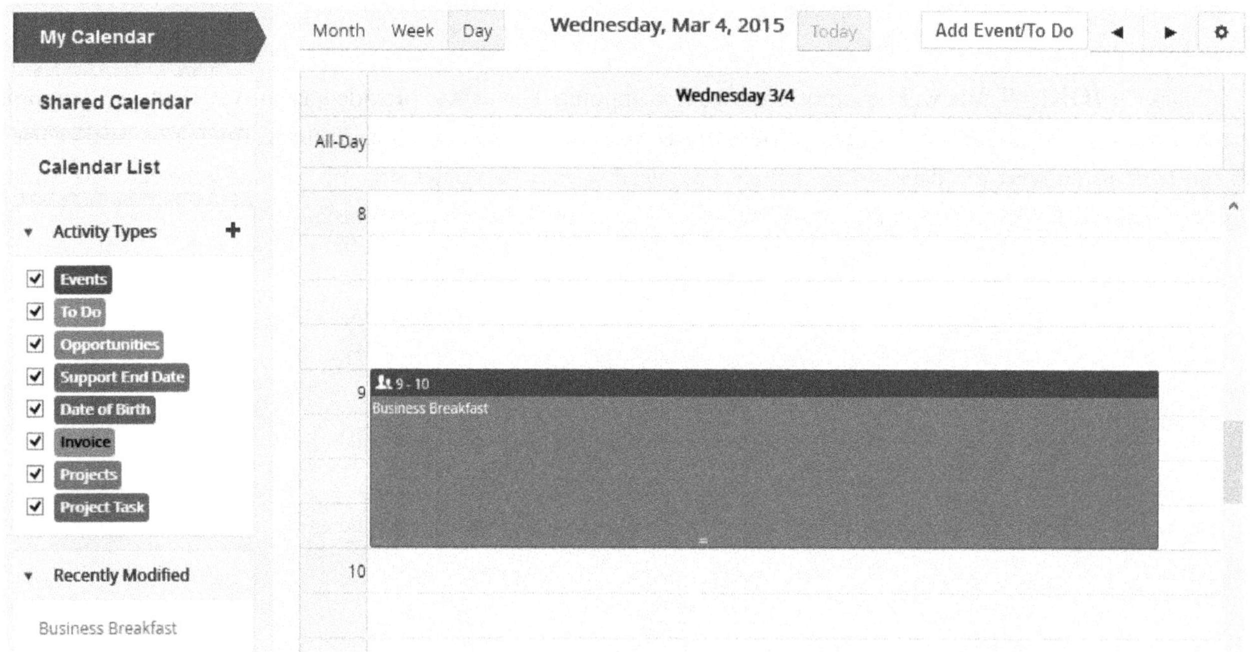

Figure 3-6: Calendar Hour View

3.2.1 Calendar

If you want use the calendar to schedule an event or task, click on either on the calendar menu at the navigation area. A new window will open which will display, depending on your system setup, either the calendars list or the hour view. The hour view is shown in Figure 3-6. A calendar is displayed in the browser-defined language. If you see the calendar in a wrong language, please check your browser settings.

At this view, all events scheduled for a particular day are displayed. You can switch to a weekly, monthly or yearly view by clicking on the appropriate icon at the top of the daily calendar. You can also switch to a list view or to the calendar of one of your coworkers. You will probably get the best view on your calendar if you make the weekly view to your standard view.

Adding an Event to the Calendar

In order to enter the schedule of a meeting, call or one of your own event types click in a time field and select your event type. A popup window within the calendar will open as shown in Figure 3-7.

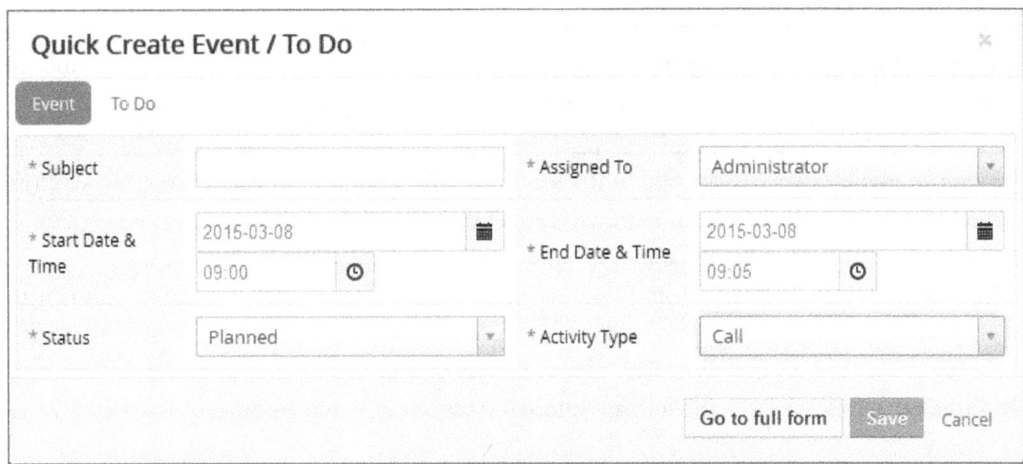

Figure 3-7: Event Edit View

Here you can enter your event information. The following table explains the field types.

Table 3-1: Overview event information

Entry Field	Description
Subject:	This is a mandatory field and you must provide a name for the activity.
Assigned to:	By default the creating user is the owner of the event. You can change it if necessary.
Start Date/Time and End:	Every event has a beginning and an end. You can choose to have an end date a number of days later. This is for instance the case if you have business trip of several days.
Status:	By default the status for a new entry is set to **Planned**. If the status is set to be planned you can only make entries which are dated in the future. If you want to make entries for the past, set the status to **Held** or **Completed**.
Activity Type:	Select a call or meeting or other custom activity types as defined by the CRM administrator.
Description:	This field is available in the full form. You can add a short description of this event when you plan this event. After the event, you can use this space to enter goals, action items, or meeting minutes.
Related To:	These fields are used to link calendar entries with other module entries. Once linked a calendar entry will show up at the related activities list of the connected entry.
Priority:	You can set a priority for an event. Each priority has its own color.
Send Notification:	If you mark this check box, an email with the actual event information will be sent to the owner of the event. You can use this function for instance if the event owner changes.

Entry Field	Description
Start Date/Time and End:	Every event has a beginning and an end. You can choose to have an end date a number of days later. This is for instance the case if you have business trip of several days.
Invite:	You can invite other CRM users to this event by following the instruction displayed. Note that these users will receive an automatic email with the event information as content.
Visibility	You can mark your calendar entry as public or private. Private entries are not shown to other CRM users.

You can click on the **[Reminder]** checkbox, to schedule an automatic reminder email to be sent by the CRM as shown in Figure 3-8.

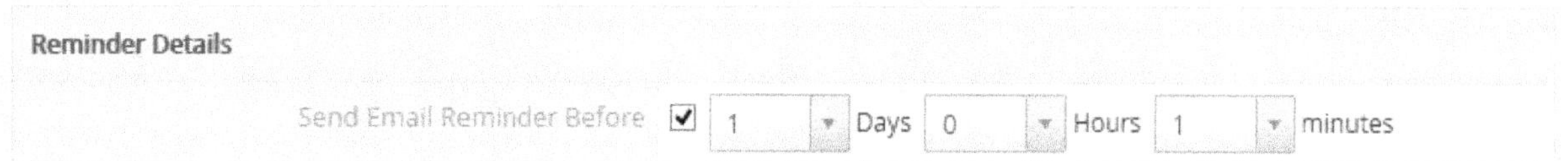

Figure 3-8: Set Calendar Reminder

For the reminder message you have to enter the time. The current version does not allow you to change the email address. The mail gets send to the event owner.

In addition, the CRM allows you to schedule events which occur on a regular basis. Click on the **[Repeat]** checkbox in order to make your settings. The dialog is shown in Figure 3-9.

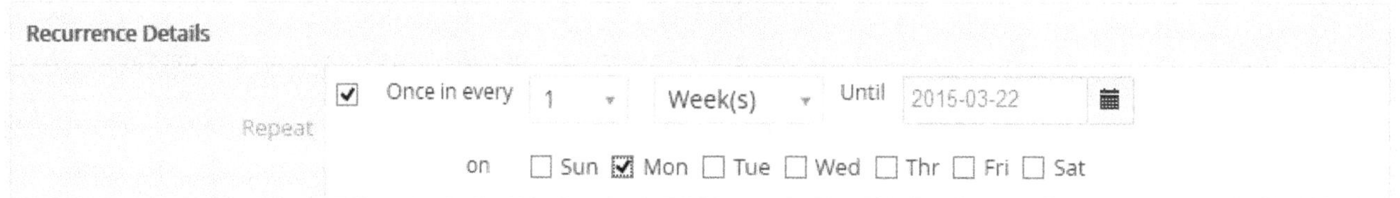

Figure 3-9: Repeat Calendar Entries

Finally, click on **[Save]** in order to transfer the event schedule to the CRM. As a result you will see the event listed in your calendar.

Calendar Sharing

By default, every user's calendar is set to private. That means that other users can see that you have an event scheduled but do not get access to detailed information. You can add other user's calendar by clicking on the ✚ icon as illustrated in Figure 3-10.

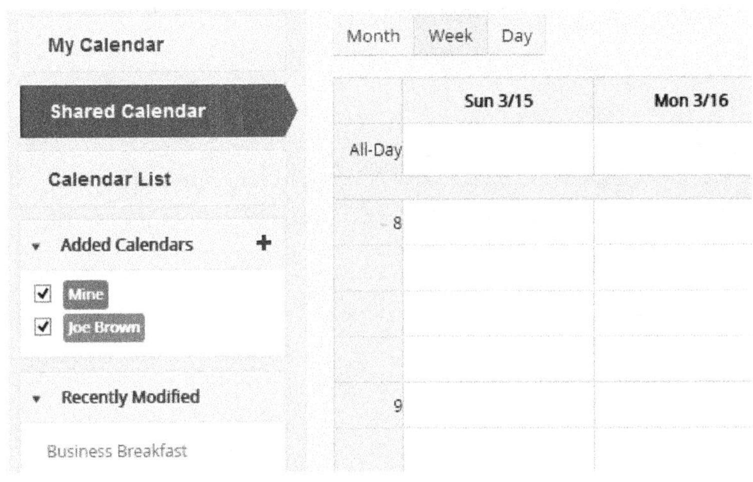

Figure 3-10: Calendar Sharing

Other users in the role-based hierarchy can also view specific events at another user's calendar if these events have been made public. In order to make a particular event public, mark the **[Public]** checkbox when you create a new event. A user with a role above in the hierarchy can always see the calendar of subordinates.

Tasks and To Dos

The CRM system helps you to schedule tasks which are also sometimes called ToDos. Tasks are always assigned to one CRM user or Group and do not have an end time but a due date. You cannot invite other users to tasks nor can you link more than one contact with tasks. However, you can transfer tasks to others by changing the owner.

There are many places in the CRM where you can enter tasks. You can enter tasks at any detail view of steps in your sales process or in the calendar. The edit view window as shown in Figure 3-11 will open and you can enter your task information. Please note the mandatory fields.

Creating New To Do

Save Cancel

To Do Details

* Subject: Create Slides — * Assigned To: Administrator

* Start Date & Time: 2015-03-15 08:00 — * Due Date: 2015-03-15

Campaigns: Type to search — Contact Name: Type to search

* Status: Not Started — Priority: Medium

Send Notification — Location

Description Details

Description: we need a new presentation

Figure 3-11: Task Menu

When you are finished, click on **[Save]** in order to store the task in the CRM system.

3.2.2 Calendar Setup

Click on the icon on the calendar's view in order to call up the settings menu. You can configure the time your calendar starts and the time format and some other default settings as illustrated in Figure 3-12.

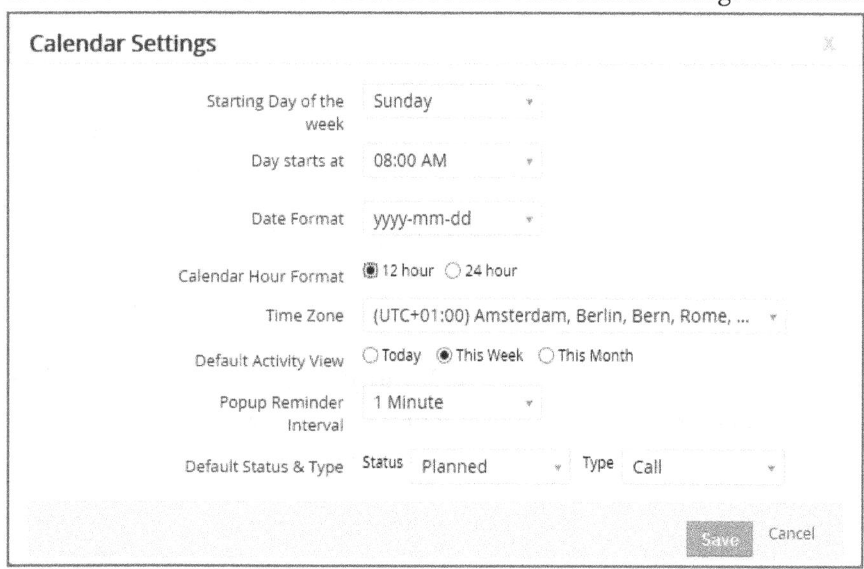

Figure 3-12: Calendar Settings

3.2.3 Calendar List View

If you want to see all activities in one list you can click on the **[Calendar List]** button at the calendar menu as shown in the example below in Figure 3-13.

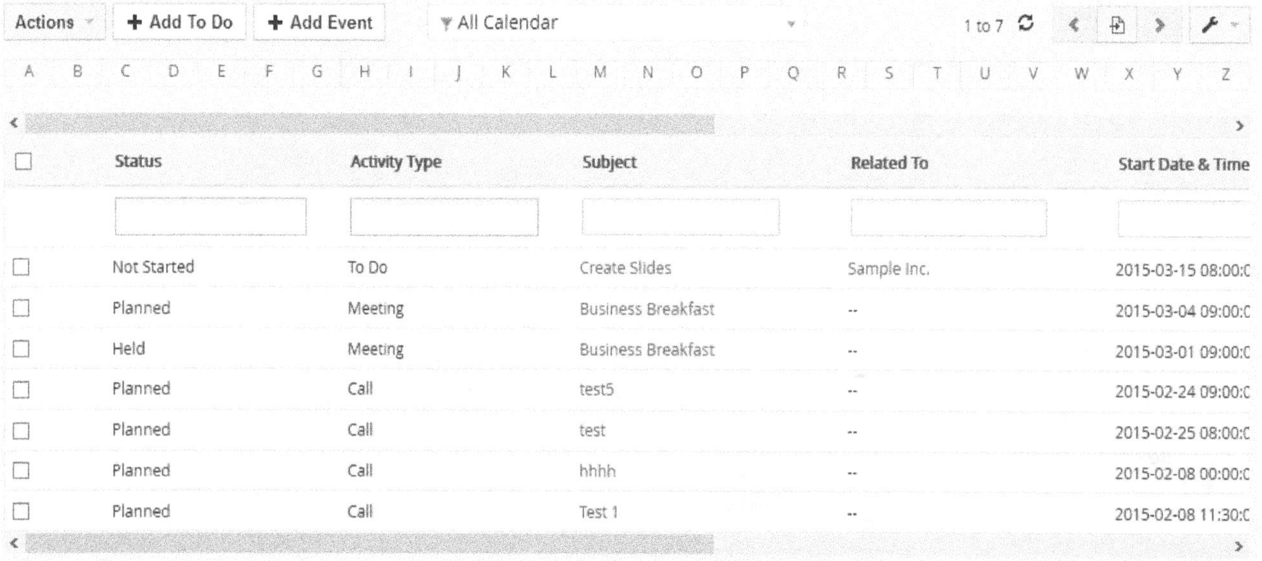

Figure 3-13: Calendar List View

You can change the list according to your own criteria by the filter functions. Please refer to chapter 2.2.3.2 for further instruction on how to customize the list view for your specific purposes.

3.2.4 Import and Export of Activities

Using the calendar's **[Action]** menu, you can export or import activities in the so called iCal format. This format is supported by many other office applications.

The CRM comes with a set of extensions to be installed on your computer for automatic export or import operations. This includes an Outlook plug-in for Windows computers or a Thunderbird & Mozilla extension for Windows, Mac or Linux. For further information on these extensions, please consult the relevant manuals as listed in the manual's appendix.

3.3 The Sales Process

You can use the CRM system to drive your entire sales process from the first contact with a prospective customer to after-sales services. The CRM system can accommodate the different data and feature requirements at various points along the process. The following sales process phases are offered by the CRM and explained in the following sections:

- Leads
- Opportunities (sorted by different stage, priorities and other criteria
- Quotes
- Sales and Purchase Orders
- Invoices
- Help desk with ticket system and FAQ

The sales phases are connected closely with the contact and activity management, product and service catalogues and powerful reports.

Keep in mind that as your contact data progresses from a lead to an opportunity, the CRM system will automatically transfer the requisite data during the progression from one sales phase to another. However, if you find that you need to "jump ahead," going directly to the contact, account or opportunity phase, the CRM allows this.

3.3.1 Customer Contacts

The effective administration and utilization of customer contacts is the most important element of a customer relationship management system. Ultimately, all business activities are targeted to customers. The CRM system distinguishes three different contact types:

- Leads
- Contacts to single persons
- Contacts to an organization, such as legal entities, groups, agencies etc.

The CRM enables entering information about each of these contact types and allows linking individuals to organizations, and organizations to one another, as appropriate. While working with the CRM system, contacts will be categorized in accordance with their stage in the sales process, such as leads (earliest stage), opportunities (pre-sales stage) or help desk (post-sales stage).

The following example describes a typical sales procedure:

- Contact information for a potential customer before any business has been discussed, and often before any contact has been initiated, is a **Lead**. At this sales stage it is not clear whether there will be a business opportunity.
- The **Lead** status of this contact will be maintained until contact has been established and there is a concrete business opportunity. All activities related to this **Lead** will be tracked within the CRM.
- Once a business opportunity emerges, the lead can be converted in to an opportunity. At this time, the data contained within the lead are automatically split out into a contact and an account and the **Lead** is

deleted. All the information collected for the **Lead** is still available but is now split between **Contacts, Accounts** and **Opportunities.**

By using this procedure, only those contacts and accounts which represent potential business are tracked separately. In order to prevent the CRM system from becoming overloaded with useless data, less concrete leads are segregated and aggregated in a more compact fashion.

It is not necessary to go through the lead conversion process for every contact and account, however. You can enter new accounts or contacts directly if they are not suitable for the described procedure. This might be true for your own employees, existing customers, partners of your company, personal contacts etc.

3.3.2 Leads

Leads are the first phase in establishing a customer relationship and most likely the best starting point for you to enter customer data into your CRM system. Your company can get leads from marketing activities such as trade shows, advertisement or PR efforts. At this phase, you do not know whether this first contact will lead to a business opportunity.

Usually (and unfortunately), most of your leads will not generate any business. The CRM system considers this by treating leads differently from all other contact information stored in the CRM. It is sensible to avoid useless leads burdening the CRM system unnecessarily. For this reason leads are not linked to other account or contact

If you create a lead, you can capture the following customer related data:

- Contact data to a single person or organization
- Description for a lead
- Assessment of value of a particular lead for your company

This data will be stored as master lead data within your CRM. Your administrator can modify the type and amount of master data necessary for your business.

If you think a lead provides a business opportunity you can convert a lead to a sales opportunity as explained in Section 4.2.1.

3.3.3 Sales Opportunities

In the sales process, sales opportunities are the logical successors to leads. Therefore, you can create a sales opportunity from a lead and transfer all information available for the lead to the new sales opportunity.

You can also create a sales opportunity directly. In essence, a sales opportunity is an immediate opportunity to do business with a potential or existing customer. The sales department would expect that an offer could be made for this potential customer in the near future.

Analogously to leads, you are working with a sales opportunity as you have already done it with leads. Enter all of your activities, save possibly contract documents, create quotes, etc. The goal is that your opportunity data contain all the information belonging to a specific business.

For each new business you create a new opportunity.

3.3.4 Quotes

The CRM system supports you in the creation of quotes for potential customers. The creation of a quotation is based on your product and/or service catalog and the associated price lists. This means that you must have saved your products, services in the CRM system before you can make an offer.

It also recommended that you have already the following information available:

- • mailing and shipping address information for the related contact or company
- • a related contact with proper salutation
- • a related opportunity
- • a price book with at least one entry

You can use one of the following methods to create a quote:

- You can use the detail view of a sale opportunity to create a quote by clicking on the **[Add Quote]** button at the related list. You can choose this way for an automatic transfer of the potential's master data to a quote.
- You can also create a quote directly by clicking on the **[Add Quote]** icon at the quote list view. This will require that you have to set all references, for instance to a sales potential, manually.

Most data entry fields for quotes are self-explanatory. Therefore, in the following, only the fields that require special attention or which are provided with functionalities, and which do not reveal themselves at first glance are considered.

Quote Details

Table 3-2: Quotes - special default master data entry fields

Entry Field	Description
Subject:	You have to give the quote a name. It is practical for a search function to have the customer's name mentioned, e.g. Sample Inc. - 1st Quote.
Quote No:	The quote number is generated by the CRM automatically based on the CRM administrator's setup. Please refer to section 5.5.5 for more information.
Valid Till:	Enter the expiry date of this quote. This information will become a part of the PDF output.
Inventory Manager:	If you use the CRM to maintain your inventory, you can select the inventory manager here. The inventory manager will receive an automatically-generated email by the CRM system that informs about this quote as soon you hit the [Save] button.
Organization Name:	You must refer your quote to an existing account. The CRM will receive the address information from this account and will automatically fill in the corresponding fields at this entry page.

Address Details

You must have billing and shipping addresses as part of your quote.

Item Details

In the case of quotes, the CRM system considers all type or discounts which can apply to the offer of products or services. These can include local, state or federal taxes as well as special taxes. These taxes can be calculated individually for each product or service, or calculated for the whole. Before you select products for your quote, you need to decide what tax mode applies to your offer.

The CRM system supports an **Individual** and a **Group** tax mode.

The Figure 3-14 displays an example for the entry details for products calculated with the **Group** tax mode. With this tax mode you can set one tax which applies for all items you offer.

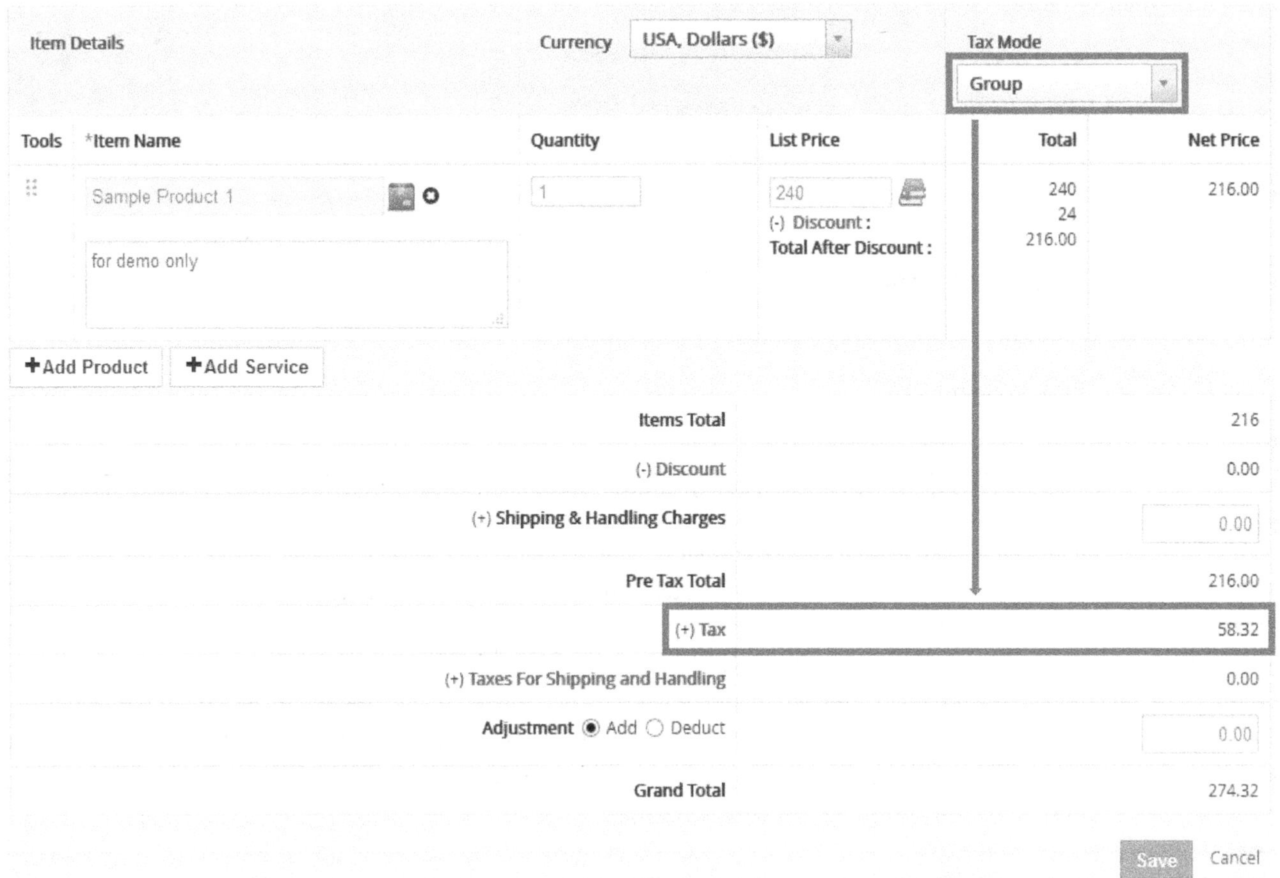

Figure 3-14: Quotes - Group Tax Mode

In Figure 3-15 you see the entry details with the **Individual** tax mode. Here the tax is calculated for each individual product. The tax can be different for different items.

You can add further products or services by clicking on the **[Add Product]** or **[Add Services]** button.

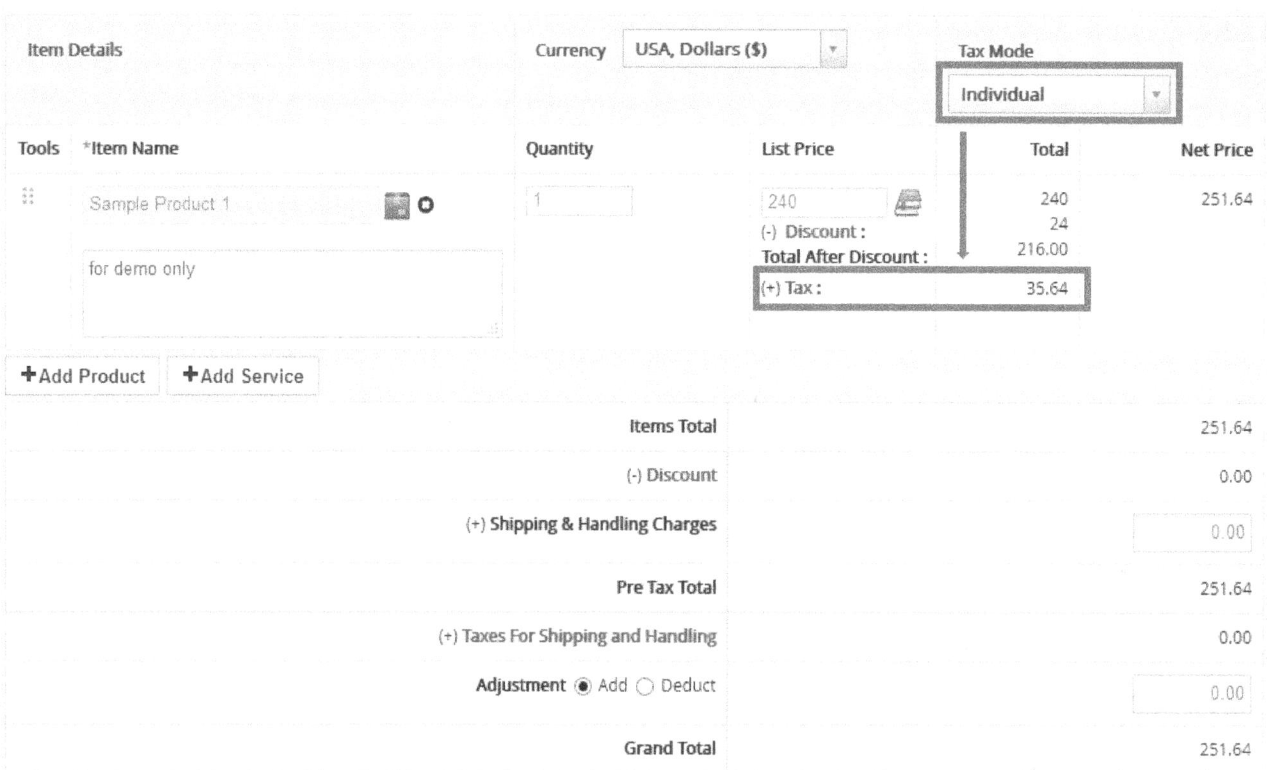

Figure 3-15: Quotes - Individual Tax Mode

Table 3-3: Quotes - Product Entry Fields

Field Entry	**Description**
Item Name:	You must have created a product or service catalog before you can create a quote. Here you have to use the special icon to select a product or service. You can add an additional comment for each individual product you offer.
Quantity:	You have to select a quantity of products or services you offer.
List Price:	Here you enter the customer price. Please note that you can use the icon to select the price from your price book entries. That is especially useful if you maintain various price lists for different customer types.
Discount:	You can select a discount for each individual line item or a discount for the whole. This discount can be in percent (%) of the list price or can have a fixed value.
Tax:	The CRM calculates your taxes on the basis of the tax information on your product or service catalog. You can modify the calculation for a quote without changing the product catalog entry if required. Tax types and values which apply to your business are set by the CRM system administrator.
Shipping & Handling Charges:	You can add additional shipping charges if applicable.

Field Entry	Description
Taxes For Shipping and Handling:	You can add additional shipping taxes if applicable.
Adjustment:	Finally you can make an adjustment to the quote by adding or deduction a fixed amount.

Product Currency

All price calculations are done in the default currency assigned to a specific user. The currency assigned to a specific product or service is also considered.

You can change the currency by selecting a different currency from the list located on top of the product list. If you change a currency the prices for goods or services are being converted to the new currency automatically. The currencies which are available and their conversion rates are defined by the CRM administrator as explained in section 5.5.4.

Finally, the CRM will add up all your entries and will calculate the sub total. You can add further taxes or adjustments. Please note that the terms and conditions can be defined by your CRM administrator can define default terms and conditions as described in section 5.5.3.

Click on **[Save]** in order to transfer your quote to the CRM.

PDF Output

In order to provide a PDF copy of your quotes, you must have set your company information in advance as described in section 5.4.1. Such a PDF copy can be created and mailed by making the appropriate selection at the **[More]** button displayed at a quote's detail view.

3.3.5 Sales Orders

Sales orders are orders you receive from customers. Such orders of goods or services are usually presented as a paper copy received by fax or mail. It makes sense to capture such orders also in the CRM. A sales order can differ from your quote and you should have such information available in the CRM system.

You can create a sales order from a previous quote by opening the detail view of the corresponding quote and clicking on the **[More]** button and making the appropriate selection. This will automatically transfer your quote information to the new sales order.

Most data entry fields for sales orders are also self-explanatory or explained in the previous manual section already. Therefore, in the following only the special entry fields of this menu are considered.

Table 3-4: Sales Orders - Special default master data entry fields

Field Entry	Description
Subject:	You have to give this sales order a name. It is advised to make it unique and to include the account name.
Sales Order No:	The sales order number is generated by the CRM automatically based on the CRM administrator`s setup. Refer to Section 5.5.5 for more information.

Address Details

As soon you pick a contact or an account name, the address information is taken from the contact or account and included automatically.

Create Recurring Invoices

As illustrated in Figure 3-16, you can add recurring invoice information to a sales order. This means that an invoice will be generated automatically every time the conditions set at this sales order are met. This will be done by a time-based job scheduler that usually runs once every day at your CRM.

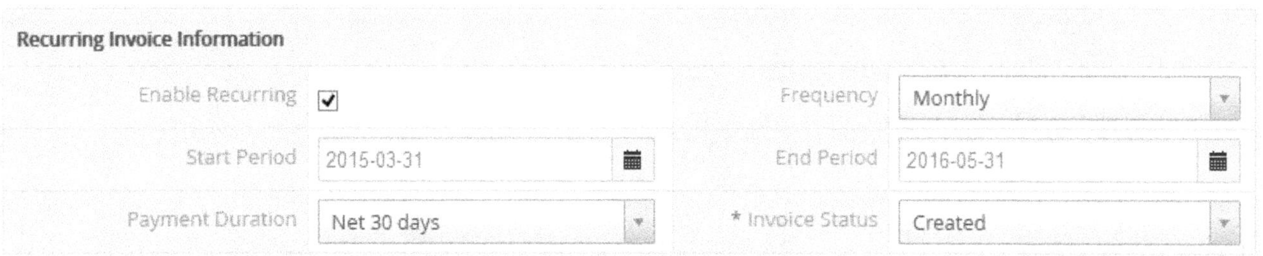

Figure 3-16: Sales Order - Recurring Invoice Information

Item Details

Here the ordered goods and services ordered are listed. Please refer to the item details description in Section 3.3.4 for more information.

PDF Output

In order to be able to provide a PDF copy of your quote, you must have set your company information in advance as described in Section 5.4.1. Such a PDF copy can get created and mailed by making the appropriate selection at the **[More]** button displayed at an order's detail view.

3.3.6 Purchase Order

The CRM supports you also in purchasing goods or services. That might be helpful if you have to order something to fulfill a customer sales order or to maintain your company operation. Before you can enter any purchase orders, you must have the vendor in the vendors list. This is explained in Section 3.5.4.You must also have the products or services to be purchased in your price book.

Most data entry fields for purchase orders are also self-explanatory or explained in the Section 3.3.4 already. Therefore, in the following only the special entry fields of this menu are considered.

Table 3-5: Purchase Order - Special default master data entry fields

Entry Field	Description
Subject:	You have to give a purchase order a name. It is advised to make it unique and to include the vendor name.
Vendor Name:	You have to select a vendor name already stored in your CRM system. This will automatically fill in the address information entry fields.
Purchase Order No :	The purchase order number is generated by the CRM automatically based on the CRM administrator`s setup. Refer to Section 5.5.5 for more information.

PDF Output

In order to be able to provide a PDF copy of your order, you must have set your company information in advance as described in section 5.4.1. Such a PDF copy can get created and mailed by making the appropriate selection at the **[More]** button displayed at an order's detail view.

3.3.7 Invoices

You can use the CRM system to create customer invoices manually or automatically from a sales order.

Most data entry fields for invoices are also self-explanatory or explained in the Section 3.3.4 already. Therefore, in the following only the special entry fields of this menu are considered.

Invoice Information

Table 3-6: Invoice - Special default master data entry fields

Entry Field	Description

Entry Field	Description
Subject:	You must give your invoice a name. It is advised to make the name unique and to include the customer's name.
Invoice No.:	The system automatically proposes an invoice number every time you create a new invoice by incrementing from the last existing invoice number. Therefore, you cannot have an invoice number twice and the CRM maintains consecutive numbers. You can define your own standard numbering format for your company as explained in Section 5.5.5.
Terms & Conditions :	This information is taken from the CRM administrator settings as explained in Section 5.5.3.
Invoice Date:	Every invoice must have a date. You can pick it here.

You can create recurring invoices from sales orders as explained in section 3.3.5.

PDF Output

In order to provide a PDF copy of your invoice, you must have set your company information in advance as described in section 5.4.1. Such a PDF copy can get created and mailed by making the appropriate selection at the **[More]** button displayed at an invoice's detail view.

The CRM does not allow you to use an invoice number again. Therefore, in the majority of cases it is not recommended to delete an invoice once it has been created. Set the amount to 0.00 or, what would be better, create a credit invoice, by selecting it at the status field, instead.

3.4 Campaigns

The CRM supports your marketing efforts with a **Campaign** module. You can use a campaign, for example, to send serial emails or letters to multiple recipients. You can then also trace in CRM, who had been the recipient of your activities.

Click on the **[Add Campaign]** button at the campaign's list view in order to open the create view as shown in Figure 3-17.

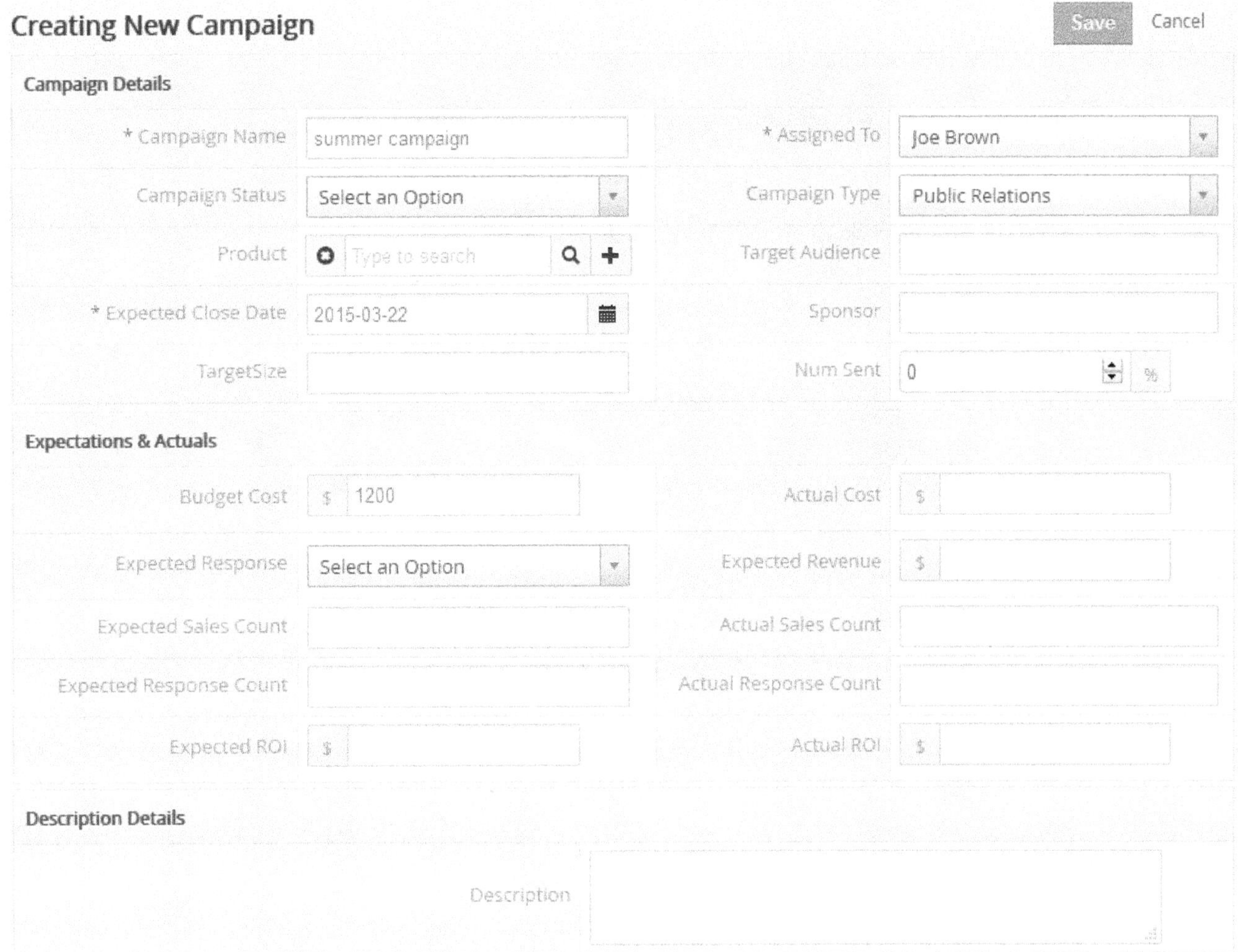

Figure 3-17: Campaign Create View

The following table gives you an overview about special entry fields:

Table 3-7: Campaigns - Special default master data entry fields

Entry Field	Description
Campaign Name:	You must give your campaign a short and unique name

Entry Field	Description
Campaign No:	The system automatically proposes a campaign number every time you create a new campaign by incrementing the previous campaign number. You can define your own standard numbering format for your company as explained in section 5.5.5.

Click on **[Save]** in order to transfer your campaign data to the CRM.

You can add individual contacts, leads, opportunities to your campaign. Alternatively, you can load existing contact lists or lead lists to your campaign by making the proper selection. These lists must already exist as a customized list view in your lead or contact module. Therefore, it is recommended that you create your list views at the leads and/or contacts module before you start a campaign. These lists should include the data sets you want to consider in a campaign.

In Figure 3-18 you see the related contact list, as an example. You can add:

- Single contacts from your CRM by clicking on the **[Select Contacts]** button
- A new contact entry by clicking on the **[Add Contacts]** button
- A list of contacts by clicking on the **[Select to Load List]** field

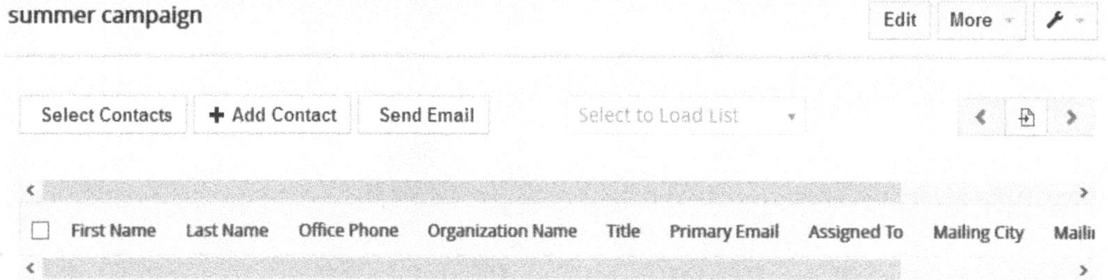

Figure 3-18: Campaign Related Contact List

You can also add opportunities or activities to your campaign at the appropriate related lists.

Once you have your campaign filled with contacts, you can send a mass mail with substitute fields. In section 4.1.5 it is explained how you can setup a mailing template with substitute fields which are automatically filled with CRM data.

3.5 Product Related Entries

The CRM uses the term **product** as a comprehensive term for all kinds of goods your company might offer. Similar to a catalog, the CRM provides functions with which to capture and to categorize your products with various prices and vendors and maintains an inventory list if needed. However, for some companies it might be necessary to distinguish clearly between products and services. For this purpose a CRM service extension is available as described in section 3.6.

3.5.1 Products

The CRM allows you to link product information with your sales process. In order to be able to enter a new product, simply click on the **[Add Product]** at the **[Inventory] > [Products]** menu for the full set of options. A new window will open as shown in Figure 3-19.

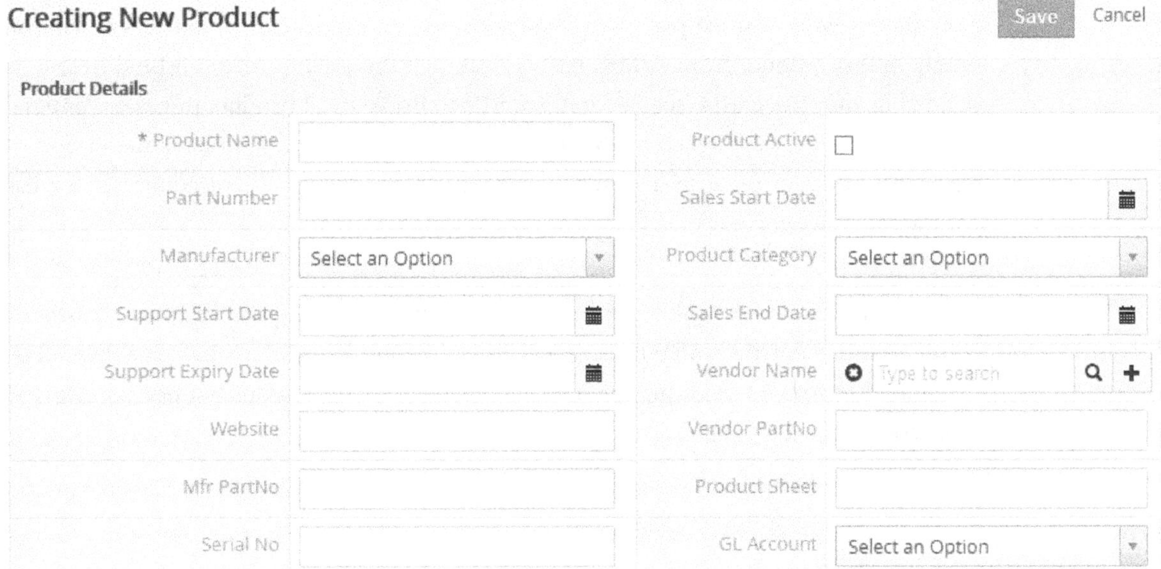

Figure 3-19: Product Create View

The following tables explain the special entry fields for the product's master data.

Product Details

Table 3-8: Products - Special master data entry fields

Entry Field	Description
Product Name:	You have to give each product a name which should be unique.
Product No:	The product number is generated by the CRM automatically based on the CRM administrator's setup. You can define your own standard numbering format for your own company as explained in Section 5.5.5.
Part Number:	You should give each product a unique order code. This could be a combination of letters and numbers. Customers should use this code with their orders.

Entry Field	Description
Product Active:	By marking this check box, a product becomes active and is available for selection in quotes, orders and invoices.
GL Account:	This entry refers to a General Ledger Account and could be useful if you do imports/exports with your accounting program. Each account in your General Ledger usually has a number for reference.

Pricing Information

Table 3-9: Products - Special default master data entry fields for pricing

Entry Field	Description
Unit Price:	You should enter a price per unit. This price can be the list price you pay when you purchase this product from a third party. Note that the selling price can be different as defined in your price lists (see Section *3.5.3* Price Books). All product prices are entered with the currency as assigned to the user who enters the prices. You have the option of entering a product price in a different currency if the CRM system administrator has configured other currencies.
Tax Class:	You can enter a tax in % that applies to a product. Note that your CRM administrator configures the tax types and rates as explained in section 5.5.6. Only tax types defined by the administrator will be displayed. You can change the tax amount but not the tax type if necessary.

Stock Information

The CRM supports you in maintaining a stock of goods.

Table 3-10: Products - Special default master data entry fields for stock information

Entry Field	Description
Qty in Stock:	You can enter the quantity in stock. This information is used by the CRM when making quotes, orders or invoices. You can use a workflow to control your stock as described in section 5.5.8. If you do not intend to use the inventory management features of the CRM system, it is recommended that you set the quantity information to a high number, e.g. 100,000 to avoid low inventory warning messages.
Handler:	You should assign a responsible person with the responsibility for maintaining the stock. This person will automatically be informed by the CRM system when goods are sold or when the stock levels become critical.
Reorder Level:	Here you can enter the minimum quantity of goods you want to keep in stock. If the CRM system detects during the sales process that the actual quantity in stock gets close to the minimum amount, the person in charge of the stock will be notified by email.

Entry Field	Description
Qty. in Demand:	Here you can note the quantity of goods you usually buy.

Product Image Information:

You can add up to 6 product images to your product. The image must be in .jpg, .gif or png format and have file extensions with small letters (jpg, gif, png). You should keep the image size as small as possible in order to avoid time consuming downloads every time you display this CRM page. If you add more than one image, your images will be displayed as a slide show at the detail view.

Description Details

Here you have a space for further product information if required. This information can get included with the PDF output of quotes, orders or invoices.

Click on **[Save]** in order to transfer your product information to the CRM system.

After saving, the detail view of your product opens. You will see the master data you have just entered. At the related lists, you have the possibility to enter additional information or to set relations to other CRM modules.

Table 3-11: Products - Special related lists entries

Entry Field	Description
Trouble Tickets:	Here you will find all product related tickets. These tickets can be based on customer complains, product bugs, or other customer related after-sales events. You can find further information about tickets in the Trouble Ticket Section 4.2.2.1.
Product Bundles:	Here you can add sub products to your product and bundle these products together for a product selection in quotes, orders or invoices as explained in the next section. Such sub products could be, for instance, additional parts you are selling in relation to your main product.
Parent Product:	The CRM lists the main product if your product is already part of a product bundle.

3.5.2 Product Bundles

You can create product bundles from your existing product listing but not from services. This feature allows the building of a hierarchical products order where you have sub products related to a parent product. A product can be a sub product to an unlimited number of products but a parent product can never become a sub product.

The initial bundle set up is no different to creating a new product or service. Click on the **[Product Bundles]** button of a parent product's detail view for the creation of a new related sub product. Enter the product information and save your new product.

In order to access your product bundles for quotes, orders or invoices, open the product selection menu. The new window opens with a list view of your parent products. Click on **[Sub Products]** in order to see a list of related sub products as illustrated in Figure 3-20.

Only activated products are available for selection. If you do not see a product in the selection list, you can check the product status by opening the detail view of this product.

Figure 3-20: Select Products from Bundle

3.5.3 Price Books

The CRM allows you to work with an unlimited number of different price lists, called price books. This is very helpful, for instance, if your company has different types of customers which require different pricing. You can use special retail, distribution, end customer price lists or others.

Create Price Books

In order to create a new price book, **[Add Price Book]** at the **[PriceBooks]** menu. A new window will open as shown in Figure 3-21.

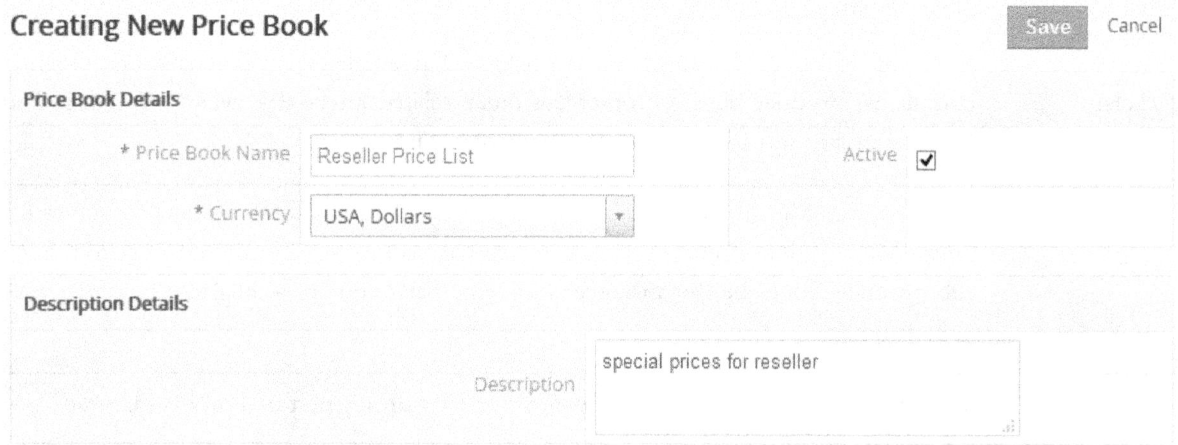

Figure 3-21: Price Book Create View

You have to give this price book a unique name and a currency. You can add a description for future reference. Mark the check box **[Active]** if you want to have this price book available for quotes, orders and invoices. Click on **[Save]** in order to create this new price book at your CRM system.

Edit Price Books

In order to add a product to your price books, click on the related list **[Products]** or **[Services]** into the detail view. The new window opens as shown in Figure 3-22. You can add the products you want to this price book by going to the **[Select Products]** menu.

You can also set a list price for the product as it is selected for orders, quotes or invoices by clicking on the ✎ icon.

The entered list price is only valid for this price book. The unit price as set in the product catalogue is shown as a reference.

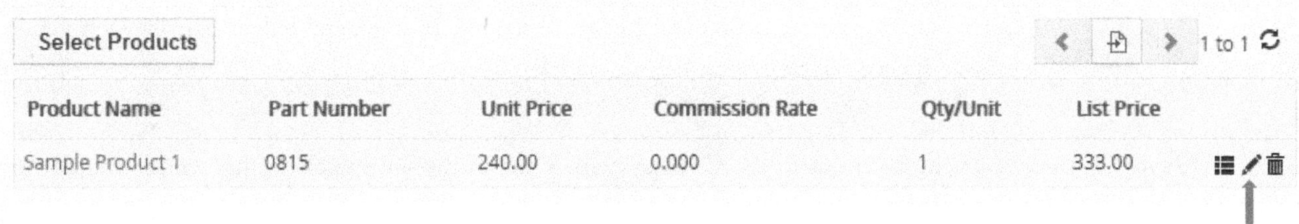

Select Products

1 to 1

Product Name	Part Number	Unit Price	Commission Rate	Qty/Unit	List Price
Sample Product 1	0815	240.00	0.000	1	333.00

Figure 3-22: Price Books Product Selection

3.5.4 Vendors

The CRM allows you to enter an unlimited number of vendors which provide goods or services to your company or to your customers. Such vendors are stored separately and not part of the contacts or accounts lists.

In order to enter a new vendor, click on the **[Add Vendor]** button at the **[Vendors]** menu. A new window, as shown in Figure 3-23, will open.

Creating New Vendor

Save Cancel

Vendor Details

* Vendor Name	Vendor A	Primary Email	
Primary Phone		GL Account	305-Sales Other
Website		Category	
* Assigned To	Joe Brown		

Address Details

Street		PO Box	
City		State	
Postal Code		Country	

Description Details

Description: for demo

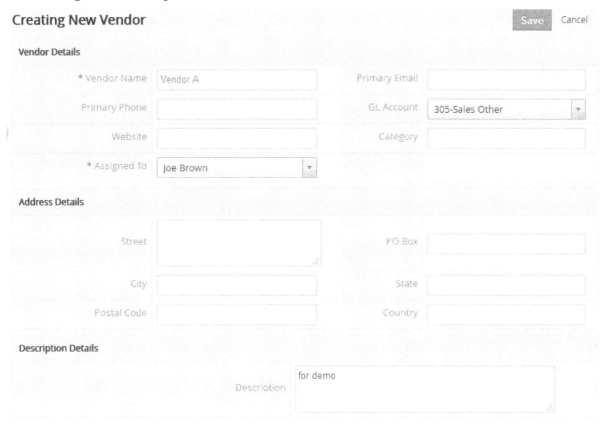

Figure 3-23: Vendor Create View

Table 3-12: Vendors - Special default master data entry fields

Entry Field	Description

Entry Field	Description
Vendor Name:	You have to provide a vendor name and should use the vendor corporate name.
GL Account:	This entry refers to a General Ledger Account. In a general ledger usually each vendor has a special reference number

Click on **[Save]** in order to create a vendor in the CRM system. Your menu will switch to the vendors detail view which contains all the information you just entered.

At the vendor's related list that can be accessed via the detail view, you can link a vendor with other records.

3.5.5 Product Import and Export

By the export and import functions, you can exchange data between the CRM and a large number of programs on your computer. All product data can be exported or imported.

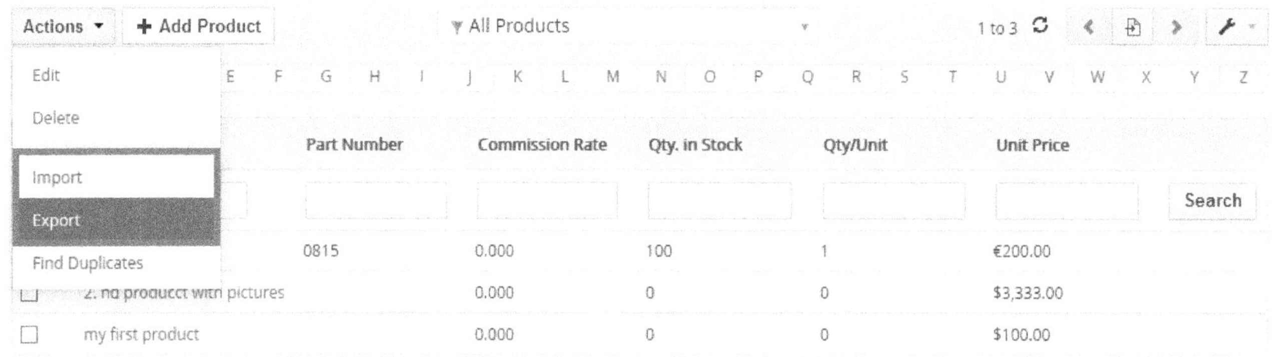

Figure 3-24: Product Import and Export Selection

In order to start to import or export, please go to the list view, click on the **[Actions]** button as illustrated in Figure 3-24 and make your selection.

Please refer to section 3.1 for further export and import instructions. Use the description of the contacts import procedure accordingly for your products. You can find sample import data in Section 3.1.1.

3.6 Service Related Entries

You can use **Service** for all your company offers which are not related to products. Similar to a catalog, the CRM provides functions to capture and to categorize your services with various prices and vendors. There is no inventory list for services. Services can get combined with product offerings as described in the previous section.

3.6.1 Services

In order to enter a new service, click on the **[Add Service]** button at the **[Services]** menu. A new window will open, as shown in Figure 3-25.

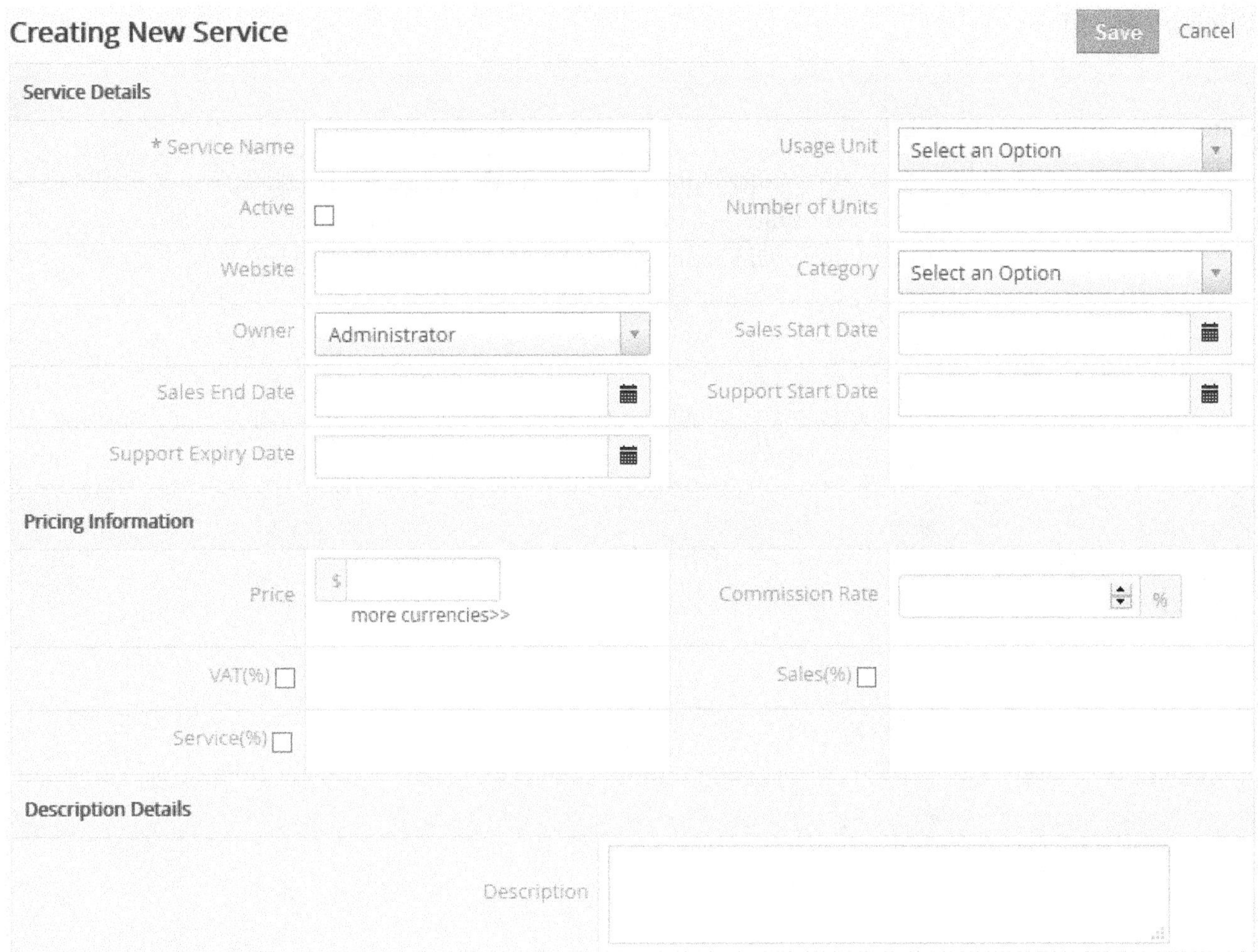

Figure 3-25: Service Create View

Most data entry fields are self-explanatory but some serve special purposes:

Service Details

Table 3-13: Services - Special default master data entry fields

Entry Field	Description
Service Name:	You have to give each service a unique name.
Service No.:	The service number is generated by the CRM automatically based on the CRM administrator's setup. Refer to Section 0 *Other* Settings - *Customize Record Numbering* for more information.
Usage Unit:	Select the usage unit. Please note that the CRM administrator can change the content of the pick list.
Description	This entry can get provided to quotes, orders and invoices.

Pricing Information

Table 3-14: Services - Special default master data entry fields for service pricing information

Entry Field	Description
Price:	You should enter a price per unit. All service prices are entered with the currency as assigned to the user who enters the prices. You have the option to enter a service price in a different currency if the CRM system administrator has configured other currencies as described in the section: Currencies.
Tax Class:	You can enter a tax in % that applies to a service. Please note that your CRM administrator configures the tax types and rates as explained in the section: Tax Calculations. Only tax types defined by the administrator will be displayed. You can change the tax amount but not the tax type if necessary

Click on **[Save]** in order to transfer your service information to the CRM system.

After saving, the detail view of your service opens. You will see the master data you have just entered.

3.6.2 Services Contracts

In order to enter a new service contract, click on the **[Add Service Contract]** button at the **[Service Contracts]** menu. A new window will open as shown in Figure 3-26.

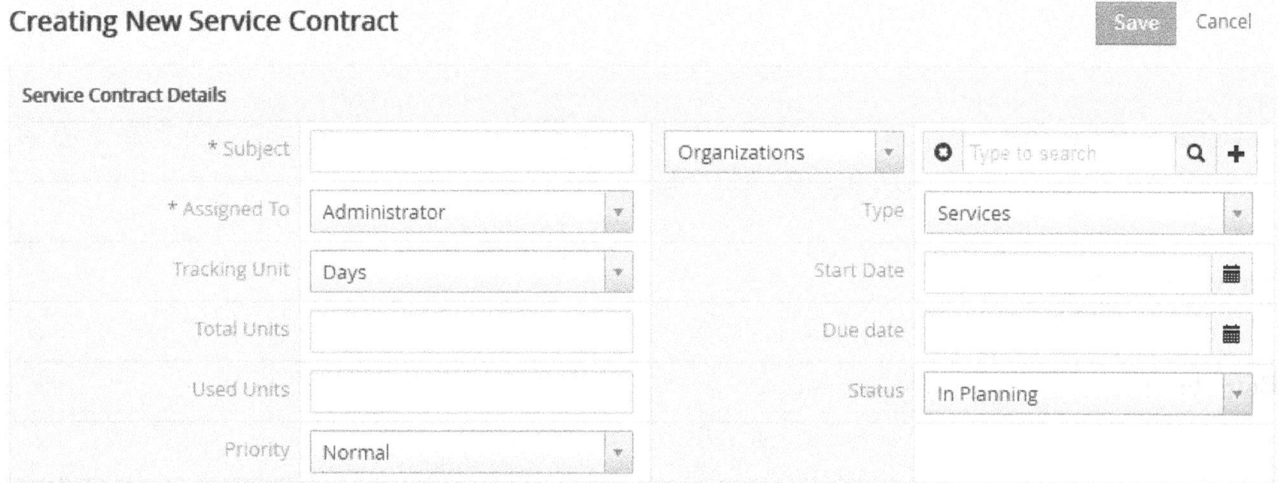

Figure 3-26: Service Contract Create View

Most data entry fields for quotes are self-explanatory but some serve special purposes:

Service Contract Information

Table 3-15: Service Contracts - Special default master data entry fields

Entry Field	Description
Service Name:	You have to give each service a unique name.

Entry Field	Description
Related to:	You should assign the contract either to a contact or to an account already stored at your CRM.
Tracking Unit:	Select the usage unit. Please note that the CRM administrator can change the content of the pick list.
Total Units:	This is the total of the tracking units which are part of the contract.
Used Units:	Here you can enter how many units has been already part of the service you provided. Please note that based on this number the percentage value for the contract completion at the Service Contract List view will be computed.

Click on **[Save]** in order to transfer your service contract information to the CRM system. After saving, the detail view of your service opens. You will see the master data you have just entered.

3.7 Asset Management

If you deliver goods which require special follow up services, the CRM's asset module provides the necessary tracking functions related to serial numbers or other product attributes. In order to enter a new asset, click on the **[Add Asset]** button at the **[Asset]** menu. A new window will open as shown in Figure 3-27.

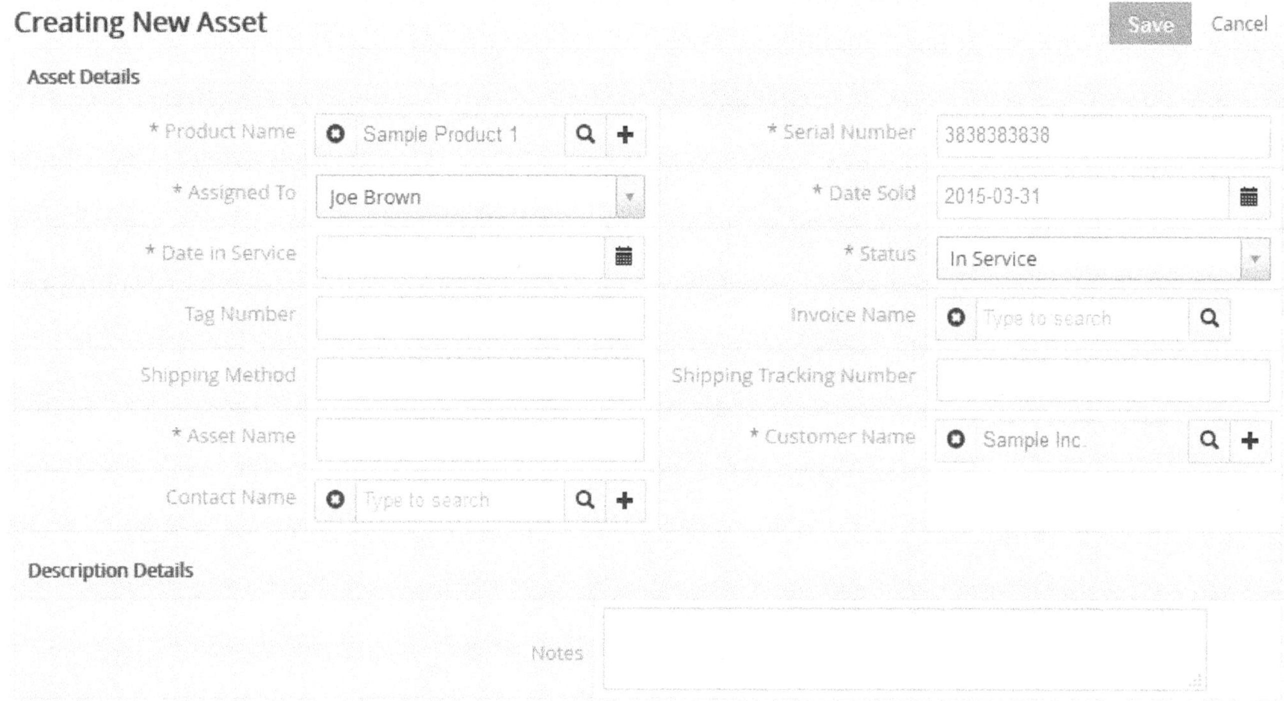

Figure 3-27: Asset Create View

The offered standard fields are self-explanatory but some have a special purpose.

Asset Details

Table 3-16: Assets - Special default master data entry fields

Entry Field	Description
Product Name:	You have to provide the related product name. This information is needed to link assets and product information.
Asset No:	The asset number is generated by the CRM automatically based on the CRM administrator's setup. Refer to Section 5.5.5 for more information.
Serial Number:	Provide the serial number of this product.
Asset Name:	You can use this field for asset classifications.
Date in Service	You have to provide a date which sets the start of service.

Click on **[Save]** in order to transfer your asset information to the CRM system.

3.8 Project Management

This menu is only available if you have installed the appropriate optional CRM package. The CRM can support you in your project management by providing all the information necessary to plan, organize and managing resources for a successful completion of specific project goals and objectives. The CRM's project management is focused on collecting project specific data and it is related to milestones and tasks. It will help you to keep track of the progress project and its related sales process.

3.8.1 Projects

In order to create a new project, click on the **[Add Project]** button at the **[Projects]** menu. A new window will open as shown in Figure 3-28. The offered standard fields are self-explanatory but some have a special purpose.

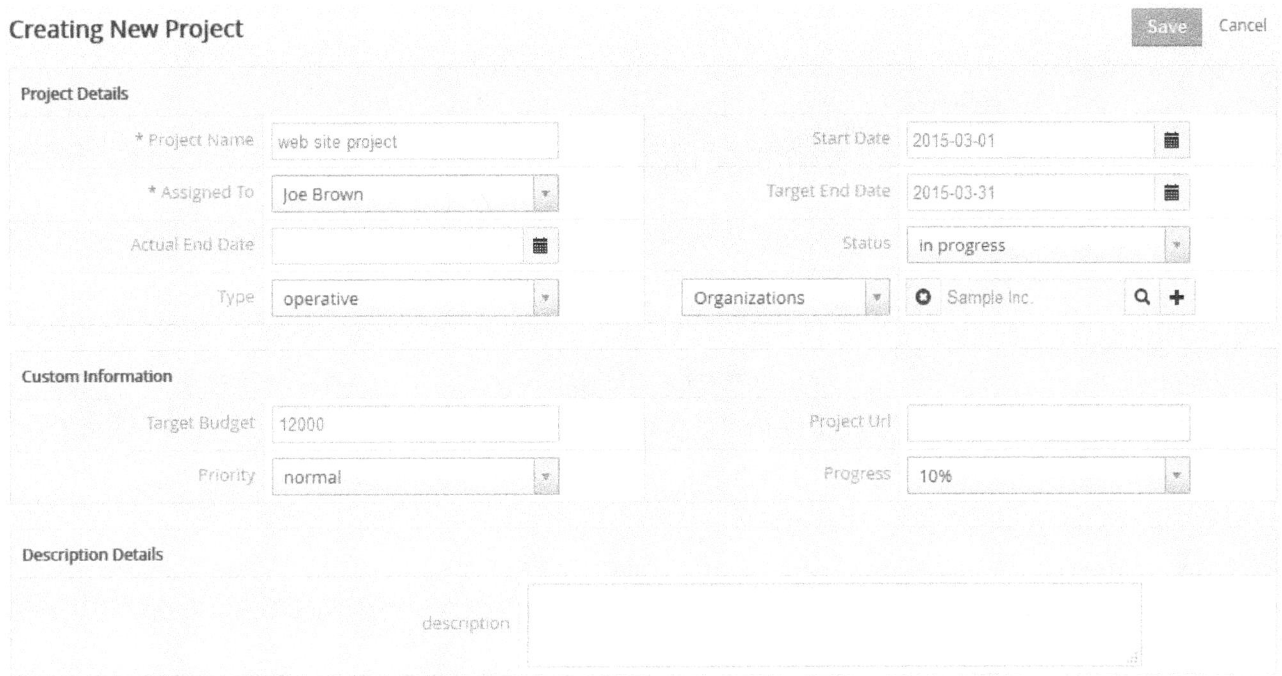

Figure 3-28: Project Create View

Project Details

Table 3-17: Projects - Special default master data entry fields

Entry Field	Description
Project Name:	You have to give each project a unique name.
Project No:	The project number is automatically generated by the CRM based on the CRM administrator's setup. Refer to section 5.5.5 for more information.
Start and Target End Date:	Set the time period for the project. This will be considered in the graphical presentation.

Entry Field	Description
Progress:	Set the project progress in %.

Click on **[Save]** in order to transfer your project information to the CRM system. After saving, the detail view of your project opens. You will see the master data you have just entered as well as the related data from project related milestones, tasks and documents as shown in Figure 3-29.

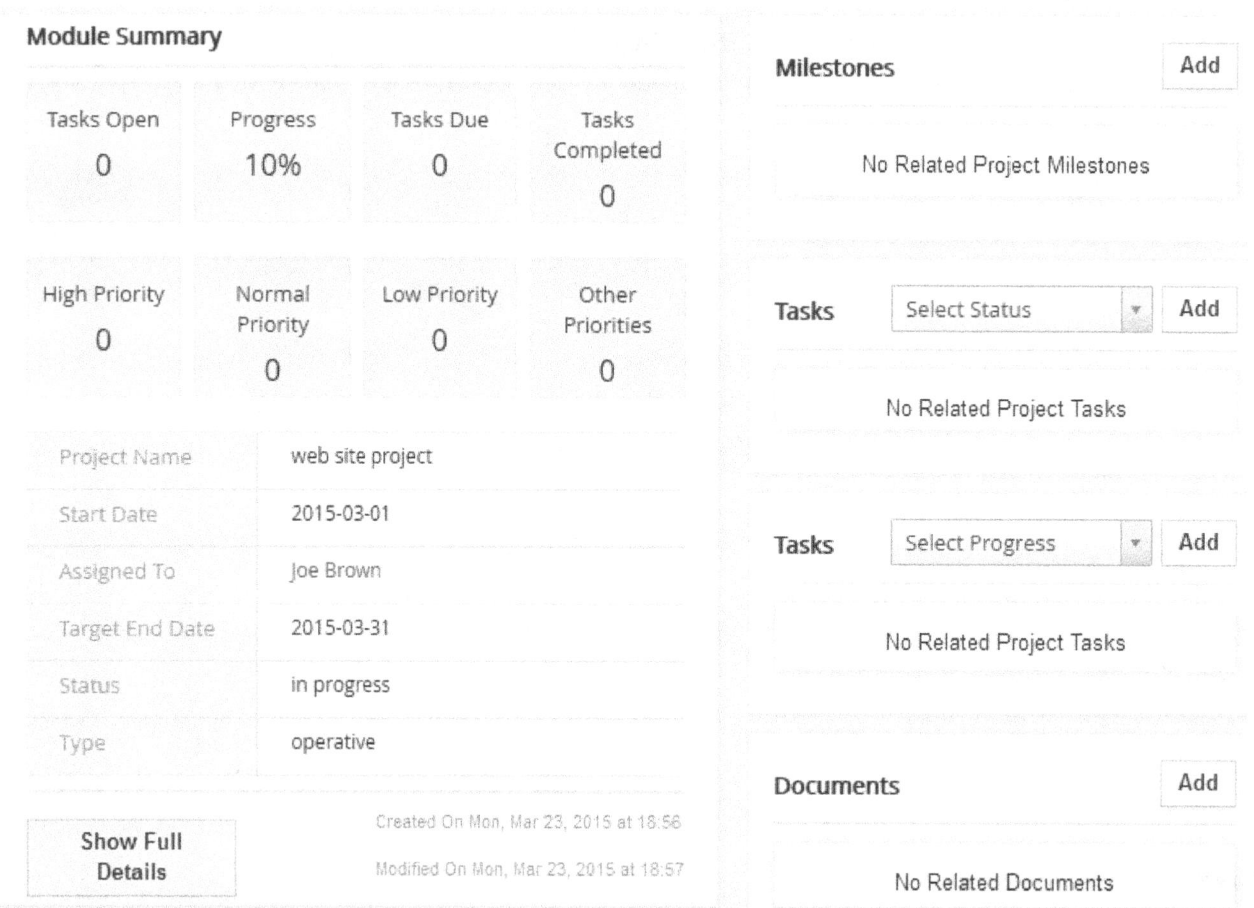

Figure 3-29: Project Detail View

In the next sections it is explained how you can create related project information.

3.8.2 Project Milestones

Each project has milestones. The simplest case is having milestones with a start and an end date only. In the case of larger projects, however, it is recommended that additional milestones be set in order to keep track of the project's development, the resources involved and to compare the project's progress with the original plan.

In order to add milestones to your project, open a project's detail view and click on the Milestone related **[Add]** button. You will be presented with the milestone menu as illustrated in Figure 3-30.

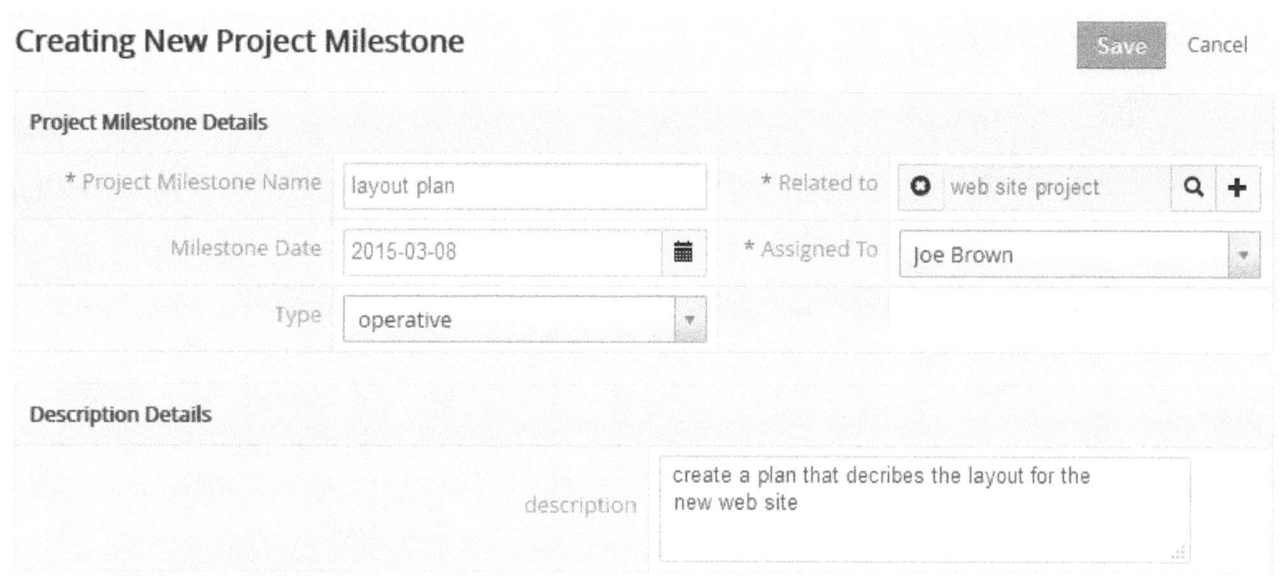

Figure 3-30: Project Milestone Create View

Table 3-18: Milestone - Special default master data entry fields

Entry Field	Description
Milestone Name:	You have to give each milestone a unique name.
Milestone No:	The milestone number is automatically generated by the CRM based on the CRM administrator's setup. Refer to Section 5.5.5 for more information.
Related To:	This field links a milestone with a specific project.
Milestone Date:	This is the day on which the milestone becomes valid.

Click on **[Save]** in order to transfer your milestone information to the CRM system. After saving, the detail view of your milestone opens. You can add additional milestones as needed or move back to the project.

3.8.3 Project Tasks

Everything that needs to be done for a project should get collected in separate project tasks. Click on the **[Add Task]** button at a project's detail view in order to enter a new task as shown in Figure 3-31. All fields are self-explanatory.

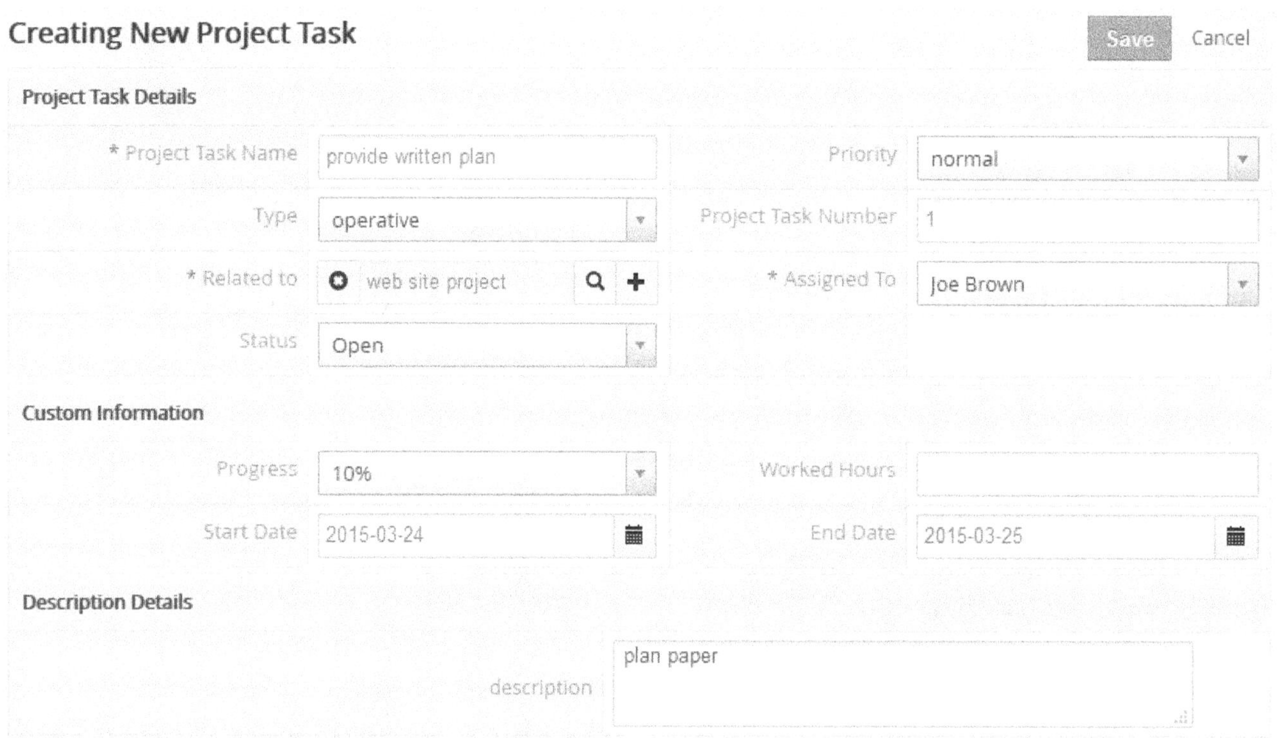

Figure 3-31: Project Task Create View

Click on **[Save]** in order to transfer your project task information to the CRM system. After saving, the detail view of your task opens. You will see the master data you have just entered. You can add further tasks or go back to the project's detail view.

4 Working with the CRM System

This chapter explains how to work efficiently with the CRM system. It includes usage hints relating to the sales process from a leads stage to after-sales services.

4.1 General Remarks

4.1.1 Tag Cloud

Tag Clouds are designed to improve the usability of the CRM. They help you categorize CRM entries based on the user's judgment or rating, independent from categories set by the CRM system.

Tag Clouds are based on the assumption that humans tend to pool objects subjectively or for other values. Such a pooling is in fact a new categorization of data stored in the CRM system. In order to meet such a requirement for categorization, the **Tag Clouds** provide users the capability to build categories which are not limited to a single CRM module. These categories are independent from the categories defined in the master data of each CRM entry, usually the pick list entries.

For instance, a sales person can consider a meeting, a customer and a service request as **important**. These new categories or groups can be defined freely. You can use any terms such as **important, Proposal, Berlin, private** or **Spring**. You can add such a term with the **[Tag this Record]** button to any CRM entry that can be considered to be in the same category.

Tags are always single words! Do not use sentences or combined expressions.

A tag cloud entry is shown in Figure 4-1. The more CRM entries are labeled with the same tag, the bigger this tag will be displayed in the tag cloud.

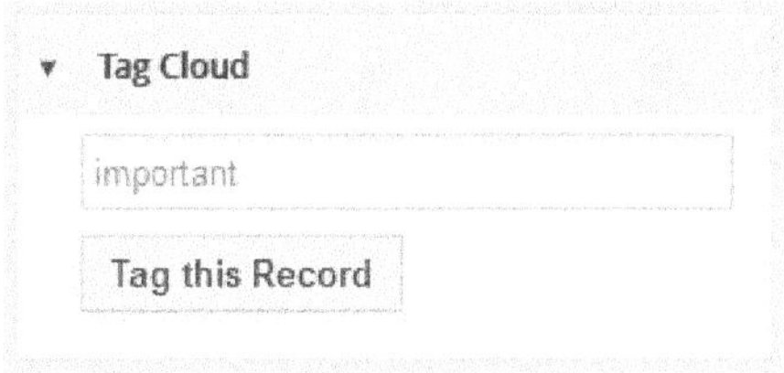

Figure 4-1: Tag Cloud

Use the term listed in the **Tag Cloud** to find all CRM entries which have the same tag. On the homepage, all the tags will be displayed if you add the **Tag Cloud Widget. Tags** for a corresponding entity will only be displayed in the detail view. On clicking on the tag, in both the detail view and the homepage, the entities tagged with the corresponding tag will be displayed. You can delete the tag from the detail view tag cloud. You can also delete a tag by deleting the entity.

Tag Cloud entries are assigned to the user who made the entry. You can't share **Tag Cloud** entries with other users.

4.1.2 Duplicates Handling

Data duplicates are dangerous for the CRM usage. Imagine you have entered for instance the same contact twice and one of your sales staff is using the first entry while the other sales representatives are working with the second entry.

Since both contact entries do not relate to each other, your sales staff does not get valid information about the contact's history or future plans.

In order to prevent duplicates, in some cases the CRM checks for already-existing entries. For instance, if you try to enter a new account with an account name which already exist you will receive a warning message.

However, the CRM software can't avoid duplicates completely. For instance, you can get duplicates from data imports or synchronization (e.g. Outlook Plug-in) or by users with different access privileges.

In order to remove duplicates, the CRM provides a function in the list views to find duplicates for leads, contacts, accounts, potentials, products, tickets and vendors. The duplicate search is also available for custom views.

Click on the **[Action]** button and **[Find Duplicates]** on top of a list view to open the Merging Criteria Selection menu as illustrated in Figure 4-2.

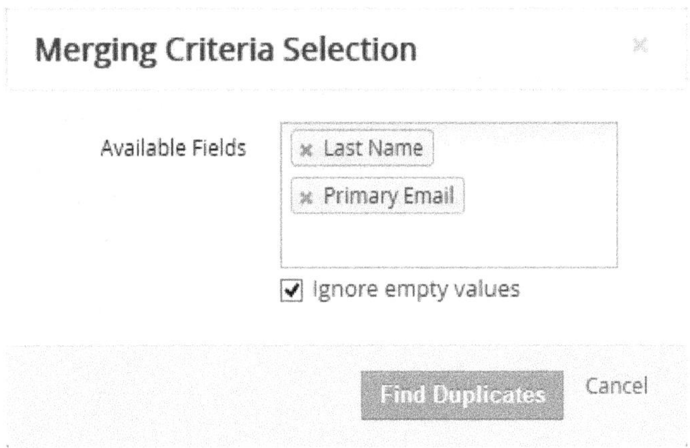

Figure 4-2: Merging Criteria Selection Menu

In the available fields field you can select the master data fields you want to use for identifying duplicates. If you uncheck the "Ignore empty values" field also empty values will be identified as duplicates. You can use this for instance if you want to find entries where a content is missing.

Hit the **[Find Duplicates]** button in order to start the search.

The opening menu displays all records which are identified as duplicates and allows you to delete entries or to merge the content of duplicate records as shown in Figure 4-3.

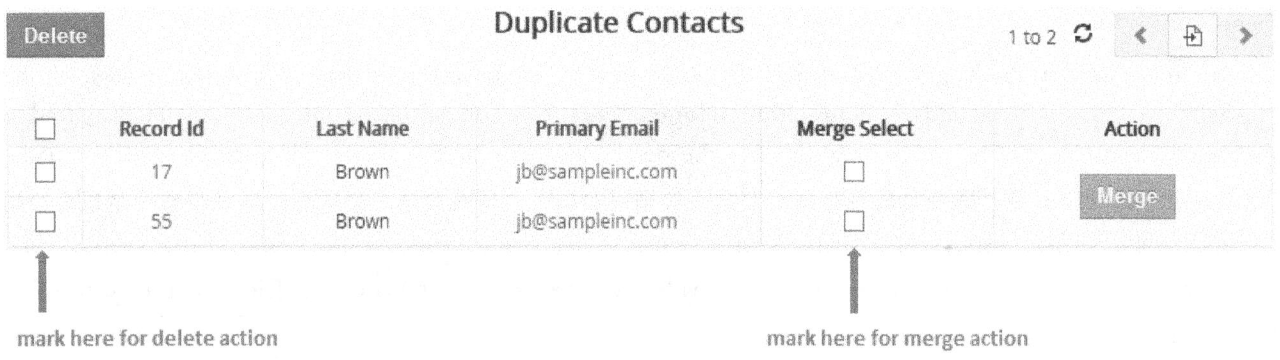

Figure 4-3: Duplicate Search Result

You can delete a duplicate record directly, but in most cases it is better to carry out a merge. If you delete a record, all related entries are going loose the relationship to this record. In the case of a merge, the related information does not get lost but moved to the remaining record. You can merge up to 3 records.

Select the records you want to merge and hit the **[Merge]** button. A new window pops up which displays the content of the records as shown in Figure 4-4.

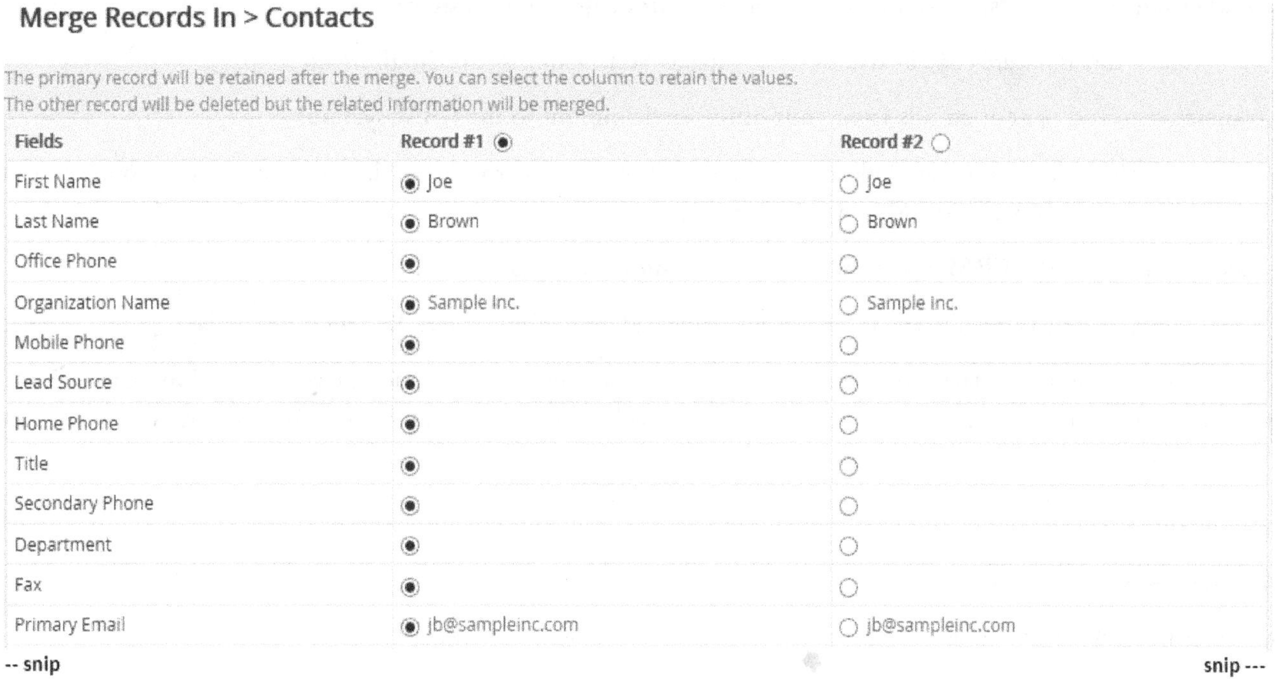

Merge Records In > Contacts

The primary record will be retained after the merge. You can select the column to retain the values.
The other record will be deleted but the related information will be merged.

Fields	Record #1 ◉	Record #2 ○
First Name	◉ Joe	○ Joe
Last Name	◉ Brown	○ Brown
Office Phone	◉	○
Organization Name	◉ Sample Inc.	○ Sample Inc.
Mobile Phone	◉	○
Lead Source	◉	○
Home Phone	◉	○
Title	◉	○
Secondary Phone	◉	○
Department	◉	○
Fax	◉	○
Primary Email	◉ jb@sampleinc.com	○ jb@sampleinc.com

-- snip snip ---

Figure 4-4: Duplicate Merge and Removal

First select the record you want to keep as the primary record. Then mark the content of the fields you want to add to the primary record. You should direct your special attention to the **Assigned To** field. If you merge pick list entries which are only accessible by users with administration privileges these entries will be displayed as "not accessible" to users which do not have administration privileges. Hit the **[Merge]** button in order to finish the process. Your primary record will be updated and the other records will be moved to the recycle bin.

4.1.3 Calendar Reminder Popup

Each user can activate an activity reminder function by setting a reminder interval on the **[My Preferences]** menu, as explained in section 2.3.1. If activated, a popup browser window will be displayed every time an activity is due. The popup window displays the time, status, and subject of an activity. It offers you the option to postpone or to close a reminder message. If postponed, the message will pop-up again after the next reminder interval until it is closed.

4.1.4 Send and Receive Emails

The CRM system offers a variety of methods for including email in your work with your customers, co-workers, suppliers and other contacts.

You can

send emails to contacts, accounts or leads directly from the CRM system:

These functions are explained in the following as **Send Emails** and **Email Mass Mailing**.

transfer received or sent emails from your office environment to the CRM system:

The CRM comes with an Outlook plug-in as well as a Thunderbird/Mozilla email client extension. You can use these additional programs on your computer.

receive emails in the CRM system from personal mail accounts

The functions offered to receive emails are explained in the following as **Receiving Emails**

In the case of outgoing emails, you have to configure a common mail server access as explained in Section 5.5.2. You will also need to configure the access to the individual receiving mail servers for each individual user as explained later in this section.

4.1.4.1 Send Emails

If you want to use the CRM system for outgoing emails you have the following options:

1. You can create an email from the detail view of one of your leads, contacts or accounts. By using the contact details already stored on your CRM system, the system makes sure that the sent emails will be stored in reference to the existing contact entries.
2. You can create an email directly at the **Mail Manager** menu. In this case, the reference to a contact has to be made manually. See Section 4.1.4.4 for a detailed description of this menu.

Before you can send any email, make sure that your outgoing mail server has been configured as explained in Section 5.5.2. One server is used for all CRM users.

The CRM provides the senders information for an email based on the logged in CRM user's information available on the **My Preferences** menu, see section 2.3.1. There you provide the name and the sender's email address and you can also create an email signature which is attached to an outgoing email automatically.

Assuming that you are in a detail view of a contact, you then click on the **[Send Email]** button in order to compose a new email. In a popup window it opens the **Compose Email** menu as illustrated in Figure 4-5. In case the popup window is not displayed, check your browser's settings and allow popups from the CRM URL.

The information required for an email are the same as you know it from other email clients. However, due to the CRM's mass mailing capacities, the **To** field is processed differently.

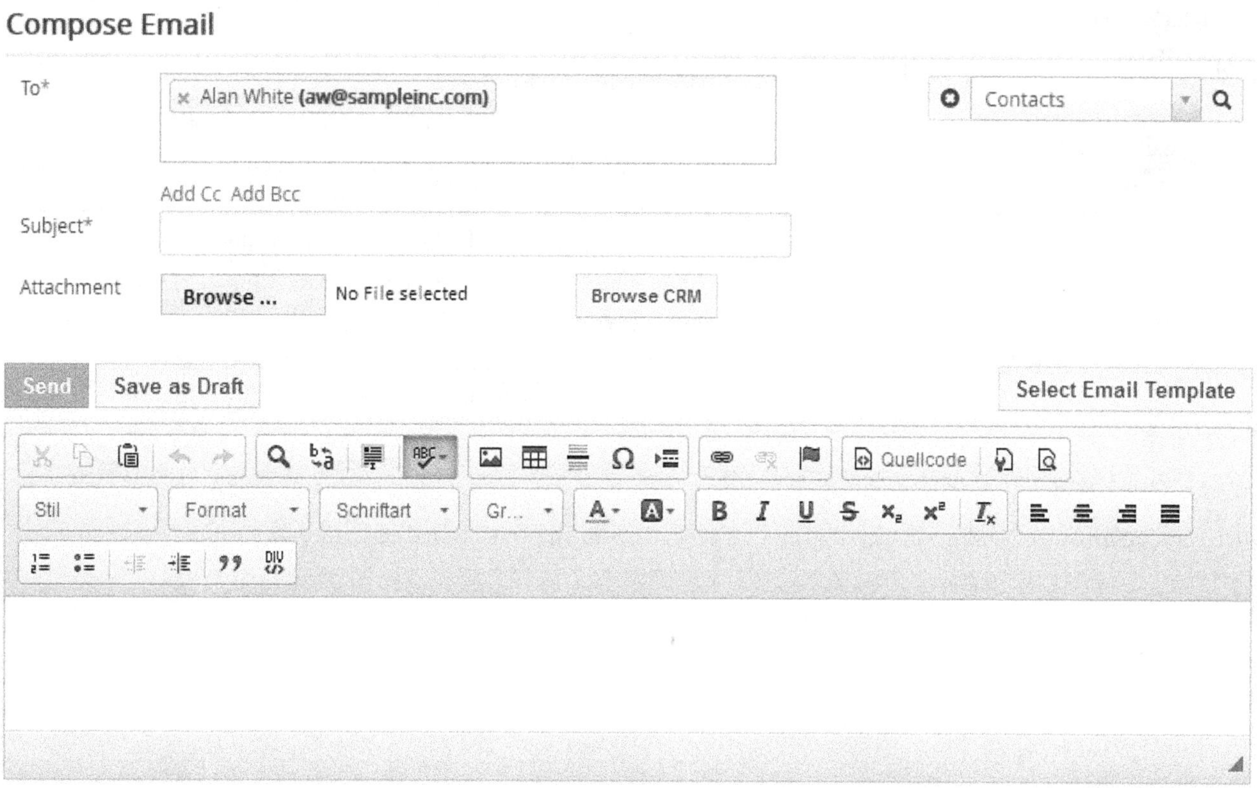

Figure 4-5: Compose Email Menu

The following tables explain the entry fields and buttons of this menu.

Table 4-1: Compose Emails – Special fields

Field	Description
To:	If you create an email from a detail view, this field is already filled. For additional recipients you can type in the name or email addresses of the recipients in order to trigger a search. **Each recipient will receive a separate email and will not be able to see other recipients if you have sent the email to multiple recipients.**
Add CC:	CC stands for Carbon Copy. The recipient entered here will receive a copy of the sent email. The CC recipient will be also visible to all recipients listed in the To field.
Add BCC:	BCC stands for Blind Carbon Copy. This means the same as CC, however the recipients entered here will be not visible for the other email recipients.
Browse for Attachment	You can add attachments to your email. The maximum size of the attachments is limited by the CRM settings and can be changed by the administrator and CRM server operator.
Browse CRM	This button opens a new popup window which allows you to select an attachment from the documents stored in the CRM.

Table 4-2: Compose Email - Special buttons

Field	Description
Select Email Template:	The CRM offers you to work with email templates. These templates must be designed and stored in the CRM system as explained in section 4.1.5.
Send:	The email will be sent. A signature will be added automatically if defined in the My Preferences menu. The email will be assigned to the sending user. A copy of the email will be automatically sent by the CRM system to the assigned user.
Save	You can save this email without sending it. The email will be stored and be listed in the recipient's detail view.

Once sent, an email is listed in the detail view of a related contact, as illustrated in Figure 4-6.

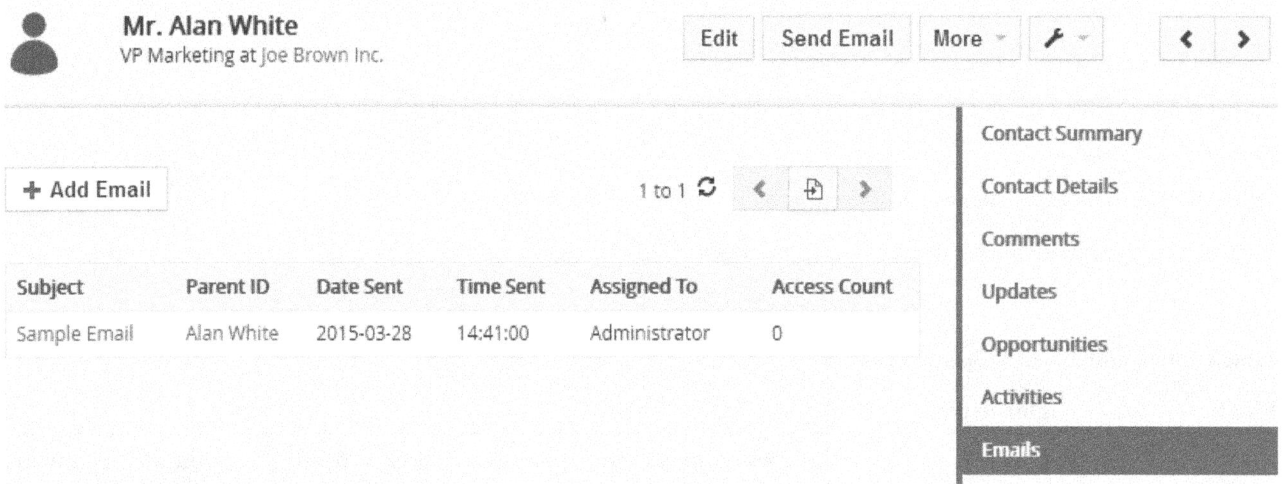

Figure 4-6: Email Listing in Detail View

Please take note the special **Access Count** column. Here you can see whether your email was read by the receiver. This information is made available in the form of a little 1x1 pixel image sent together with every email. If a receiver opens the email with an email client that is set to allow the images in emails to be displayed, a backlink to the CRM gets triggered and the display of the little image will be counted in the CRM.

4.1.4.2 Mass Emails

You can send a common email from the CRM to several people at the same time. You can use this function for mass mailings to your customers or to other contacts saved in your CRM system. For mass mailing it is recommended to create an email from the list view or to use the campaign modules as explained in Section 3.4.

For a list view operation, you should use the following steps:

- Create a customs view of your leads, contacts, or accounts. Use the filter operations to select the desired contacts. It is also recommended to add to the filter conditions that only data sets with email addresses are to be selected.

- Save the custom view.
- Display the custom view. Select the contacts which are going to receive your mass mailing. Click on the **[Actions] -> [Send Email]** button in order to call the Compose Email menu as shown in Figure 4-5 in the previous section.
- Compose and send your email.

As already mentioned in the previous section, each recipient will receive a separate email and does not see the other recipients as listed in the **To** field.

A reference to a copy of the sent emails will be stored at each individual contact and is displayed at the detail view.

The same process applies for a campaign based mass mailing.

4.1.4.3 Receive Emails

If you generally receive your email at your office, you can use the Outlook Plug-in or the Thunderbird extension to transfer selected emails to the contacts stored in your CRM system.

In addition to that, you also have the possibility to receive emails directly in the CRM by the **Mail Manager** as explained in the next section.

All emails are received in unprotected mode. That means that the CRM does not check for any viruses or other threats frequently transmitted by email. Even though these threats can not cause any damage to the CRM, it is advised to take protective action at the receiving mail server, especially if you plan to download email content to your computer.

4.1.4.4 Mail Manager

Mail Manager Setup

Before you can receive any email via your CRM, you must have configured the access to your receiving email server. When you go to the **Mail Manager** menu the very first time a menu is displayed which ask you for your mail server access data. You do not need administrative privileges for this operation.

You can select one of the pre-defined mail account types or use **Others** to get the full set of options, as illustrated in Figure 4-7. You have to enter all configuration data as described in the following table. Please ask your email service provider for the necessary access information.

Entry Field	Description
Mail Server Name or IP:	You must enter the address of your email server. You can use a name or the IP address but you have to use a server which supports the IMAP protocol.
User Name & Password:	You must enter the user name and the password you use in order to access the email server.
Protocol:	In the current CRM version, only IMAP is supported and fully functional as your email protocol. The POP protocol can become available in the future.

Entry Field	Description
SSL Options:	You must select whether you want encrypted communication with your email server.
Certificate Validations:	If you use encryption to access the mail server, you should select whether the certificate is validated.
Refresh Timeout:	You can change the refresh rate on which the CRM looks for new mails.

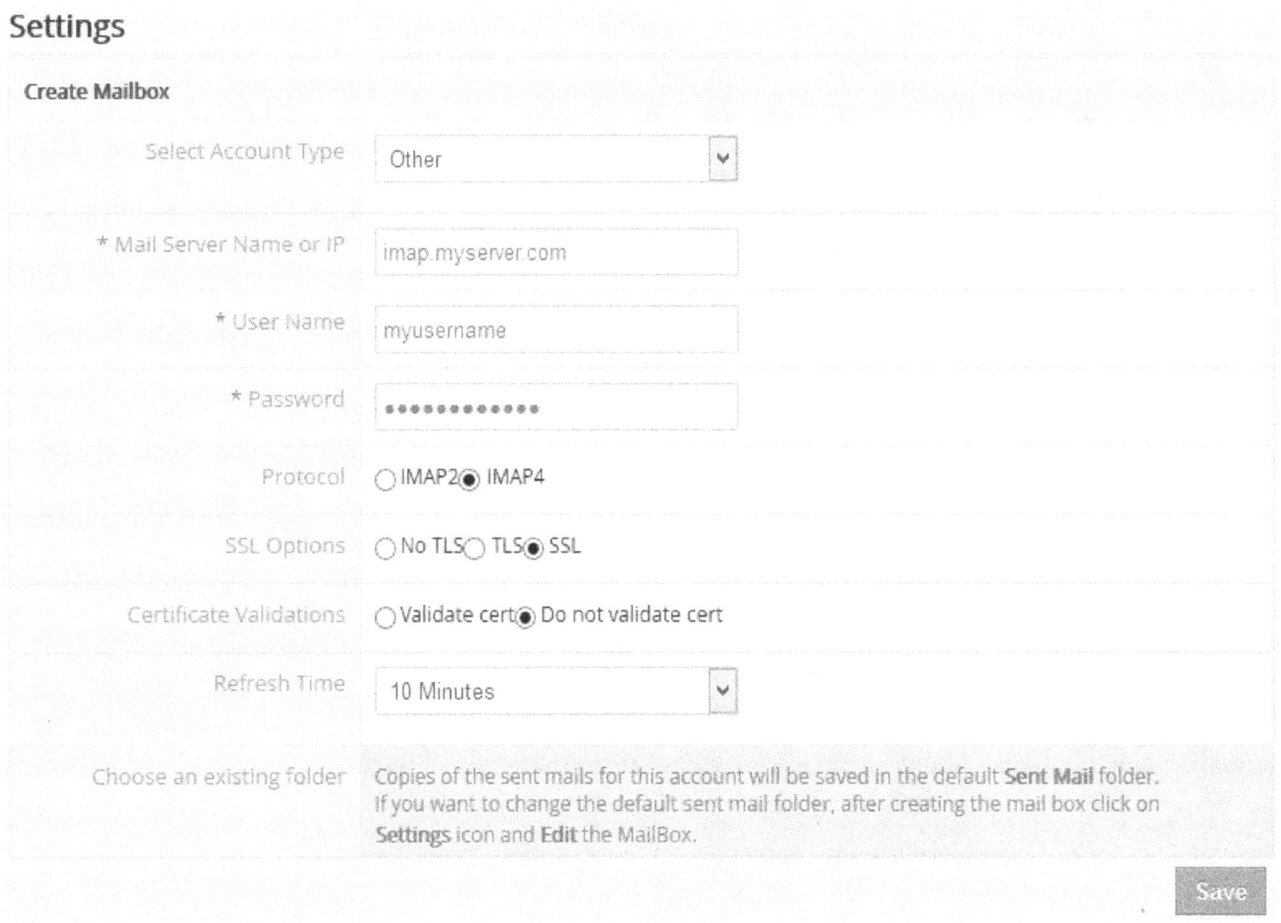

Settings

Create Mailbox

Select Account Type	Other
* Mail Server Name or IP	imap.myserver.com
* User Name	myusername
* Password	●●●●●●●●●●●●
Protocol	○ IMAP2 ◉ IMAP4
SSL Options	○ No TLS ○ TLS ◉ SSL
Certificate Validations	○ Validate cert ◉ Do not validate cert
Refresh Time	10 Minutes
Choose an existing folder	Copies of the sent mails for this account will be saved in the default **Sent Mail** folder. If you want to change the default sent mail folder, after creating the mail box click on **Settings** icon and **Edit** the MailBox.

Save

Figure 4-7: Mail Manager - Server Settings Menu

Click on **[Save]** in order to configure the mail function in the CRM system and to connect to your mail server and to download the headlines of existing mails from your server's INBOX.

Email Display

The CRM looks up the server's folders and all folders will become organized for display in the same way as they are organized at your email server as illustrated in Figure 4-8. If you want to modify the folders name or the amount of folders displayed, you have to do this on your email server.

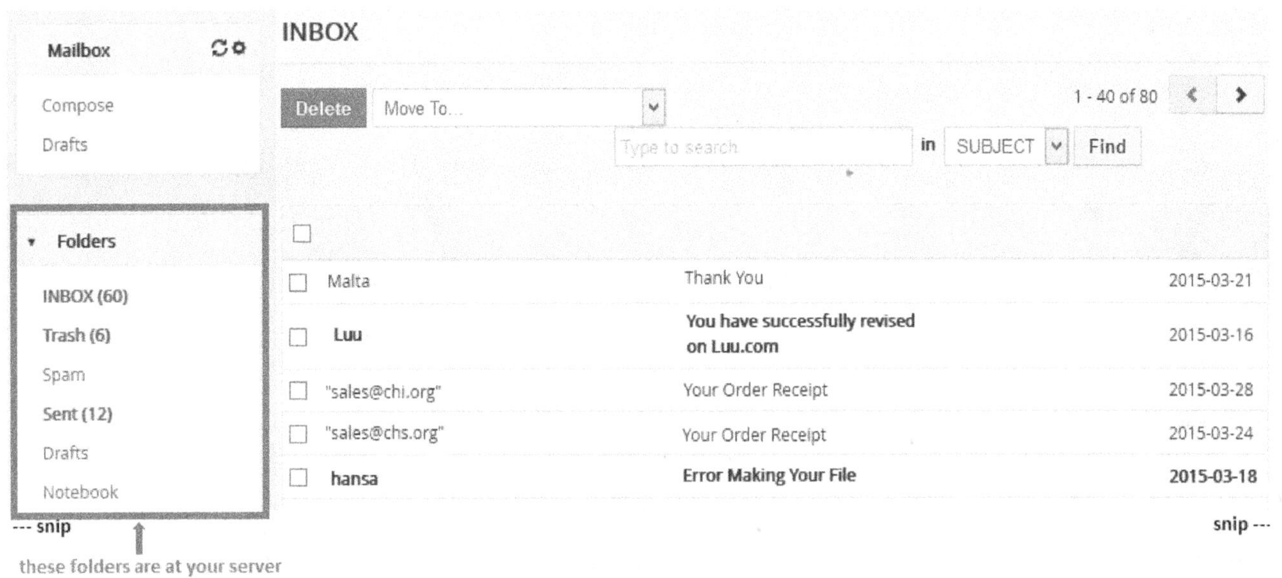

Figure 4-8: Mail Manager - Email List

The mail manager displays only the email headers. As soon you click on an email, the CRM downloads the content from the server and stores the email in the CRM system for future reference and in order to speed up the process.

Following the mail download, the CRM looks up the sender's email address. If a CRM entry is found the reference is shown in the detail view as illustrated in the example of Figure 4-9.

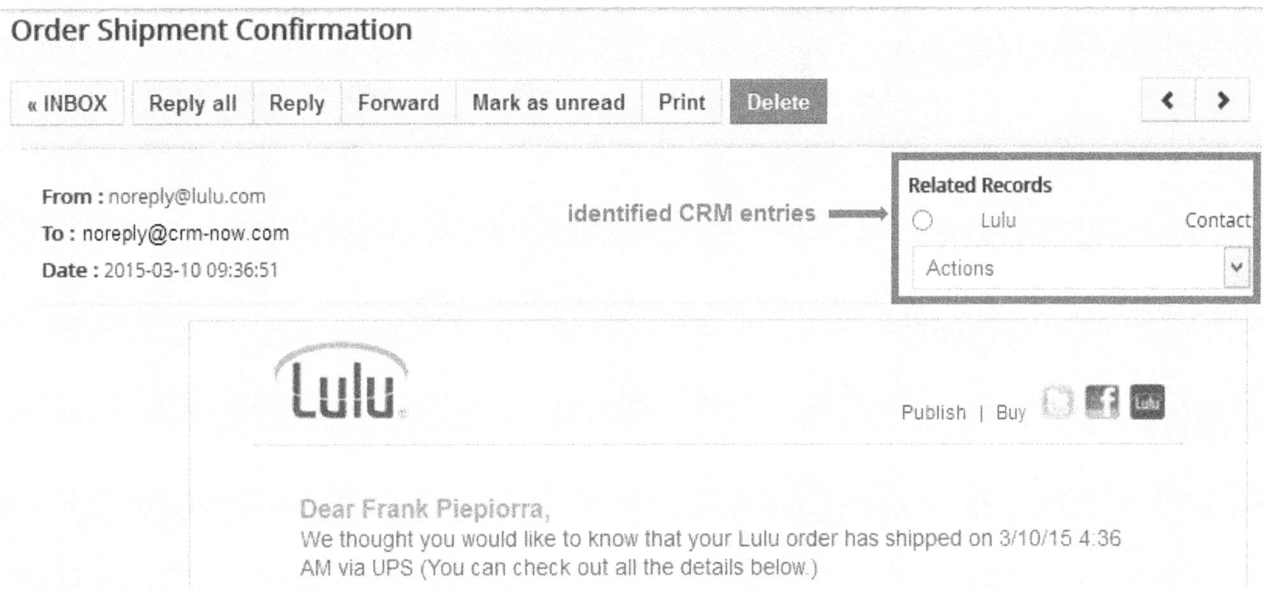

Figure 4-9: Mail Manager - Detail View

You can decide that you want to relate this email to one or more of your existing CRM entries. Depending on the identification result: the actions drop down list differs, as illustrated in Figure 4-10.

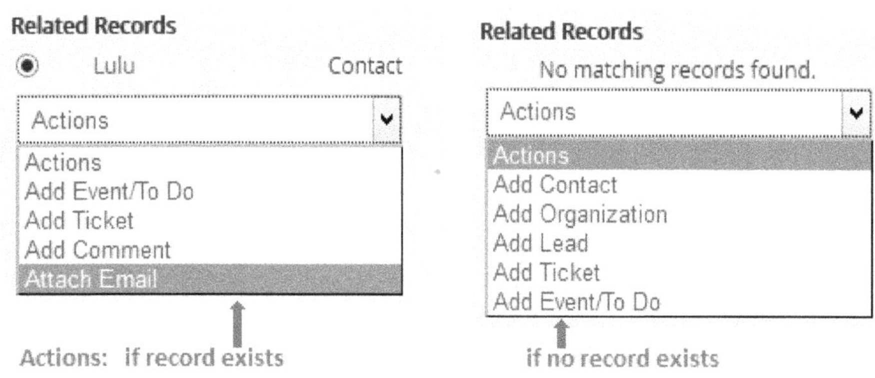

Figure 4-10: Mail Manager - Actions Menu

If the email sender was not found, you can add a new CRM record as contact, organization, lead or ticket by means of an action. While you create such an entry, the email is attached to this new record automatically.

Be aware, that every email you open gets stored in the CRM, irrespective of whether you set a reference or not.

All the buttons at the top of Figure 4-9 provide functions as you know them from other email clients.

4.1.5 Email Templates

If you frequently use the CRM for sending standard emails, it is most helpful to have such emails available as templates. In order to see any existing email template list, please click on the **[Email Templates]** menu.

The CRM comes with templates as listed in Figure 4-11. You can modify existing templates or create an unlimited number of new templates. Please note that there are public and private templates. Public templates are available to all CRM users. Private templates are only provided to particular users.

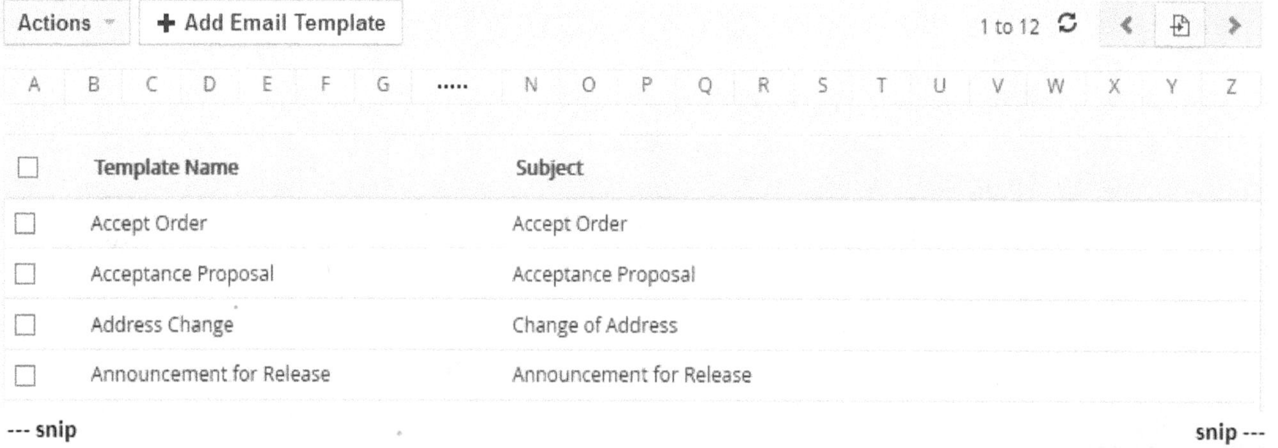

Figure 4-11: Email Templates List View

Click on a templates name in order to see the detail view of an existing template. An example is shown in Figure 4-12.

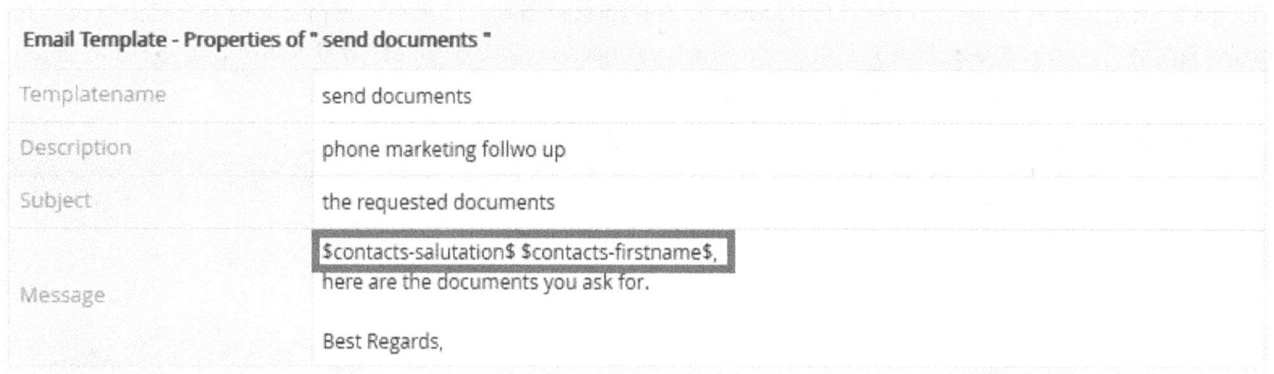

Figure 4-12: Email Template Detail View

Please note that the merge field values highlighted in this figure. Merge field values are used to dynamically include CRM data into the email.

In this example email, the merge field values **$contacts-salutation$** and **$contacts-firstname$** represent the salutation and the first name of a contact.

You can include dynamic merge fields into your template on the edit view as shown in Figure 4-13.

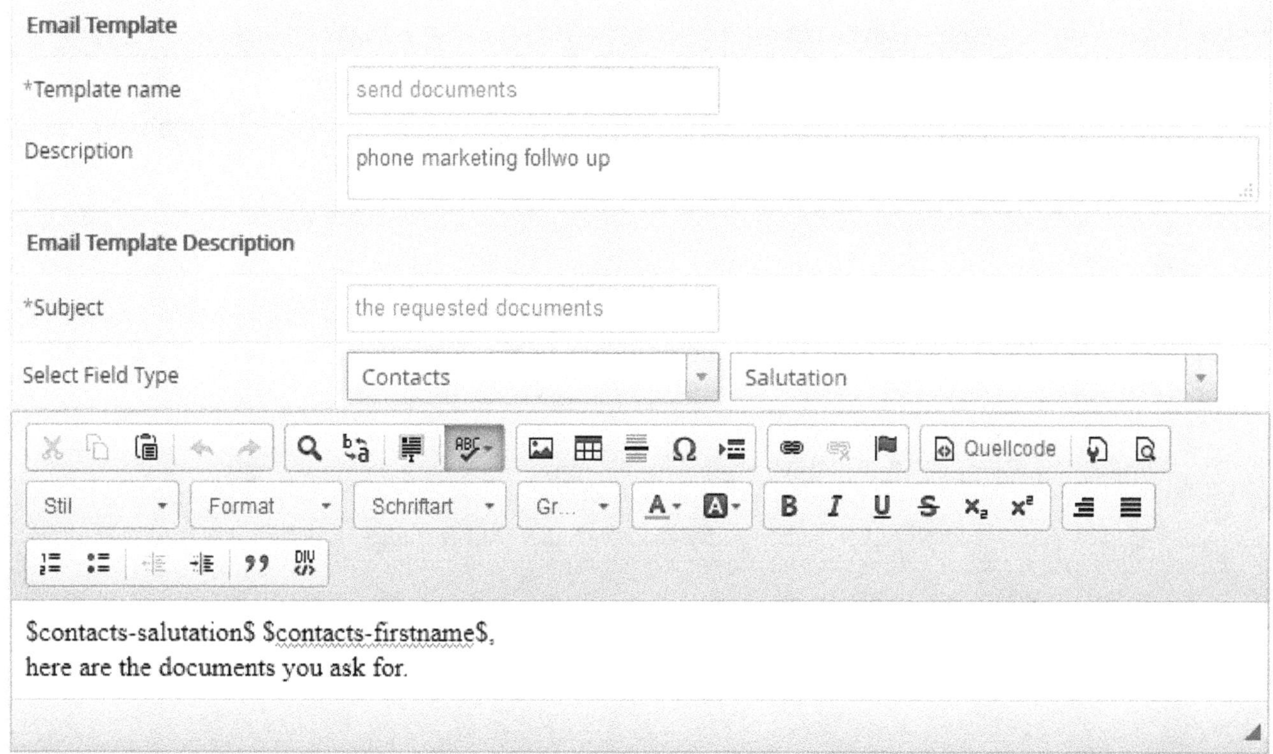

Figure 4-13: Email Template Edit View

The **Select Field Type** drop downs support you in defining the merge field syntax. You can include standards as well as custom fields as merge fields. As soon as you select a field from you master data, it is included in the mails body at the current cursor position.

You shall not mix field codes from different modules. For instance, if you use **"Contact Fields"** as shown in the figure, you shall not add **"Account Fields"** to this template.

All emails are going to be sent in the HTML format. You can use the HTML editor functions in order to design a special layout. You can also include HTML code which has been created by an external editor. But please be careful and test your results, not all HTML code options are supported.

Click on **[Save]** in order to transfer your template to the CRM system.

4.2 Sales process procedures

The CRM system has been designed in order to support you in all phases of a sales cycle, from a lead to closed business, by integrating all relevant data. Sales processes are defined differently in each enterprise, yet there are common principles for the work flow, which the CRM system represents. The most common scenario for goods or services with longer sales cycles could be:

- When you have your first contact with a prospective customer, create a lead. At this particular point in time you cannot know whether this contact has serious interest in the goods or services your company offers. You can collect as much information about this contact as possible.
- Sales activities will now start with this lead. You can schedule meetings, make phone calls or send emails until you know whether a business opportunity exists or not.
- If you find out that this lead does not go any further, you can set the lead status to lost and forget about it. If this lead looks promising for your business, you can convert it to a sales opportunity.
- During conversion, the CRM will create a sales opportunity, an account and a contact, using the data you have already collected. The lead will be deleted.
- Now you can start working with the opportunity. You indicate the progress by setting different sales stages.

The contact and account information relating to your sales opportunity are the foundation for you and your co-workers to build a relationship with a potential customer. You can use this information for scheduling and controlling activities, distributing tasks, forecasting revenues, understanding the purchase decision process of a customer, and much more besides.

4.2.1 Lead Conversion

A lead represents the first stage of the sales process and is therefore the starting point for many activities.

In the sales process, opportunities are the logical successors to leads. Therefore, you should create a sales opportunity from a lead and transfer all information available for the lead to this sales opportunity.

In order to create a sales opportunity based on an existing lead, you must switch to the lead detail view. On top of the lead's details you can hit the **[Convert Lead]** button as shown in Figure 4-14.

Figure 4-14: Call Lead Conversion

A new popup window will open as shown in Figure 4-15. In this menu you can give the CRM instructions of how to perform the lead conversion.

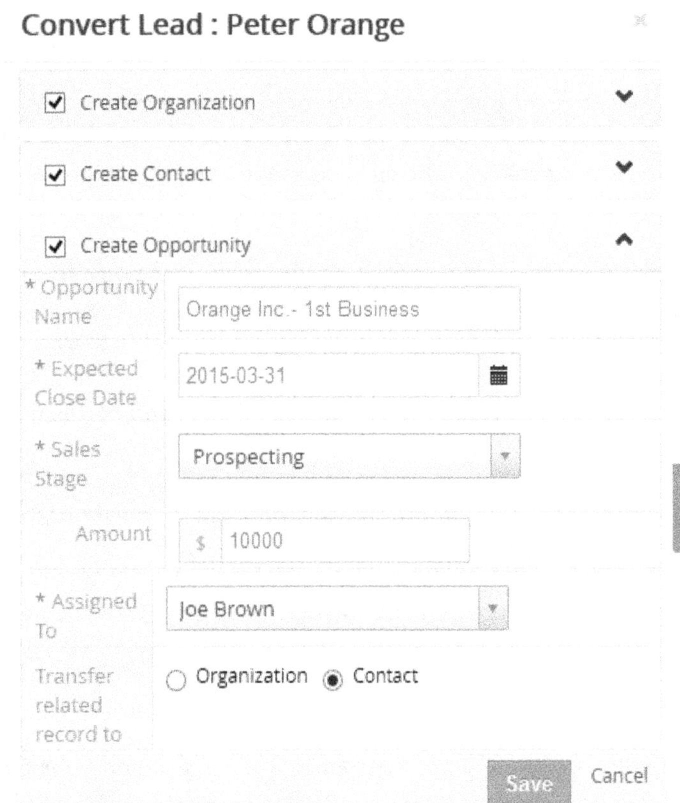

Figure 4-15: Lead Conversion Settings

Field Entry	Description
Create Organization / Contact:	Here you can choose whether you would like that CRM creates these records. The related fields are already filled by the corresponding lead data.
Create Opportunity:	If you do not tick this check box, only new entries for an account and for a contact will be created by the conversion. There will be no opportunity related to it. You can use this function if you intend to store account and contact information which is not related to an upcoming business but important enough to be listed in the CRM system.
Opportunity Name:	Here you must enter a unique name for your new potential. It makes sense to include the account name in order to maintain a clear name structure.
Expected Close Date:	Pick a likely closing date for this potential business. You will be able to change it later if necessary. This is particularly useful information for creating forecasts.
Amount:	You can enter the potential amount of the business you expect. You can change this later. This amount can be used for forecasts.
Sales Stage:	You must enter a sales stage for the opportunity. The available sales stages can be defined and changed by the CRM administrator.

Field Entry	Description
Assigned To:	Here you can choose a new owner for the converted data.
Transfer Related Records To:	Here you decide where the content of the related lists of the corresponding lead will be located after the conversion.

With the lead conversion, the following operations are performed automatically by the CRM system:

- Creation of a new opportunity.
- Creation of new entries for **Accounts** and **Contacts** and linking both to each other and to the new potential.
- Transfer of all data from the lead to the new created entries.
- Assignment of the created account, contact and potential to the selected user or group.
- Deletion of the lead.

Please note that a lead conversion cannot get reversed.

4.2.2 Working with Support

The CRM system offers extensive functionality to maintain the valuable customer relationships after sales. Why should you use the support functions?

- Above all, the support functions help you to collect and sort customer requests, inquiries and disturbances, problems etc. related to sold goods or services.
- The support functions, keep CRM users and customers informed about the status reached with respect to the response to customer's messages.
- Support staff has a very effective tool to keep track of customer complaints or requirements relating to customers or products or both.
- Sales staff and management can get a quick overview of support activities related to customers or products or both.
- CRM users or customers have convenient access to frequently asked questions (FAQ). This can help your company keep the service requests low and maintain standard procedures in responding to customer's requests.

The CRM's capabilities to provide FAQ as well as tickets are extended by the **Customer Portal** functions as explained in the **Customer Portal** manual.

4.2.2.1 Tickets

In CRM terminology, tickets are any kind of customer service request as they occur after sales. However, this menu can also serve as a storage place for your company tasks which do not have a due date or which are not yet planned.

In order to create a new ticket, click on the **[Add Ticket]** button at the **[Trouble Tickets]** menu and it opens the create view as shown in Figure 4-16.

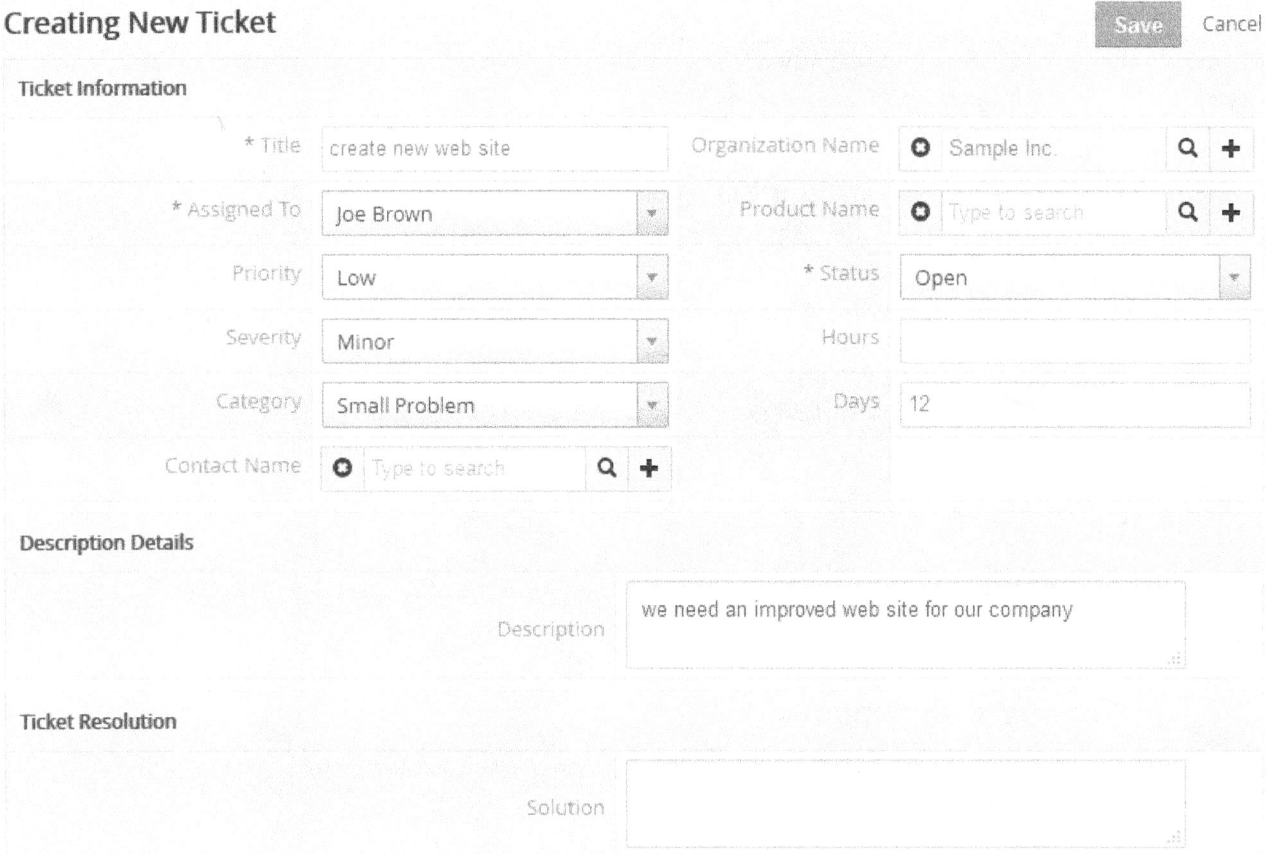

Figure 4-16: Ticket Create View

You should enter as much information as possible. Use the **Priority, Severity** and **Category** to weight the ticket. Your CRM system administrator can add additional custom field to your tickets or change the contents of the drop down lists.

Table 4-3: Trouble Tickets - Special default entry fields

Entry Field	Description
Assigned To:	You can assign the ticket to a person who is listed as CRM user or to a user group. This user or group will be responsible for answering to the customer's request and will be notified by email about any changes to a ticket.
Title:	You should give each ticket a unique name.
Contacts, Accounts:	If you link a ticket to a specific contact or account and you have not disabled the automatic email distribution for such a contact or account an email will be send to the related contact automatically any time the content of the ticket changes.
Hours, Days:	If you link the ticket to a service contract, this information is used to calculate the content of the total amount of time in the field at the related service contract.

As CRM administrator please look up the workflows for tickets, see Section 5.5.8, and make sure that the automatic email distribution for a ticket is set to your needs. If the workflows were not changed after the CRM installation, each and every ticket entry will generate an email message that automatically goes to the ticket owner as well as to the related contacts or accounts!

4.2.2.2 FAQ

The CRM system can help you create a **Frequently Ask Question** (FAQ) list. FAQ refers to questions and answers, all supposed to be frequently asked in some context, and pertaining to a particular issue. You can use this, for instance,

- as a knowledge base with which to inform your customers about your products, services or procedures,
- for your employees to inform on internal business procedures,
- for your service staff to discuss procedures for helping customers, and much more besides.

You can reach the FAQ list by means of the **[FAQ]** menu. Click on the **[Add FAQ]** button on top of the list in order to enter a new FAQ. In Figure 4-17 you see the screen for a new FAQ entry.

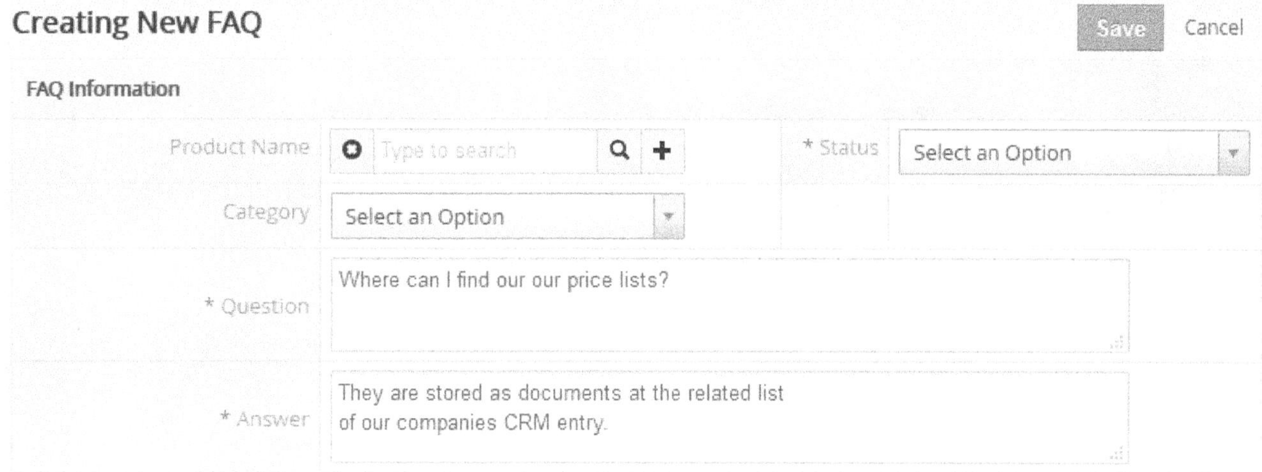

Figure 4-17: FAQ Edit View

You can enter a question and an answer. In addition, you can

- link this entry to a product or service your company offers,
- assign a category for this entry,
- set a status for the entry.

FAQ with the status **Published** will be visible at the customer portal.

Click on **[Save]** in order to transfer your FAQ to the CRM system.

4.2.3 Reporting and Analysis

The CRM provides you with several possibilities for evaluating your data according to criteria you have selected beforehand. You can summarize the data stored in the CRM using reports. There is a set of predefined reports available with which you can customize to your requirements.

You can get a report for almost any data you have stored in your CRM at the **[Reports]** menu as shown in Figure 4-18.

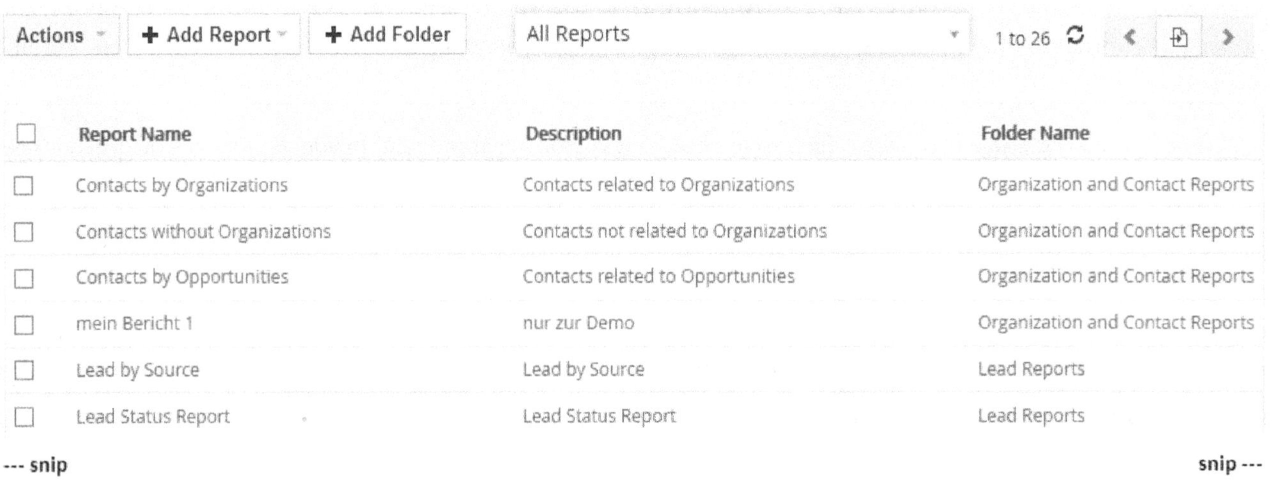

Figure 4-18: Reports List View

You can click on any report on the list in order to see the result of a report operation.

The following explains how to modify reports by using the **Contacts by Organization** report. Click on the report name. The report gets exercised and the report results are shown, as displayed in Figure 4-19.

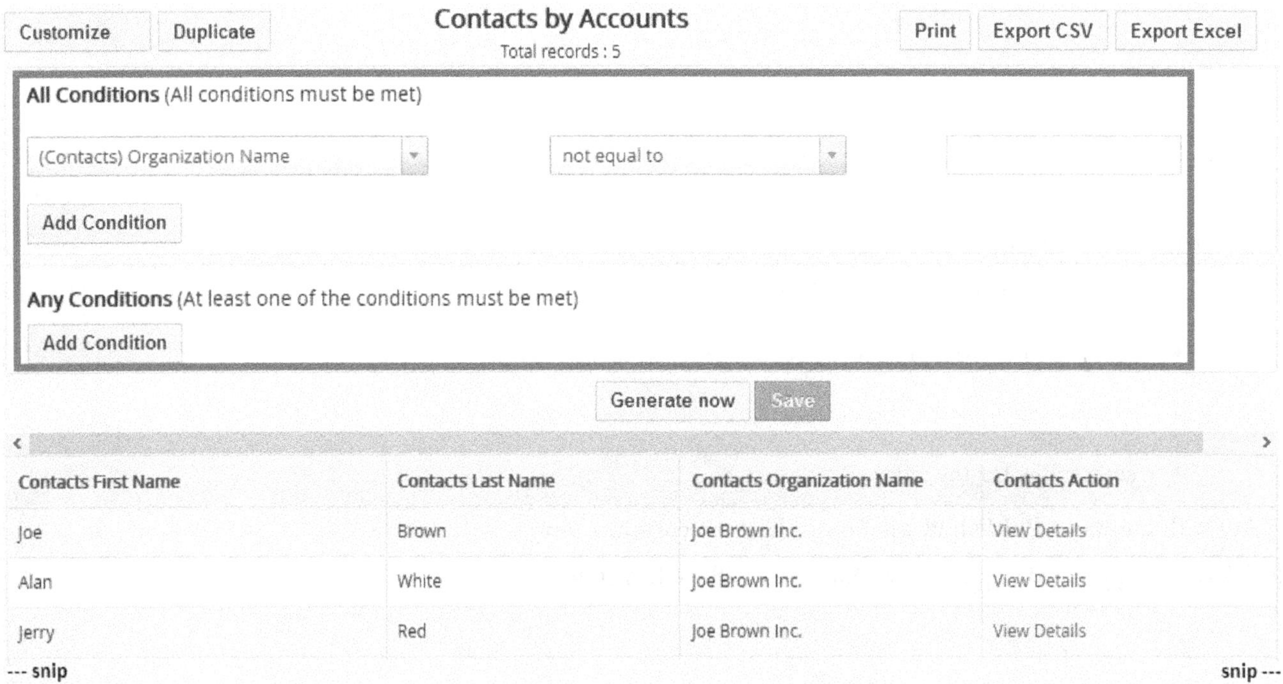

Figure 4-19: Report Filter and Results

The upper part of the screen show the filters used, the lower part displays the report results. You can modify the filter criteria and generate the report once again by considering the following:

Permanent Report Changes

If you click on the **[Save]** button the current filter settings is saved and available the next time when you open this report.

Temporary Report Changes

If you click on the **[Generate Now]** button the current filter settings are used to generate a new report, but not to save it. When you exercise the report again later, the original filter setting is used.

Filters are based on logical AND or OR operators. The following Figure 4-20 illustrates an example.

Figure 4-20: Filter Example

A report with this filter will show all contacts in the sample report which are related to *Joe Brown Inc.* **OR** *Beauty Inc.*

Create a new report

The adaptation of a report can be a relatively complex task when many criteria and filters should be used. It is therefore appropriate to start with a simple report. Additional criteria should be gradually introduced and systematically reviewed until the desired content is displayed in a report.

For a report you can decide on the following report parameters:

- Which modules are selected for a report?
- Do you want to include calculations with groupings?
- What data are requested for each report column?
- How are the data filtered?
- Which CRM user has access to the report?
- Do you want to receive reports by email automatically?

In order to create a new report, click on the **[Add Report]** button at the report list view. The menu for the first step opens as shown in Figure 4-21.

First you are asked for a unique report name. Then you have to select a report folder.

You must select the primary module for your report. Based on this selection, the content of the filed Select Related Modules is generated. You should add a report description for future references.

You can schedule an automatic report by making the Schedule Reports check box. This report will generate an email at the set date and time to the listed CRM users.

Click on the **[Next]** button to go to the second step as illustrated in Figure 4-22.

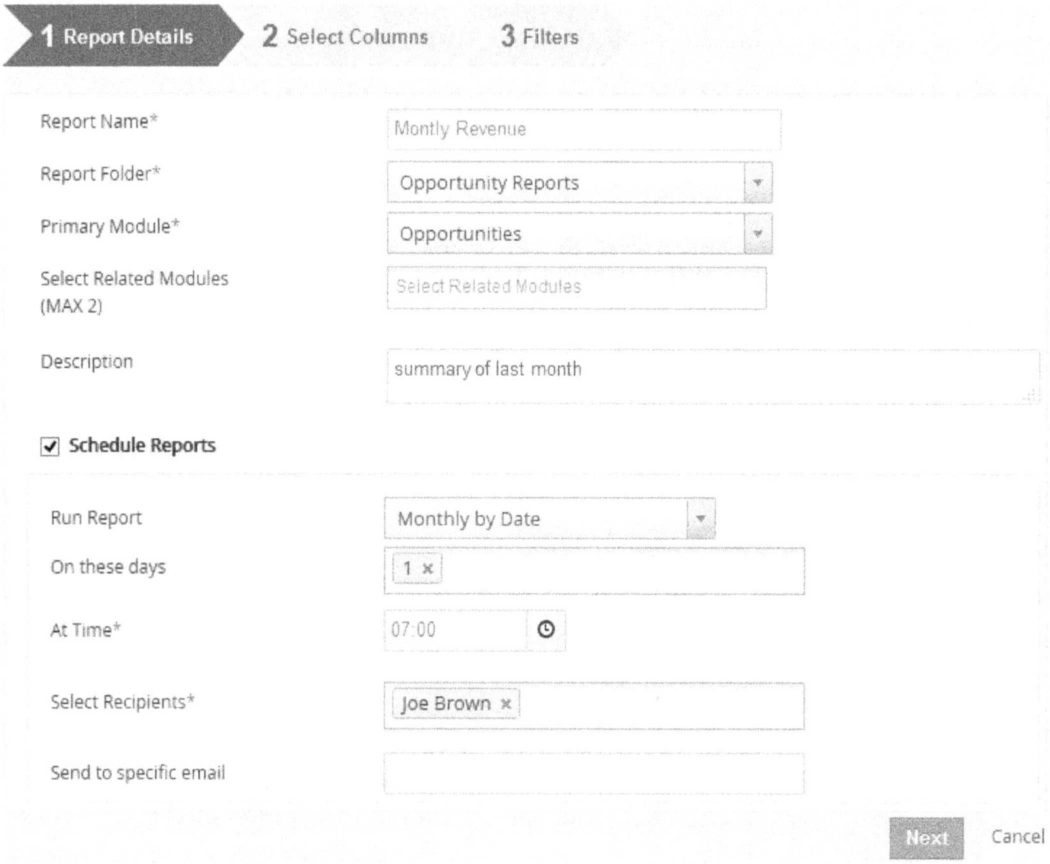

Figure 4-21: Report Creation Step 1

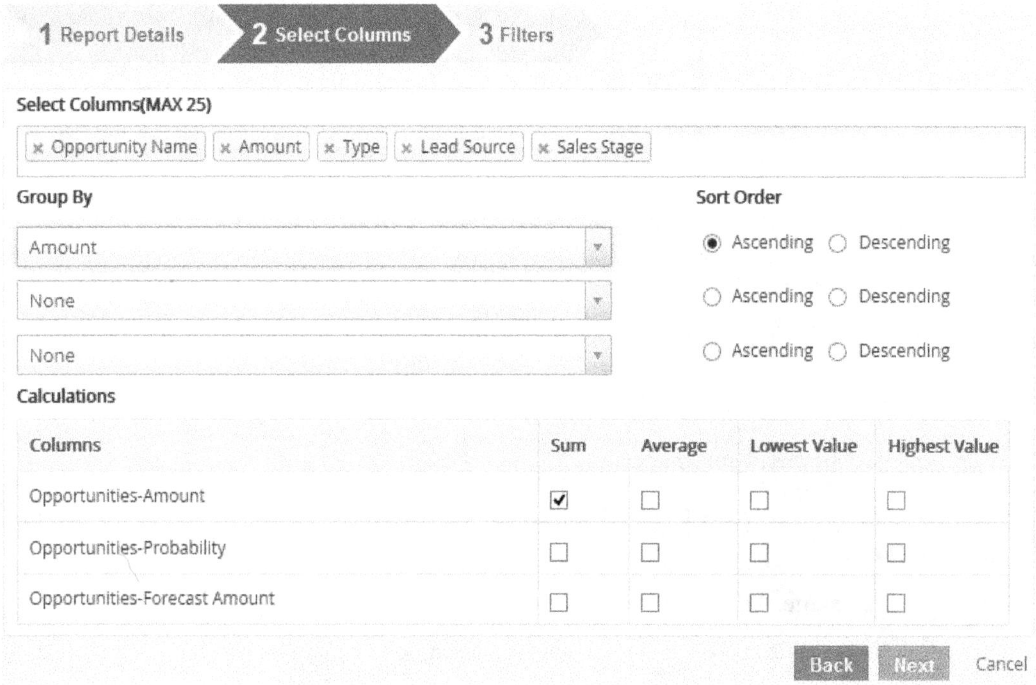

Figure 4-22: Report Creation Step 2

Based on your selection for the primary and related modules at the first step, the fields available for the reports are selected by the CRM system and displayed in the **Select Columns** field.

Select the fields for the columns you want to have in the report. In case one of your fields is a number or currency field, you can add a calculation.

At step 3 you add a filter to your report. Click on the **[Generate Report]** button in order to run and to show your new report.

Then you

- can see the report on your screen,
- can export the report as PDF or Excel file, and
- print the report, and
- make a duplicate as a copy.

Customized Report Folders

In order to create your own report folder, click on the **[Add Folder]** button at the reports list view. In the new popup window, you can give this folder a name and a description. You could use this folder in order to store your own or modified reports. The new folder will be listed at the reports detail view. You can also move existing reports to the new folder by means of the **[Actions]->[Move Reports]** button.

4.2.4 Synchronizing CRM with Google™

The CRM has an extension module that connects with your Google account. With this can synchronize your calendar and contacts. If your CRM administrator has installed this extension module, your Google™ account was setup to provide an API and the Google™'s credentials were applied to your CRM, you can use the synchronization function as illustrated for contacts in Figure 4-23.

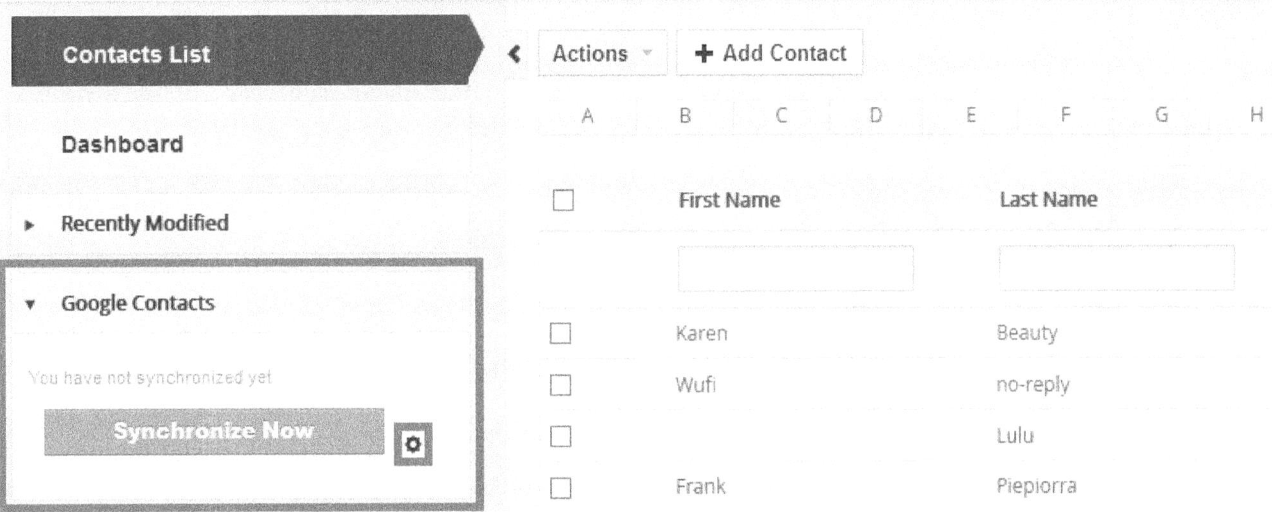

Figure 4-23: Google Contacts Synchronization

Click the setting icon ⚙ to configure your fields used by the Google™ connection.

When you make your synchronization the very first time follow these steps:

- Click the [Synchronize Now] button. You'll be redirected to start-up page.
- Sign into your gmail account.
- After signing in click on Grant Access.

This will start the synchronization process and may take a little while. As a result you will get a short report display.

The synchronization functions is also available at your calendar's list view.

Since the synchronization will transfer information from the CRM to Google™ it is recommended that you make yourself familiar with Google's Privacy Policy.

4.2.5 Synchronizing CRM with Office Environment

The CRM comes with a set of programs which enhance the functionality of your office environment by linking your desktop computer with the CRM system.

Thunderbird Extension

The **Thunderbird/Mozilla** email client is an **Open Source** program that runs with Windows, Mac and Linux operating systems. It allows you to send and receive emails and it also contains an address book. You can think of it as a free version of Outlook. With the help of the **Thunderbird Extension** program you can:

- send emails you have received, to the CRM and store them in reference to the appropriate contact
- send contact information from your email client to the CRM
- receive contact information from your CRM

Please consult the **Thunderbird** extension manual for further information.

Outlook Plug-in

Microsoft Outlook is very common in office environments. The Outlook plug-in enhances the functionality of Outlook and allows users to synchronize data between Outlook and the CRM system. In detail you can:

- transfer any email to the CRM system and attach it to the appropriate contact
- synchronize your calendar
- synchronize your contacts
- synchronize your notes
- synchronize your tasks

Please consult the Outlook Plug-in manual for further information. Note that there are additional and improved Outlook Plug-in versions available as community contributions from the vtiger Extension site.

5 Administrative Tasks

This chapter explains how the CRM system can be configured and managed by users with administrative privileges. It is very important that a CRM system administrator is capable of configuring the CRM in accordance with the intended purpose and the company's business processes. Any skilled CRM administrator knows that understanding how things work is as important as knowing how things are done. If you want to make yourself familiar with the so called **Role Based Security** as used by the CRM, please read Annex B first.

5.1 CRM Administration

This section explains the administrative tasks required to manage the CRM system. It describes:

- The user administration and role based security settings,
- The configuration of standard and custom entry fields,
- The templates and the configuration of other preset tools, and
- The basic system configuration.

For users with administration privileges, the CRM system displays an additional icon in the navigation bar as shown in Figure 5-1. By clicking on this button, a CRM configuration window will open which is only available to administrators.

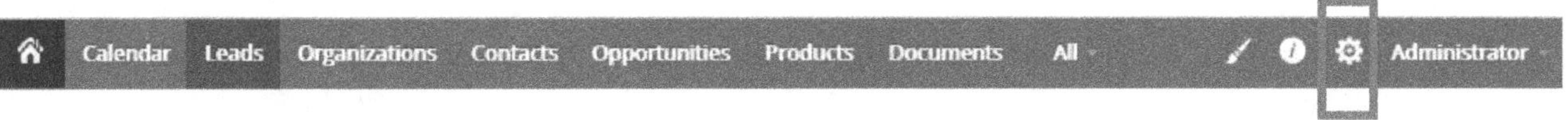

Figure 5-1: Additional Settings Icon

It is advised that only one or a very limited number of users receive administration privileges.

5.2 User Access & Control

The user management functions are the core of the security management of the CRM system. They control the access to the CRM system based on the user's privileges. The following sections will explain in detail the purpose of these functions and the features available. You can look up the simple organization setup examples in the appendix C for further reference.

User Administration Basics

From the organization point of view, user administration means administration of privileges. Essentially, the use of privileges depends on the number of users and the company structure. Few users in small enterprises have few requirements for privilege administration. In the case of an increasing number of users, the complexity of the relations between the users increases and usually develops the need to assign and administer privileges.

The CRM system offers a privilege system that is based on the following simple looking rules:

- Who can see what data?
- Who can change what data?

- Who can delete what data
- Who can create what data?

In the CRM system, **privilege assignment primarily means the withdrawal of privileges**. In the practical work with the CRM, this is most helpful and necessary as the following examples illustrate:

- A sales co-worker would certainly not be pleased, if somebody else changed the customer's data.
- Personal information remains confidential only if other co-workers are not allowed to see it.
- The company management does not want everybody to see the revenue figures.
- Only one person is allowed to change the product or service catalog.

Therefore, it is necessary that the user privilege assignment is truly based on business requirements as described in the following examples:

- Only the sales staff is allowed to change customer related data.
- The secretary does not get any access to revenue numbers.
- Only the product manager is allowed to change prices of services or goods offered by the company.
- Only the management is allowed to see all CRM data.
- Nobody is allowed to export any contacts.

Considering the current CRM capabilities when it comes to managing user privileges, you should configure your system in the following order:

Set the Default Organization Wide Privileges:

Organization Wide Privileges should be created first. They are the basis for the privilege assignment valid for all users.

Create Profiles:

Profiles are the basis for the privilege assignment to users. In any organization, there are usually different users with different tasks, like sales-person, service-technician, secretary or CRM administrator. Depending on the user type, the privileges for accessing data and using CRM modules and functions can be assigned.

Define Roles:

Roles are based on profiles and are linked with the hierarchical order of the company. They define the overall privileges for each individual user.

Define Groups:

Larger organizations can define groups in order to improve the usability of the CRM system.

Create Users:

The privileges of individual users are defined by roles. You have to assign a role to a user.

Single users do not need any privilege management. They have and need all privileges to access and to change all data stored in the CRM. Nevertheless, it is helpful to know the basics of privilege assignment. This might be needed if additional users will be needed in the future.

A small number of users, who jointly use the CRM system, should be familiar with the simple solutions offered by the privilege assignment. This includes particular:

- To prohibit that other CRM users see confidential data.
- To prohibit that other user can delete or modify data.

In a small organization, there is usually no pronounced hierarchy between co-workers. A complex privilege administration does not have to be developed. However, if it should be necessary to granulate the privileges more finely, you should begin with the use of different profiles. Each individual user can get its own profile with certain privileges.

In order to provide a larger number of users within an organization with different user privileges, a clear structure of the privilege assignment is necessary. It is sensible to connect user privileges with the position or tasks of each individual user or user groups. The current CRM version supports a finely grained privilege management.

5.2.1 Users

In order to create or to manage users, click on the **Users** menu to open the users list as shown in the following Figure 5-2.

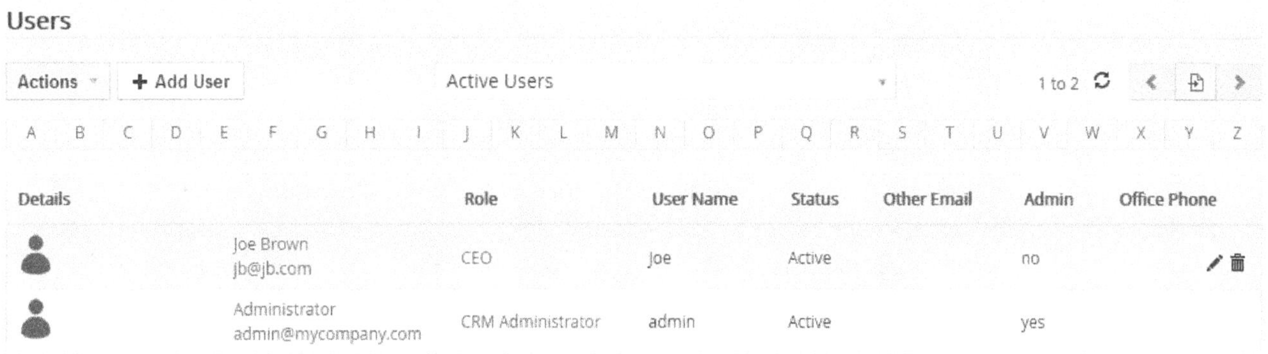

Users

Actions + Add User Active Users 1 to 2

A B C D E F G H I J K L M N O P Q R S T U V W X Y Z

Details		Role	User Name	Status	Other Email	Admin	Office Phone
	Joe Brown jb@jb.com	CEO	Joe	Active		no	
	Administrator admin@mycompany.com	CRM Administrator	admin	Active		yes	

Figure 5-2: User List View

This user list includes the user name, the role, the email address and other details for each individual active or inactive user. You can edit or delete users at this view.

If you want to delete a user, click on the icon at a user's row. This function deletes a CRM user but not the user's data. You will be asked who you want to assign as the new owner of the data. You cannot delete the admin user.

Click on the user's name in order to open the detail view of a particular user. This view includes user master data related to the login and to the user's role and other user information. User information is not visible to other users.

User privileges are not shown. These privileges are defined by the user profiles and organization-wide settings as it will be explained later.

Most of the fields in this menu are self-explanatory. The following tables explain special fields.

Table 5-1: User Login & Role - Default entry fields

Entry Field	Description
User Name:	Each user must get a unique and secure user name. Use at least 8 digits. User names once created cannot be changed by a user.
Admin Checkbox:	Check this box only if you want to create a user with administrator privileges, independent from the role.
Password:	Each user must receive a unique and secure password. User name and passwords have to be a combination of small or capital letters and numbers. It is recommended that you use at least 8 digits. The more digits you have, the more secure is the CRM access. The use of special characters such as "-","/" or umlaut (such as ä, ö, ü or ß) as they are used in other languages as well as names with empty spaces or apostrophe are not allowed. Every user has the privilege to change their own password.
First and Last Name:	Enter the user's name. The first name will be used for the welcome message. If you do not enter a first name, the last name will be used for the welcome message.
Role:	Roles define the privileges for a user. A role must be assigned to each individual user and must be created in advance.
Email:	Enter the email address of this user. This address will be used by the CRM for outgoing emails.
Status:	You can set a user as active or inactive. Inactive users are not allowed to login.
Default Calendar View:	Here you can set the default activity view and decide how activities are presented to the user on the homepage.
Default Lead View:	Here you can set the default lead view and decide how leads are presented to the user on the homepage.
Currency:	You can set the currency for this user here. Note that the currencies used by the CRM system are defined by means of the currency settings menu.

Table 5-2: More Information - Default entry fields

Entry Field	Description
Reports to:	You can select the supervisor of the user. Please note that this is only a reference and does not influence the security settings.

Signature:	You can enter an email signature. This signature will be automatically added to every email which is sent by the CRM. You can use HTML tags to give your signature a special format.
Internal Mail Composer:	This controls which mail program is used if you click on an email address. The default value is yes and this means that the CRM mail client is used. If you change it to no, the mail client installed on your computer is used for composing an email.

Table 5-3: Other User Settings Information

Entry Block	Description
Address Information	Enter the users address information.
User Photo	You can store a photo of this user. There are currently no further usages of such a photo integrated in the CRM.
User Advanced Options	The Access Key is provided by the CRM system for use by other applications in order to access CRM data and can't be changed.
Tag Cloud Display	Each user can decide whether a tag cloud will be shown at the user's CRM homepage.

If you create a new user, note that an automatic email will be sent to this user with the login data. It is advisable to inform a prospect user in advance about the purpose of this email.

It is recommended not to login with administrator privileges for daily CRM work.

5.2.2 Roles

The term **Roles** and the basics of role based security settings are explained in Annex B. Click on the **Roles** menu in order to open the hierarchical role view as shown in Figure 5-3.

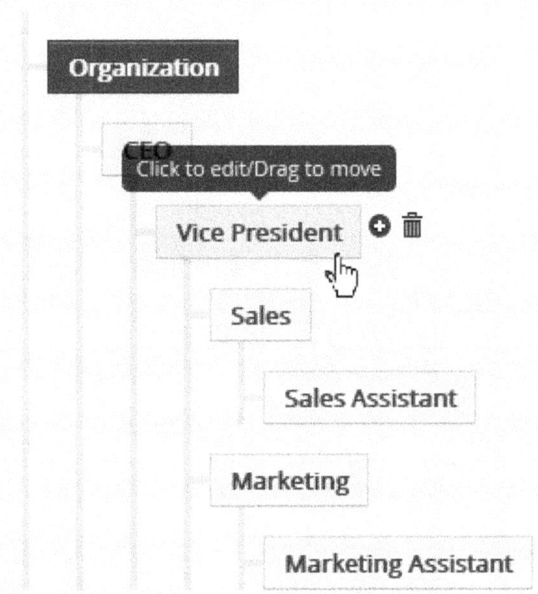

Figure 5-3: Roles - Company Hierarchy Example

On this menu you are given the opportunity to add, delete or move roles. Move your computer mouse pointer over a role entry. You will see a set of icons that allows you to perform these operations.

The ⊕ icon creates a new role which is located in the hierarchical order one level below an existing role.

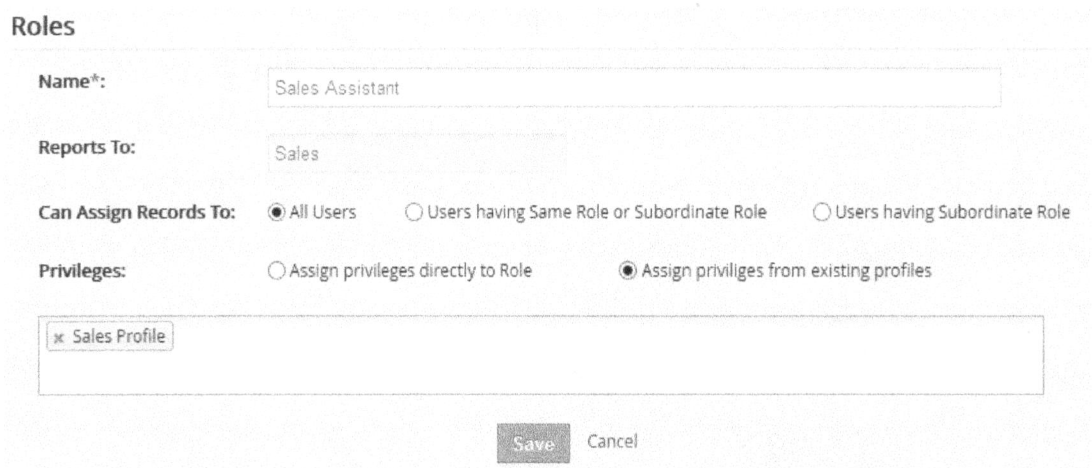

Figure 5-4: Roles Edit View

Figure 5-4 displays a sample for an edit view of an existing or new role. Each role has a unique name and privileges connected with it.

You have to first decide how the user's who are assigned to this particular role, are to be allowed to assign data records to other users. You subsequently assign the privileges. These can come from profiles or can be assigned directly.

Click on **[Save]** in order to transfer your settings to the CRM.

5.2.3 Profiles

All roles are based on profiles. With profiles you set the user privileges allowing data to be accessed, changed or deleted. The CRM system uses profiles in relation to the access privileges to modules and fields. Please note that the settings of the **Global Privileges** are always superior to the other privilege settings.

Click on the **Profiles** menu in order to open the list view of your profiles as shown in Figure 5-5. Here you see a list of all profiles that have been defined in your CRM system.

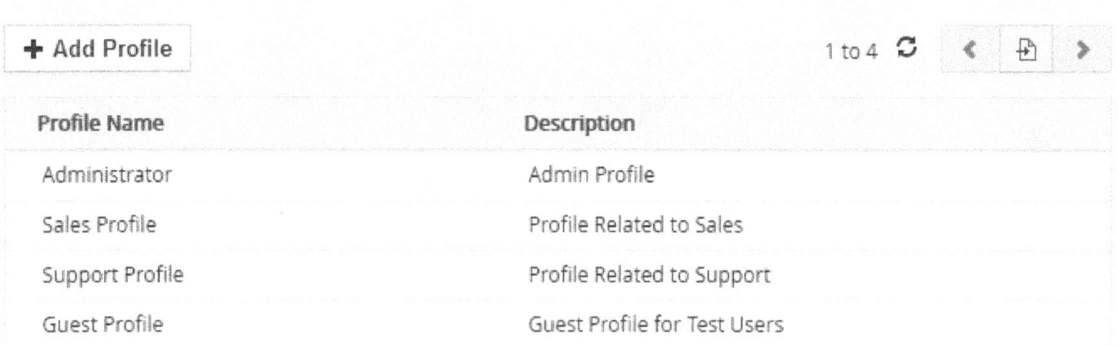

Profile Name	Description
Administrator	Admin Profile
Sales Profile	Profile Related to Sales
Support Profile	Profile Related to Support
Guest Profile	Guest Profile for Test Users

Figure 5-5: Profiles List View

Click on the name of a profile to see the details. You can change a profile by clicking on the **[Edit]** button. In order to create a new profile click on the **[Add Profile]** button at the list view.

Follow the instructions provided:

Step One:

Give the profile a unique name and description as illustrated in the next Figure 5-6.

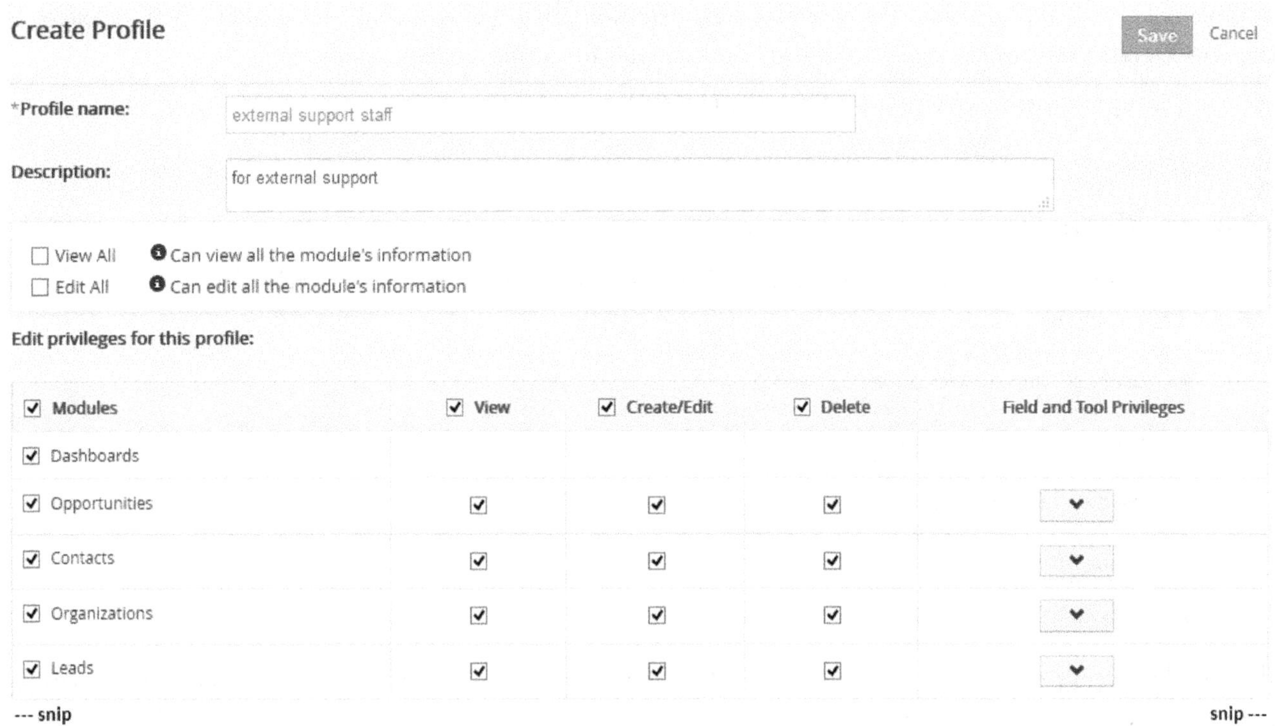

Figure 5-6: Profiles Create View

Step Two:

Configure the access privileges for all modules. You can select **Create/Edit**, **View** and **Delete** privileges for all fields. You can also configure the field permissions as illustrated in Figure 5-7.

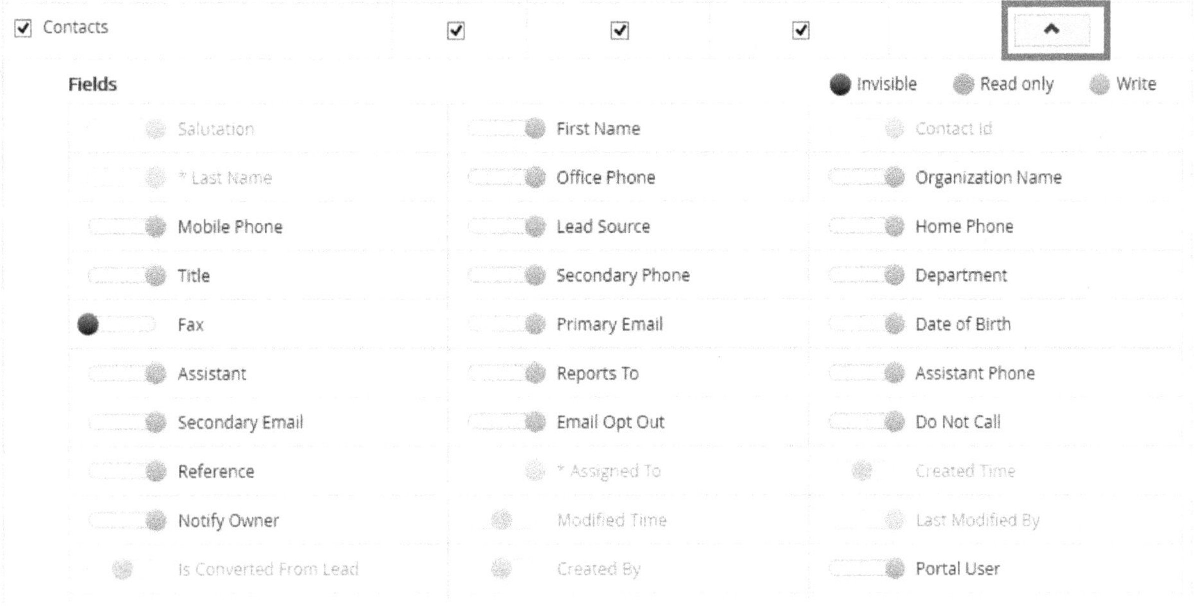

Figure 5-7: Profile Field Permission Settings

Invisible fields will only be visible to a user with administration privileges. Read only fields will be only visible on a data set's **Detail View**. In Appendix C, you will find samples for profile configurations.

Click on **[Save]** in order to save your profile in the CRM system.

5.2.4 Groups

Groups are a very effective tool in order to summarize users and privileges. Any type of relationship can be used to form a group, such as:

- users at the same location
- users with a common task
- user at the same department
- users with the same working history
- users with the same interests

Click on the **[Groups]** menu in order to open the list view as shown in Figure 5-8. You see a list of all existing groups.

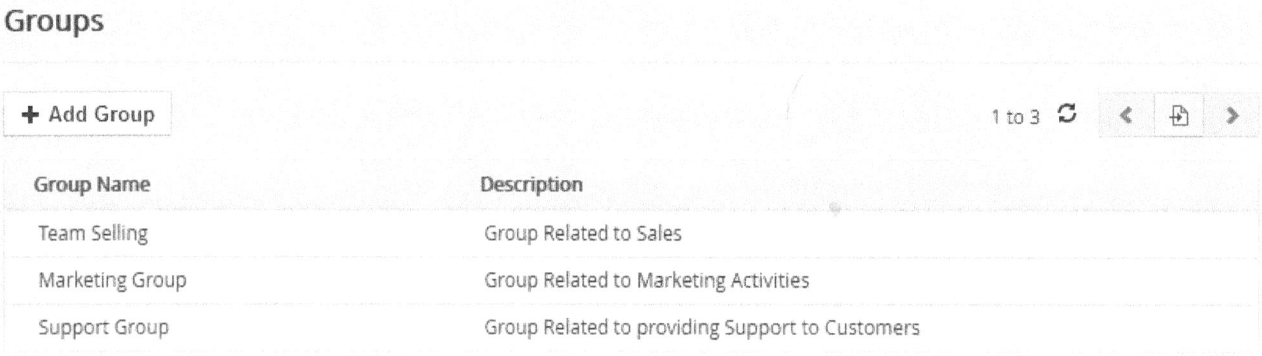

Groups

+ Add Group   1 to 3

Group Name	Description
Team Selling	Group Related to Sales
Marketing Group	Group Related to Marketing Activities
Support Group	Group Related to providing Support to Customers

Figure 5-8: Group List View

Click on the name of a group to get the details as shown in exemplary form in Figure 5-9. The detail view lists the name, the description and the members of this group. You can change the group settings by clicking on the [**Edit**] button.

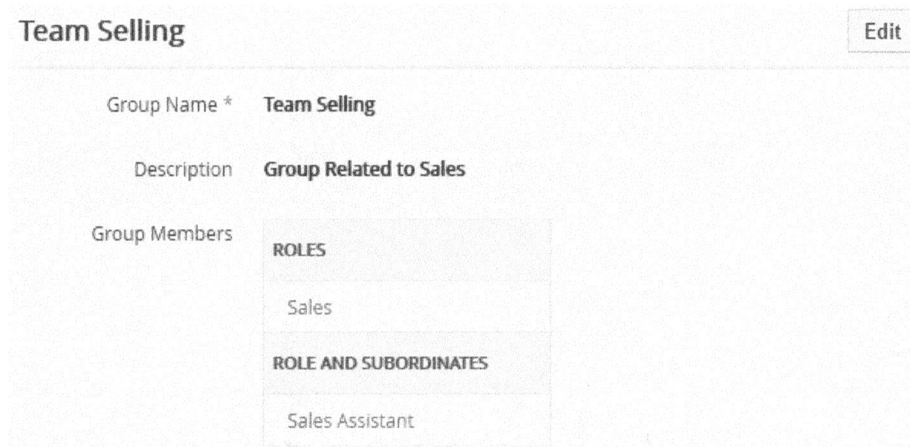

Figure 5-9: Group Detail View

In order to create a new group, please click on the **[Add Group]** button at the list view. The new entry window as shown in Figure 5-10 allows you to define the conditions for a particular group.

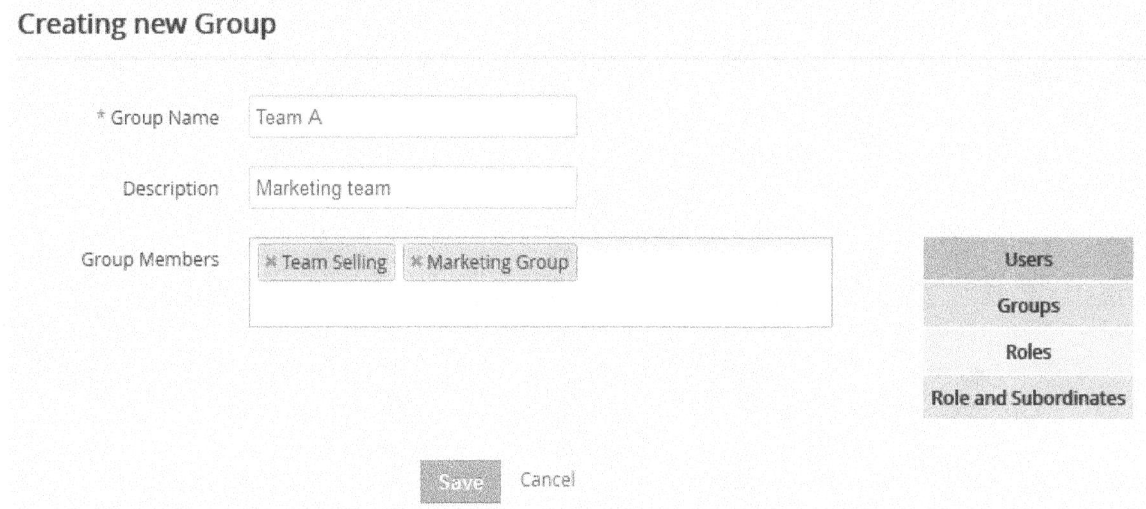

Figure 5-10: Group Create View

First, give the group a name and provide a short description. Then select the members for this group.

Click on **[Save]** in order to store your new group in the CRM system.

5.2.5 Sharing Rules

The CRM system allows you to set default privileges that are valid organization-wide. It is the purpose of this type of privilege to give an administrator tools that allow a fast overall security setting.

The **Sharing Access** privileges include **Global Access Privileges** and **Custom Access Privileges**. By default the sharing access settings allow all users to use all CRM features as long as they are not limited by profiles. In most cases there is no need to change this. However, if necessary, you can restrict the access to individual modules within your organization.

Go to the **Sharing Rules** menu in order to get an overview of the current settings. The CRM system comes with default **Global Access Privileges** for the most important CRM modules as shown in Figure 5-11.

Sharing Rules

Module	Public: Read Only	Public: Read, Create/Edit	Public: Read, Create/Edit, Delete	Private	Advanced Sharing Rules
To Do					
Opportunities					
Organizations & Contacts					
Leads					
Tickets					
Quotes					
Purchase Order					
Sales Order					
Invoice					
Campaigns					
Documents					

--- snip snip ---

Figure 5-11: Sharing Rules Menu

The following sharing permission types can be set:

Table 5-4: Sharing Permission Types

Type	Description
Private	Only the record owner, and users with a role which is above that of the record owner's role in the hierarchy, can browse, edit, delete and report on those records. That means by default that a specific user can only view the data sets that are owned by the user, owned by a group where the user is a member, owned by subordinate users, or shared with the user.
Public Read Only	All users can view and report on records but not edit them. Only the owner, and users with a role which is above that of the record owner's role in the hierarchy, can edit or delete these records.
Public Read/Write	All users can view, edit all records. Only the owner, and users with a role which is above that of the record owners role in the hierarchy, can delete those records.
Public Read/Write/Delete	All users can view, edit and delete all records.

Please note the following rules:

- Default organization sharing privileges are overridden by profile settings.
- For the activities module, the default organization sharing privilege value is set to the fixed value **Private** and cannot be altered.
- Regardless of the organization-wide defaults, users can always view and edit all data owned by or shared

with users below them in the role hierarchy if not prohibited by the profile.

- When an account has been set to **Private**, the access to related opportunities, tickets, quotes, sales orders, purchase orders, and invoices is also set to private. You must have at least a **Read Access** to a record to be able to add activities or other associated records to it.

This menu cannot be used for controlling calendar access privileges. You can configure the sharing access in the calendar settings menu.

Sharing Rules created for the **Accounts** module will automatically apply to the **Contacts** module. Please note the following general sharing rules:

- Custom sharing rules can only extend the visibility, but they cannot hide it.
- Sharing rules cannot be specified in order to allow data to be shared between two users. (If you want to do this, please refer to Appendix C, Example II.)
- Sharing rules apply to all existing data and the data which will be added in future.
- The number of sharing rules which can be defined for a single **Role, Role Subordinates** or **Group** is not limited.

In addition, you can create user defined sharing rules set by **Custom Sharing Rules** by clicking on the **[Advanced Sharing Rules]** button. These functions allow the administrators to selectively grant data access to a set of users. Custom data sharing rules can be created to share module related data between the following entities:

- From Role to Role
- From Role to Role with Subordinates
- From Role to Group
- From Role with Subordinates to Role
- From Role with Subordinates to Role with Subordinates
- From Role with Subordinates to Groups
- From Group to Role
- From Group to Role with Subordinates
- From Group to Group

A set-up of custom rules only makes sense if your sharing rules are not set to public.

Assuming that you have set the sharing rule for **Sales Orders** to **Private,** but you still want to have all users with the role sales assistant to be able to see and to edit each other's sales orders, you need to set-up a custom rule as illustrated in Figure 5-12.

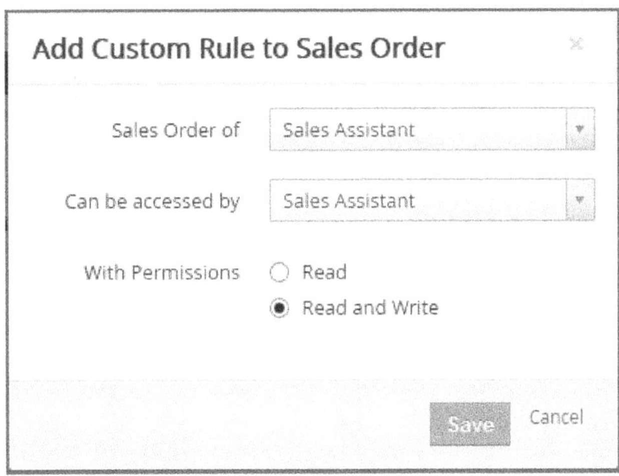

Figure 5-12: Creating Custom Sharing Rule

Sharing Rules can be created for the following modules:

Table 5-5: Sharing Rules for Modules

Module	Description
Leads:	Leads owned by the users of a given Role/Role Subordinates/Group can be shared with users of another Role/Role Subordinates/Group with Read Only or Read/Write permission. Emails related to a lead will also be shared with Read Only or Read/Write permission holders.
Accounts:	Accounts owned by the users of a given Role/Role Subordinates/Group can be shared with users of a Role/Role Subordinates/Group with Read Only or Read/Write permission. Emails related to an account will also be shared with Read Only or Read/Write permission holders.
Opportunities:	Opportunities owned by the users of a given Role/Role Subordinates/Group can be shared with users of a Role/Role Subordinates/Group with Read Only or Read/Write permission holders. Quotes and Sales Order related to an opportunity will also be shared with Read Only or Read/Write permission holders.
Trouble Tickets:	Tickets owned by the users of a given Role/Role Subordinates/Group can be shared with users of a Role/Role Subordinates/Group with Read Only or Read/Write permission holders.
Email:	Emails owned by the users of a given Role/Role Subordinates/Group can be shared with users of a Role/Role Subordinates/Group with Read Only or Read/Write permission holders.

Module	Description
Quotes:	Quotes owned by the users of a given Role/Role Subordinates/Group can be shared with users of a Role/Role Subordinates/Group with Read Only or Read/Write permission holders. Sales Orders related to a quote will also be shared with Read Only or Read/Write permission holders.
Purchase Order:	Purchase Orders owned by the users of a given Role/Role Subordinates/Group can be shared with users of a Role/Role Subordinates/Group with Read Only or Read/Write permission holders.
Sales Order:	Sales Order owned by the users of a given Role/Role Subordinates/Group can be shared with users of a Role/Role Subordinates/Group with Read Only or Read/Write permission holders. Invoices related to a sales order will also be shared with Read Only or Read/Write permission holders.
Invoice:	Invoices owned by the users of a given Role/Role Subordinates/Group can be shared with users of a Role/Role Subordinates/Group with Read Only or Read/Write permission holders.

5.2.6 User Login History

As CRM system administrator you can want to know who has accessed the system. In this menu you can retrieve the login history for each individual user. Open the menu and select a user then you will see the login details, as illustrated in Figure 5-13. Please note that the login date and time are always displayed.

The logout data are only available if a user used the logout button.

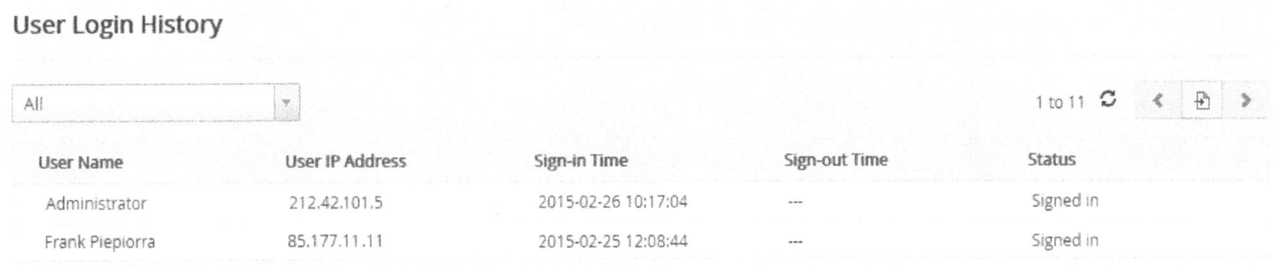

User Login History

All

1 to 11

User Name	User IP Address	Sign-in Time	Sign-out Time	Status
Administrator	212.42.101.5	2015-02-26 10:17:04	---	Signed in
Frank Piepiorra	85.177.11.11	2015-02-25 12:08:44	---	Signed in

Figure 5-13: Login History Menu

5.3 Studio

The studio allows you to customize your master data, to modify the content of the pick lists in each individual module and to add or remove CRM modules as explained in the following sections.

5.3.1 Edit Fields and Layout Editor

The layout editor allows the adding and deleting of custom fields, moving fields within a view, set and remove mandatory fields, rearranging fields as well as related lists as displayed at the **Arrange Related Tabs** tab of modules as illustrated in Figure 5-14.

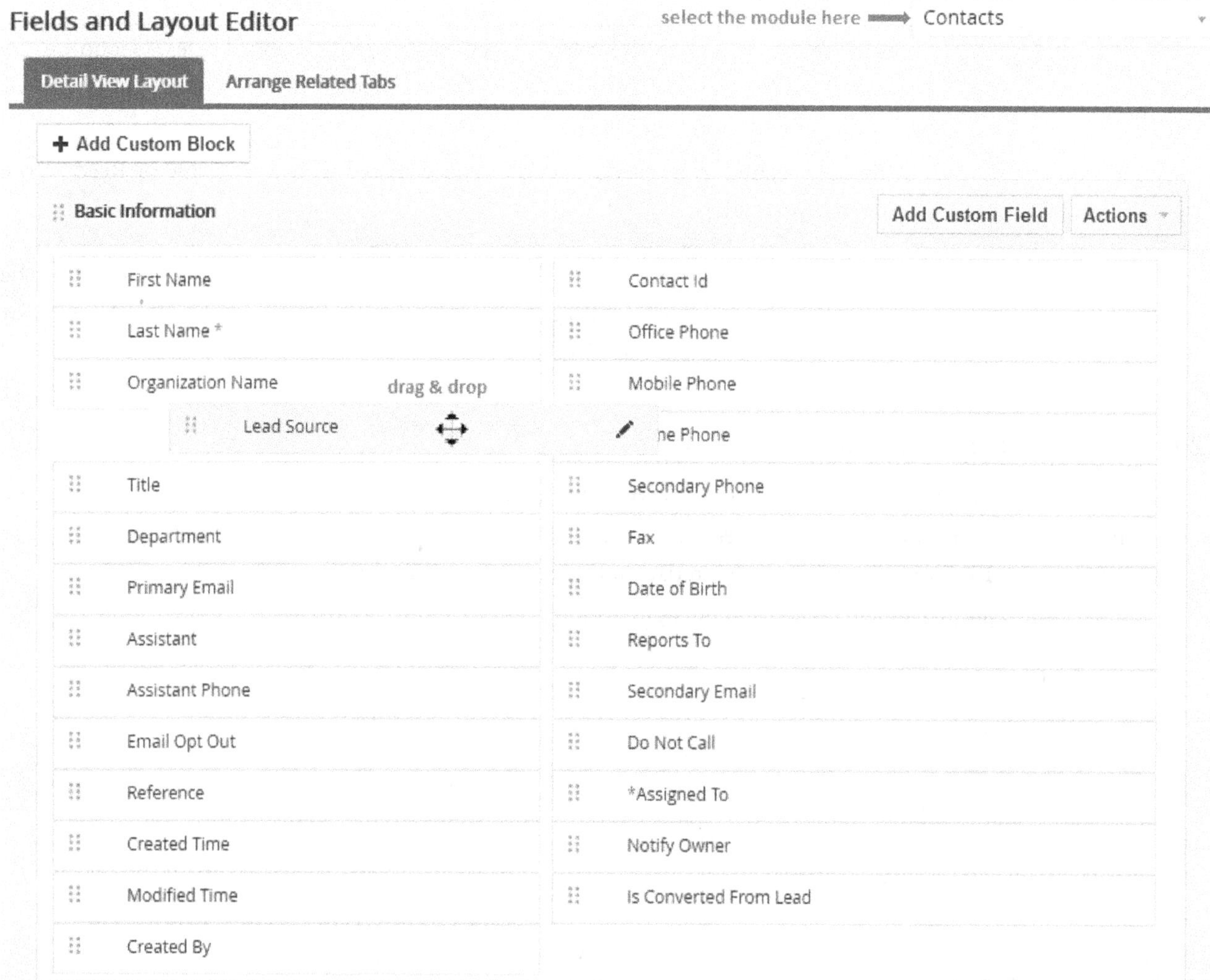

Figure 5-14: Fields and Layout Editor

In order to access the editor, please click on the **[Edit Fields]** menu. Select the module and you will see a list of all existing fields for this particular module.

Changing the field order

You can use your mouse to drag and drop fields to different locations.

5.3.1.1 User Defined Blocks

In the CRM, all information displayed is organized in so-called blocks. Each block represents an information unit. The purpose and the content of blocks are configurable. You can create additional blocks if needed as illustrated in the following Figure 5-15.

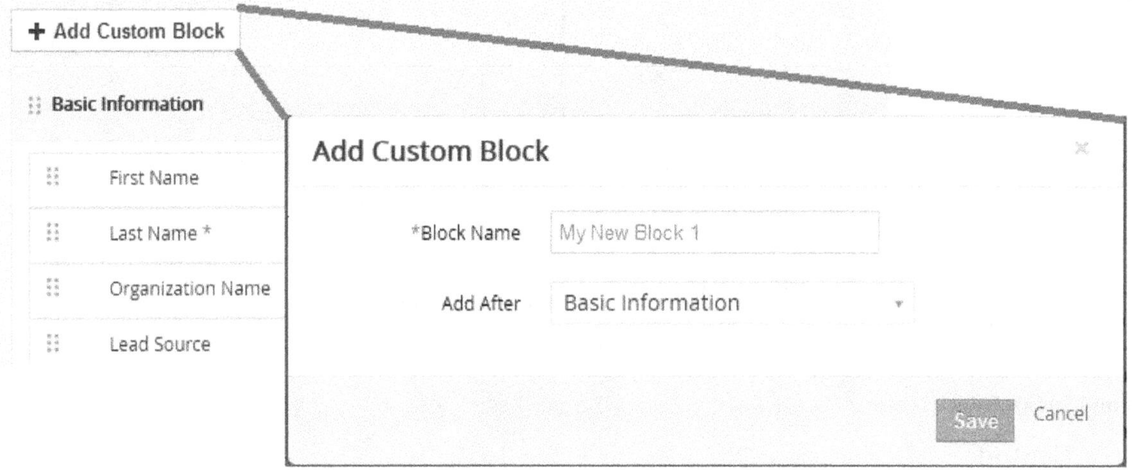

Figure 5-15: Add New Block

The following table summarizes the available functions.

Table 5-6: Layout Block Functions

Function Type	Function	Description
Block Functions	add and delete blocks	You can add a new custom block by clicking on the Add Custom Block button. You have to give this block a unique name. You can delete custom blocks only by means of the appropriate Action menu selection.
	see hidden fields in blocks	You can set fields as Active or Inactive (check box unchecked). If inactive, the field will not be displayed. If you want to see a list of the inactive fields click on the appropriate item at the Action menu.
	move blocks	You can change the order on which the blocks are displayed in a detail view by drag & drop.
	show and hide blocks	The show and hide function of the Action menu sets the default detail view for a block. Even if hidden, the blocks head line is still displayed and can be expanded to a full view if needed.

5.3.1.2 Custom Fields

You can configure your own entry fields for most of the CRM modules. By clicking on the **[Add Custom Field]** button a new window will open as displayed in Figure 5-16.

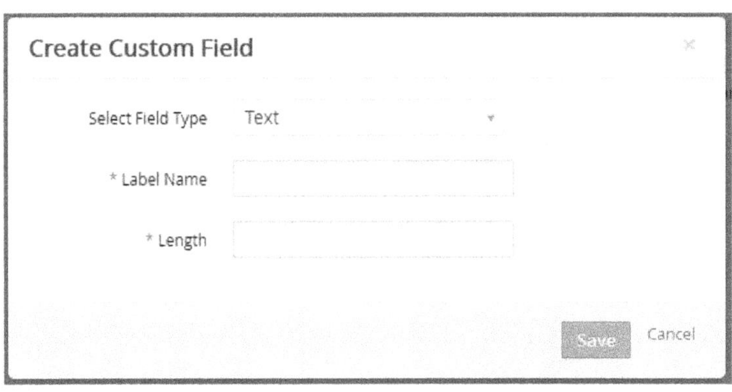

Figure 5-16: Create New Custom Field

In order to create a new field you have to select the data format as field type first. The following table lists the available formats. Make sure that each custom field is labeled with a unique name.

Table 5-7: Custom Field Definitions

Field Type	Content
Text	[Length:] Enter the maximum number of characters, e.g. 10 for ten characters. You can use up to 254 characters
Number	[Length:] Enter the maximum number of digits, e.g. 10 for ten digits; [Decimal Places]: Enter the number of decimal places you want to have, e.g. 0 has no decimal places, 1 creates one decimal place, like 55.4 and so on.
Percent	[Length:] Enter the maximum number of digits, e.g. 3 for three digits; [Decimal Places]: Enter the number of decimal places you want to have, e.g. 0 has no decimal places, 1 creates one decimal place, like 55.4 and so on.
Currency	[Length:] Enter the maximum number of digits, e.g. 6 for six digits; [Decimal Places]: Enter the number of decimal places you want to have, e.g. 0 has no decimal places, 1 creates one decimal place, like 55.4 and so on. Important: If you intend to work with multiple currencies, you must use 3 decimal places in order to avoid rounding errors.
Date	Just give the field a name.
Email	Just give the field a name.
Phone	Just give the field a name.
Pick List	You can create this pick list by using a new line for each entry. It is suggested that you use --None-- as the first entry if you do not define a default value.
URL	Just give the field a name.

Field Type	Content
Check Box	Here you can define a check box (yes/no). Just give the field a name.
Text Area	This is a field where you can enter an almost unlimited amount of text. The limit is set by your data base capacity.
Multi-Select Combo Box	You can create a list by using a new line for each entry. In contrast to the Pick List you will be able to select multiple entries at once. It is suggested that you use --None-- as the first entry if you do not define a default value.
Skype	You can use this custom field to link the CRM System with the Skype application running at your client computer. Just give this field a unique name. At your edit view of the related CRM module you can enter a Skype ID or a phone number. For more information about Skype look at http://www.skype.com.
Time	You can use this field for a time entry. Just give it a name.

Custom fields for leads are special. You can decide what will be done with the content stored in these fields when you convert a lead to a sales opportunity. Make a note of the field type and their formats if you add custom fields for leads. Please read the chapter 5.3.4.1 for further information on this.

For your fields the following functions are available:

Table 5-8: Layout Field Functions

Function Type	Function	Description
Field Functions	Create a field	You can create a new custom field by clicking on the appropriate button.
	Active and inactive fields	Click on the appropriate settings at the Action button. You can set a field active or inactive. Inactive fields will not be displayed for any user. If you want hide a field for particular users, use the profile settings for this purpose.
	Delete a field	You can delete custom fields only by clicking on the [Delete] icon. This icon not provided for CRM standard fields which cannot be deleted. If you do n need a standard field you can hide it.
	Move fields within blocks	You can change the order on which the fields are displayed by a drag & dr operation.
	Move fields between blocks	You can move a field into another block by a drag & drop operation.

Function Type	Function	Description
Arrange Related Tabs	Arrange related lists	Each detail view has related modules. You can change the display ord information by clicking on the [Arrange Related Tabs] tab.

5.3.1.3 Changing Field Properties

Each field has particular properties which you can display for each individual field by a field's property menu as shown in Figure 5-17.

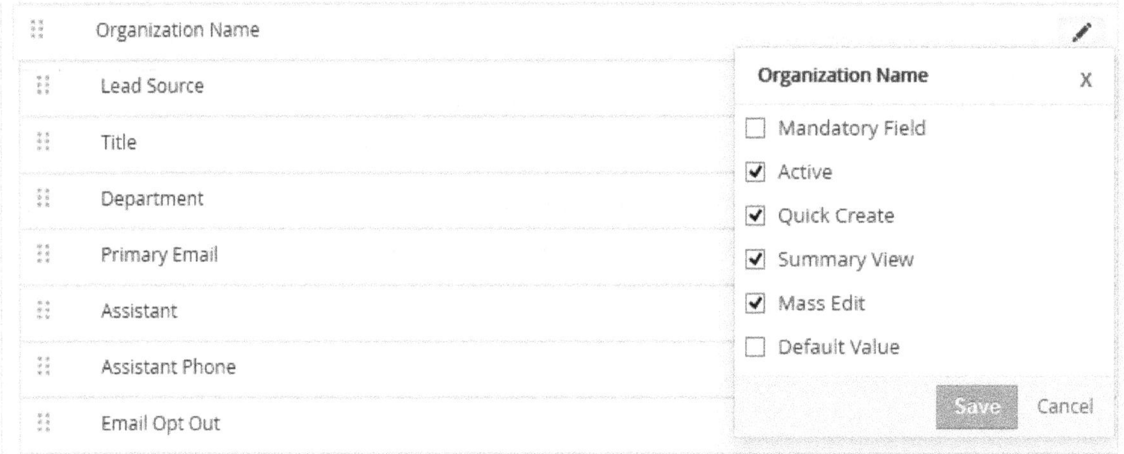

Figure 5-17: Fields Property Menu

The following table explains the possible property options.

Table 5-9: Field Properties

Property Type	Description
Mandatory Fields:	You can declare a field as mandatory for an Edit View. This means that data can only be stored if content for the field is provided. Please note that some fields are mandatory by default since they are always needed for special functions.
Active:	An active field will be displayed for the users if the profiles allow it. You can set a field as inactive if it is no longer needed. This has an advantage over the delete field option because hidden fields will maintain the data and can be restored if required.
Quick Create:	You can add any field to the Quick Create menu.
Mass Edit:	You can add or remove fields to the Mass Edit function available at List Views.
Default Value:	You can set default value for a field which applies when a new data entry is created.

5.3.2 Pick List Editor

Pick lists are drop down menus which are offered to you at the **Edit View** or **Detail View** of several CRM modules. The **Pick List Editor** menu allows you to define the content of the pick lists based on the roles assigned to the CRM users.

Click on the **[Pick List Editor]** menu in order to get to the menu shown in Figure 5-18.

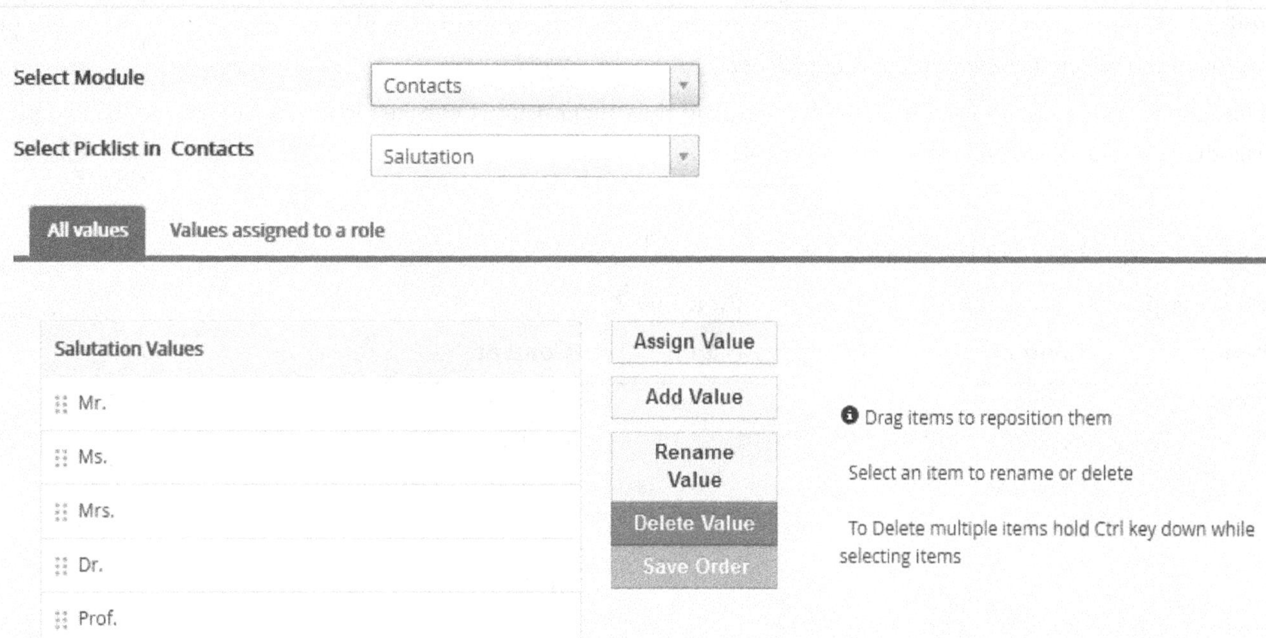

Figure 5-18: Pick List Editor

Select the module first and all pick lists of this module will become available for display at the pick-list selection menu.

Function	Description
Assign Value:	All pick lists are roles related. That means that the content of the pick list for each individual (non admin) user depends on the role which has been assigned to this user. You can use this feature for instance to create pick-lists in different languages or to restrict the users access to certain entries. Click on this button in order to select the roles to which a displayed pick list applies.
Add Value:	You can add additional pick list entries.
Rename Value:	You can add any field to the **Quick Create** menu.
Delete Value:	You can add or remove fields to the **Mass Edit** function available at **List Views**.
Dave Order:	You can drag & drop a pick list entry to change the order in the pick list. You must save your order after a modification.

Some content of the pick lists cannot be changed. This content is defined by the system settings. Please contact your CRM system provider if content is provided which does not fit to your needs.

5.3.3 Pick List Dependency Setup

Existing pick lists or pick lists which have created by the **Pick List Editor** can only be used in order to a select single or multiple entries. The **Pick List Dependency Setup** menu allows you to link contents of a pick-list with content of another pick-list. That means that you can control the content of a pick list displayed in the menu by means of the selected content of another pick list.

The following description uses an example to explain the functionality. Let us assume that we have added two pick lists to the menu as shown in the following Table 5-10.

Table 5-10: Dependency Pick List Sample

Pick List 1		**Pick List 2**	
Name	**Content**	**Name**	**Content**
Product type	--None--	Products	--None--
	Fruits		Potatoes
	Vegetables		Cabbage
	Others		Peas
			Apples
			Plum
			Pears
			Packing Crates

We would like to control the content of pick list 2 and display in pick list 2 only content which relates to pick list 1. For instance, if we select **Vegetables** in pick list 1 we would like to see only **Potatoes, Cabbage** and **Peas** in pick list 2.

Open the **Pick List Dependency Setup** menu as shown in the following Figure 5-19.

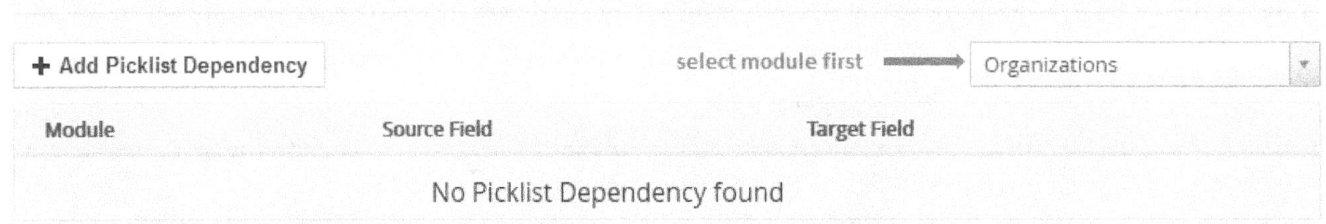

Figure 5-19: Pick List Dependency List View

Select the module and click on the button **[Add Pick List Dependency]** in order to reach the **Create View** as shown in Figure 5-20.

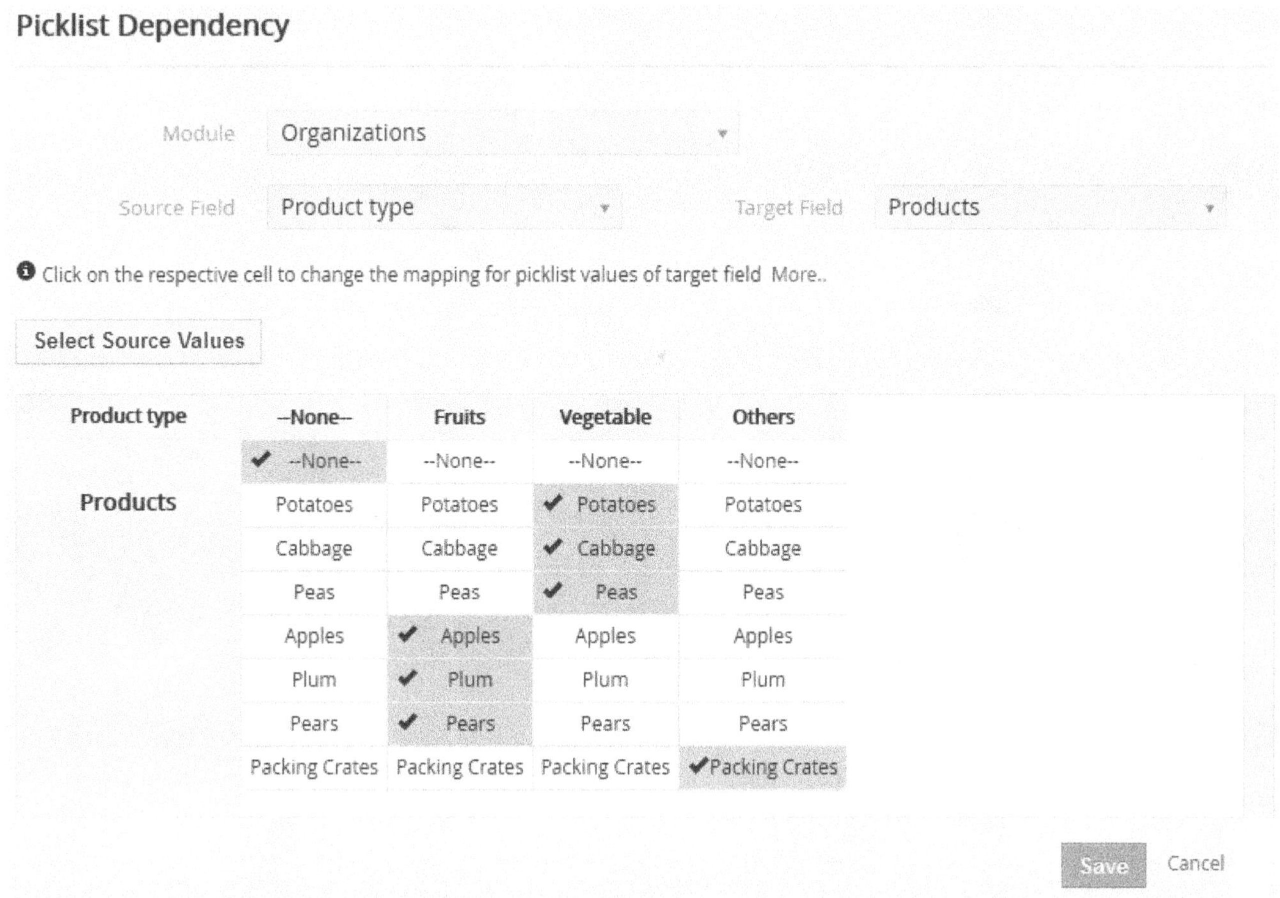

Figure 5-20: Pick List Dependency Create View

You use this menu to define the dependencies. The **Target Field** gets controlled by the **Source Field**. Select the appropriate pick lists for both fields as shown in the figure.

The menu provides you the option to set pick list fields in relations to each other. The column heading contains the content of **Pick List 1**. It is recommended that you unselect the fields column by column that you do not want to see in **Pick List 2** as shown in this example.

Click on **[Save]** in order to transfer your settings to the CRM.

5.3.4 Module Manager

The **Module Manager** allows you to configure the content and the display structure of your existing modules for all users and to add new CRM modules when available.

As illustrated in Figure 5-21 you see a list of all your CRM modules when you enter this menu.

You can disable modules which you do not need for your company by removing the checkbox mark. If you want to disable modules for particular users but not for all, you should not do it here and use the profile setting instead.

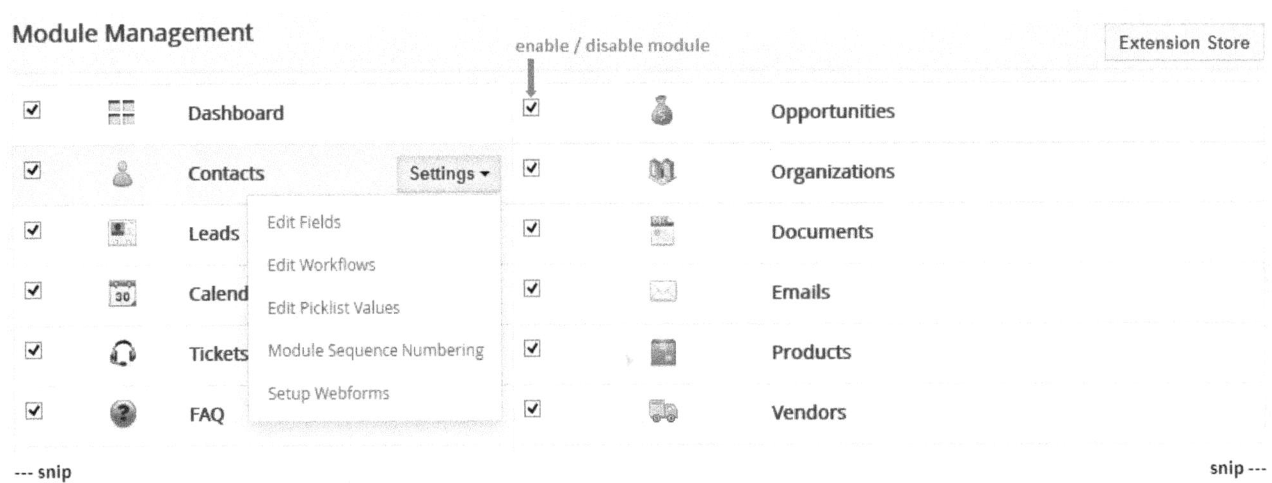

Figure 5-21: Module Manager List View

You can reach the **[Settings]** options for a particular module by moving the mouse to an entry.

Table 5-11: Module Manager Settings Options

Settings Option	Description
Edit Field:	This option opens a menu on which you can configure the fields displayed in a particular module as explained in chapter 5.3.1.
Edit Workflow:	This navigates to the Workflow module as explained in chapter 5.5.8.
Edit Pick List Values:	This navigates to the Pick List Editor module as explained in chapter 5.3.2.
Sequence Numbering:	This navigates to the Customize Record Numbering module as explained in chapter 5.5.5.
Setup Workflow:	This navigates to the Workflows module as explained in chapter 5.5.8.
Edit Field Mapping:	This navigation entry is only available for Leads and explained in chapter 5.3.4.1.

5.3.4.1 Edit Field Mapping for Leads

Custom fields for leads are special. You can decide what will be done with the content stored in these fields when you convert a lead to a sales opportunity. You can drop this information or transfer the content of these fields into the corresponding custom fields at opportunities, accounts or contacts.

The format and the type of the custom fields in leads and the corresponding custom fields in opportunities, accounts, or contacts must be absolutely identical! Please make a note of the field name and properties you have created. You will need this when you want to create references to a custom field.

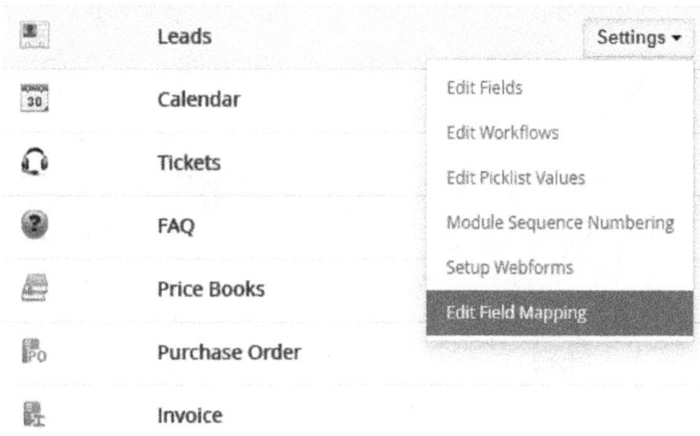

Figure 5-22: Calling Edit Field Mapping

You should adopt the following procedure in order to prepare the transfer of custom fields from leads for further use after a lead conversion:

1 Create custom fields for opportunities, accounts or contacts in reference to custom fields in leads. E.g., if you have created a custom field with the name **bank account** for leads, you should create custom fields for opportunities, called **account no**. It is recommended not to use the same name.

2 Open the **Edit Field Mapping** module (only displayed for leads) at the Module Manger as shown in Figure 5-22.

3 A new window will open. Enter the **Edit** menu as shown in Figure 5-23.

4 All fields available for leads are displayed. Select the mapping to the corresponding fields in contacts, accounts or opportunities you want to have.

5 Click on [**Save**] in order to transfer your settings to the CRM system.

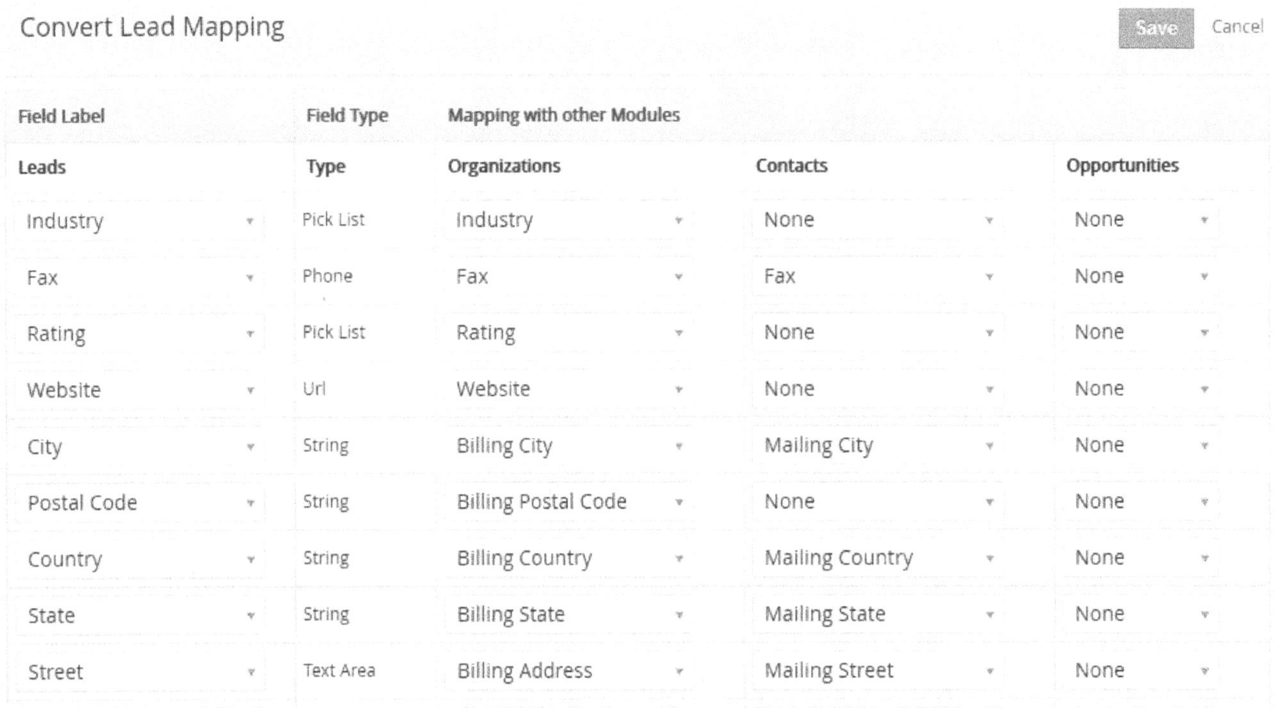

Convert Lead Mapping

Save Cancel

Field Label	Field Type	Mapping with other Modules		
Leads	Type	Organizations	Contacts	Opportunities
Industry	Pick List	Industry	None	None
Fax	Phone	Fax	Fax	None
Rating	Pick List	Rating	None	None
Website	Url	Website	None	None
City	String	Billing City	Mailing City	None
Postal Code	String	Billing Postal Code	None	None
Country	String	Billing Country	Mailing Country	None
State	String	Billing State	Mailing State	None
Street	Text Area	Billing Address	Mailing Street	None

Figure 5-23: Convert Lead Mapping - Edit View

When finished the mapped custom fields are linked and will be used when you convert a lead into an opportunity as described in Section 4.2.1.

5.3.4.2 Module Import

With **Module Manager**, the installation of CRM addons can be accomplished with a few simple clicks.

The vtiger community is providing such enhancements on its **Market Place** web site at

https://marketplace.vtiger.com

In order to find an extension this is compatible with your CRM version and supported by the Module Manager, look for the compatibility information.

In order to install an extension look for the install instructions provided with the extension module. In most cases you can use the **Extension Store** module as described in chapter 5.7.

If the extension store is not an option and you got a ZIP file the standard procedure is as follows:

- The standard file format is <module name>.zip. Do not unzip this file.
- Go to **[Module Manager]** as shown in the following Figure 5-24 and click on the **[Import from Zip]** link.
- Follow the instructions to upload the extension to your CRM. During the update the CRM verifies the file structure and compatibility of the extension and reports any possible problems. It is definitely recommended to create a backup of your existing CRM before you install any extension.

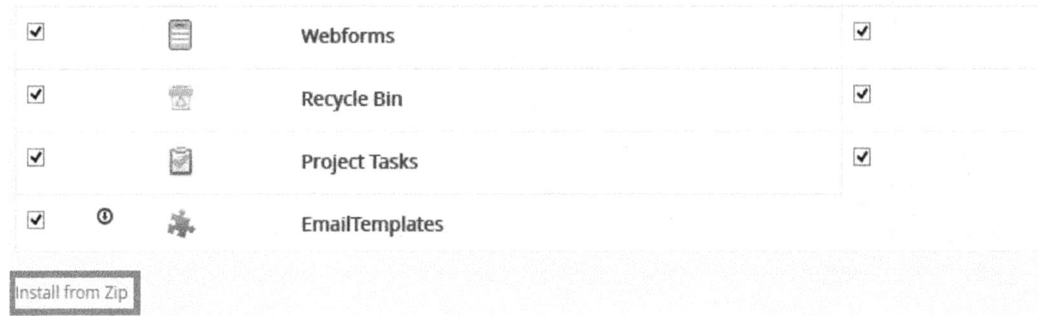

Figure 5-24: Module Import from Zip File

5.4 Communication Templates

Communication templates intend to help you to work with the CRM more efficiently.

5.4.1 Company Details

If you use the CRM to create PDF outputs for your quotes, orders or invoices, you must define the company information.

The CRM system uses the company information while creating a PDF output. If this information is not available at the time you create a PDF, an error message will be presented.

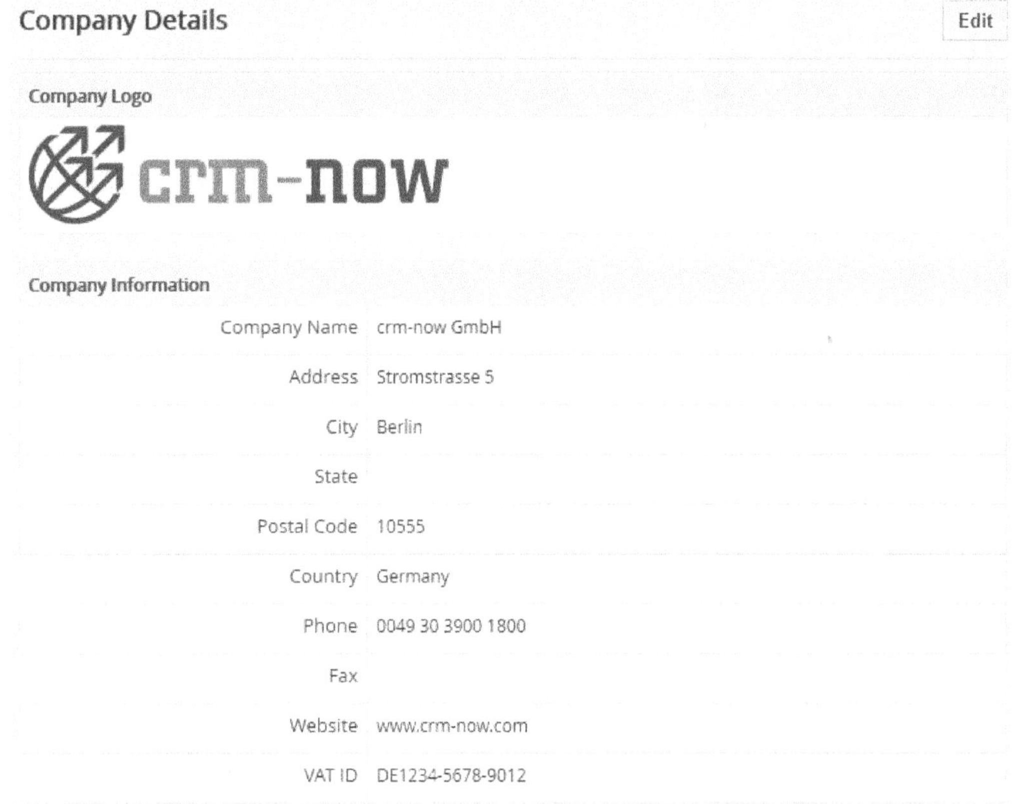

Figure 5-25: Company Details Setup

In the **Company Details** menu, click on the **[Edit]** button in order to enter company information as shown in Figure 5-25.

Make sure that the size of your company logo meets the space available for the PDF outputs. The logo must be provided in the .jpeg, .jpg, .png, .gif, .pjpeg, or .x-png file format. The recommended size is about 170 x 60 pixels.

5.5 Other Settings

With the help of the configuration functions you can specify your company information, configure the outgoing email server, your backup access, and your default currencies.

5.5.1 Announcement

System administrators or users with administration privileges are provided with a function that enables them to send announcements to all CRM users. Such an announcement will be displayed at the top of the CRM system as illustrated in Figure 5-26.

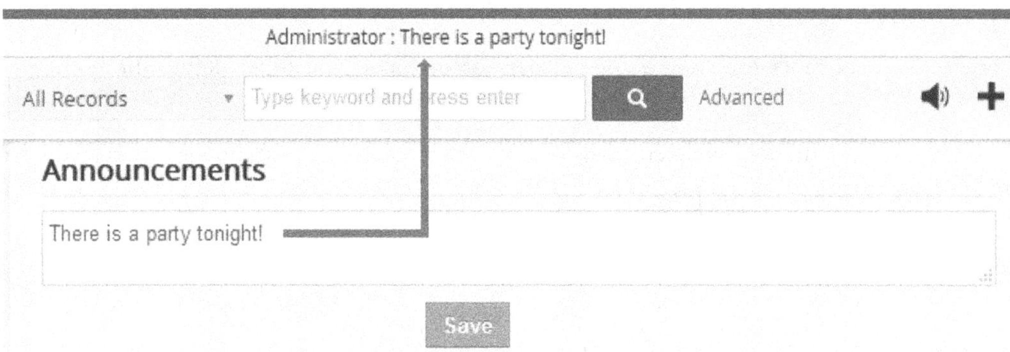

Figure 5-26: Announcement View

You can see the announcement when you leave the settings menu.

5.5.2 Outgoing Server

If you want to send emails from the CRM system or if you want to receive automatic CRM notifications, you must configure the outgoing mail server.

Click on **[Edit]** in the **Outgoing Server** menu in order to enter your email server configuration as shown in Figure 5-27. Ask your service provider for the SMTP access data. Make sure that the server can be accessed by the CRM system.

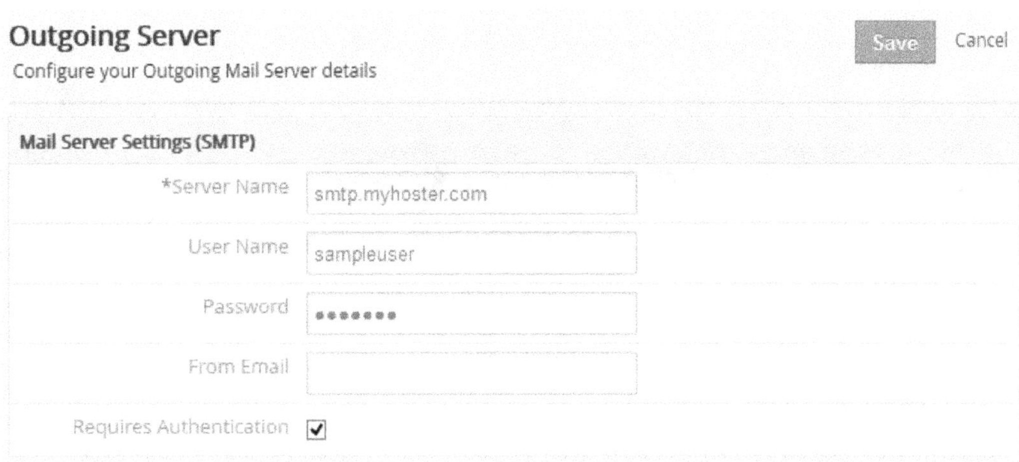

Figure 5-27: Outgoing Server Settings

All CRM users will use the same outgoing email server.

If a user sends an email by using the CRM, the user's email address as defined for each individual user at the **User & Access Control** menu will be used as the sending email address.

However, if you have made an entry in the **From Email** field, this email address will be used as a sending email address for **all** users and will be added to the **Reply to** content of your message.

5.5.3 Inventory Terms & Conditions

You can store your default company terms and conditions in the CRM. Click on **[Edit]** in the **Inventory Terms & Conditions** menu in order to open the edit view as shown in Figure 5-28.

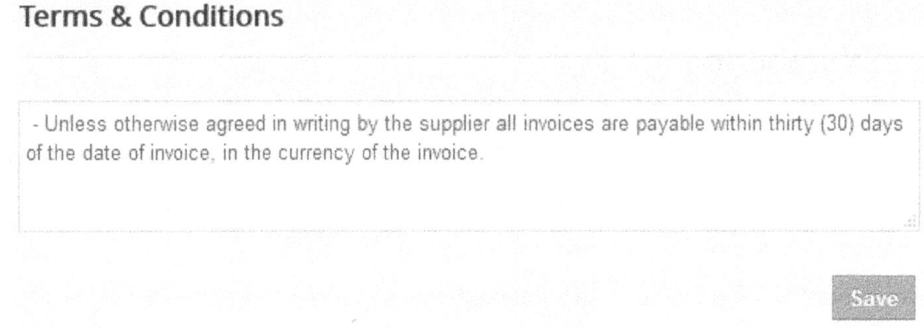

Figure 5-28: Inventory Terms & Conditions - Detail View

Enter your information. Click on **[Save]** in order to transfer the information to the CRM. These terms and conditions will be available as default entries whenever you create a new quote, order or invoice.

5.5.4 Currencies

Click on the **Currency** menu in order to set your system-wide currencies. You can add an unlimited number of currencies by means of clicking on the **[Add Currency]** button as shown in Figure 5-29. You can also delete or edit exiting currencies by clicking on the appropriate icons.

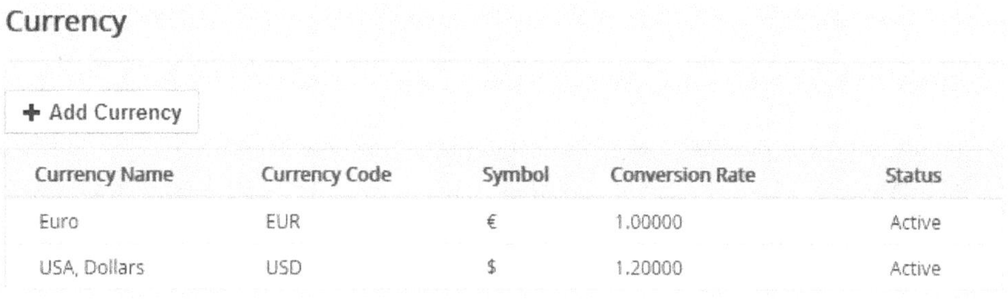

Currency

+ Add Currency

Currency Name	Currency Code	Symbol	Conversion Rate	Status
Euro	EUR	€	1.00000	Active
USA, Dollars	USD	$	1.20000	Active

Figure 5-29: Currency Setup

Table 5-12: Currency Information Fields

Type	Content
Currency Name:	The name of the currency, e.g. US Dollar.
Currency Code:	The short name of the currency, e.g. Dollar.
Currency Symbol:	Enter the symbol of the currency. This symbol will be used in the CRM for all price information, e.g. $.
Conversion Rate:	Enter the currency conversion rate in relation to the CRM basic currency. The basic currency is the first currency on your currency list.
Status:	You can set a currency as active or inactive. Inactive currencies cannot get assigned to any users.

5.5.5 Customize Record Numbering

While the CRM system uses its internal numbering system for all data, you can define your own numbering scheme for most of the modules.

You can define your numbering scheme by selecting the module first and entering your text for the prefix. Your start sequence must be a number which will increase by 1 every time you enter a new record.

Please note that the CRM controls your numbers. You cannot create a record with the same number twice. If you want to start a new sequence, you can do this by using a different **Prefix**.

Figure 5-30 demonstrates a sample for contacts.

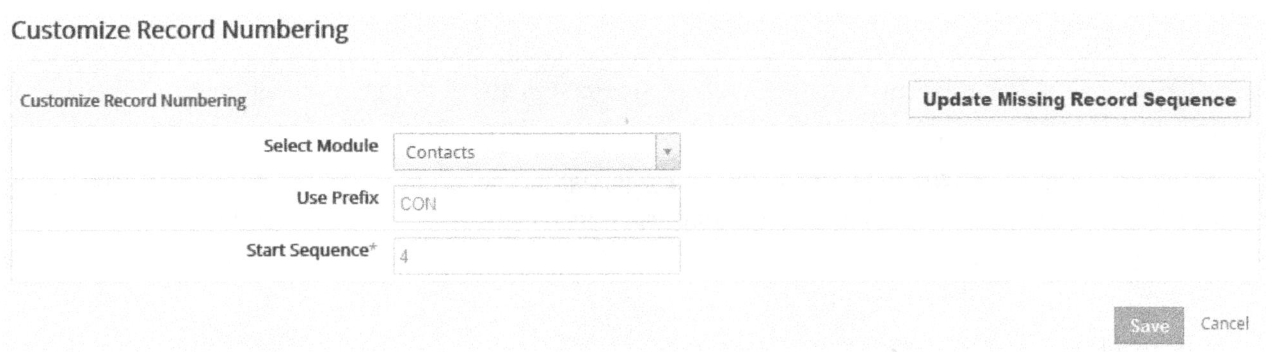

Figure 5-30: Customize Record Numbering

Click on **[Save]** in order to activate your numbering scheme.

5.5.6 Tax Calculations

In all phases of the sales process, the CRM system considers all type of taxes which can apply to the sales of products or services. These can include local, state or federal taxes as well as special taxes. These taxes can be calculated individually for each product or service to be sold, or can be calculated for the whole product-service package.

Tax Calculations

+ Add New Tax

Product & Service Taxes

Tax Name	Tax Value	Status
VAT	4.500%	☑
Sales	10.000%	☑
Service	12.500%	☑

+ Add New Tax

Shipping & Handling Taxes

Tax Name	Tax Value	Status
VAT	4.500%	☑
Sales	10.000%	☑
Service	12.500%	☑

Figure 5-31: Tax Setting - List View

You can refer to the article **Product Details** in **Quotes** for further information on the use of the tax settings. The CRM System can include taxes when calculating prices for quotes, orders or invoices. In order to change the settings of the existing taxes, click the mouse on ✎ icon in the **Tax Calculations** menu as shown in Figure 5-31.

In order to add new taxes, use the **[Add New Tax]** buttons. You can define as many additional taxes as you need. Enter your taxes in percent (%). Please note that you cannot delete the default taxes as they are provided with the CRM system. However, you can deactivate not needed taxes by clicking on the **Status Check Box**.

5.5.7 Mail Converter

The mail converter adds a capability to the CRM allowing it to scan a mail box automatically and to take action if the content of an incoming email meets certain criteria.

For example, you can have a specific email address for your support and the request that incoming emails should create a CRM ticket if these emails contain the string "support request". You can also use this scanner for mails which are generated by your web page in order to generate a contact in your CRM in case someone is interested in attaining more information about your offerings.

As a result of an email scan you have the following options:

- Create a trouble ticket: The **SUBJECT** of the email will become the title of the ticket. The **BODY** of the email will become the description of the ticket. The **FROM** email address is automatically compared with existing **Account** and **Contact** email addresses. If a match is found, the trouble ticket is associated with the existing Account or Contact.
- Update a trouble ticket: The **SUBJECT** of the email will become the title of the ticket. The **BODY** of the email will become the description of the ticket.
- Add email to a **Contact** considering the **FROM** address
- Add email to a **Contact** considering the **TO** address
- Add email to an **Account** considering the **FROM** address
- Add email to an **Account** considering the **TO** address
- Mark an email as **READ** as soon it has been scanned

In order to set-up the mail scanner, go to the **Mail Converter** menu and click on **[Create Mailbox now]**. The incoming mail box configuration menu opens as shown in Figure 5-32. Please note that this function is only available to mail boxes which provide IMAP (Internet Message Access Protocol) protocol capabilities. You can ask your Internet Service Provider for your IMAP access data and refer to http://en.wikipedia.org/wiki/Internet_Message_Access_Protocol for further information.

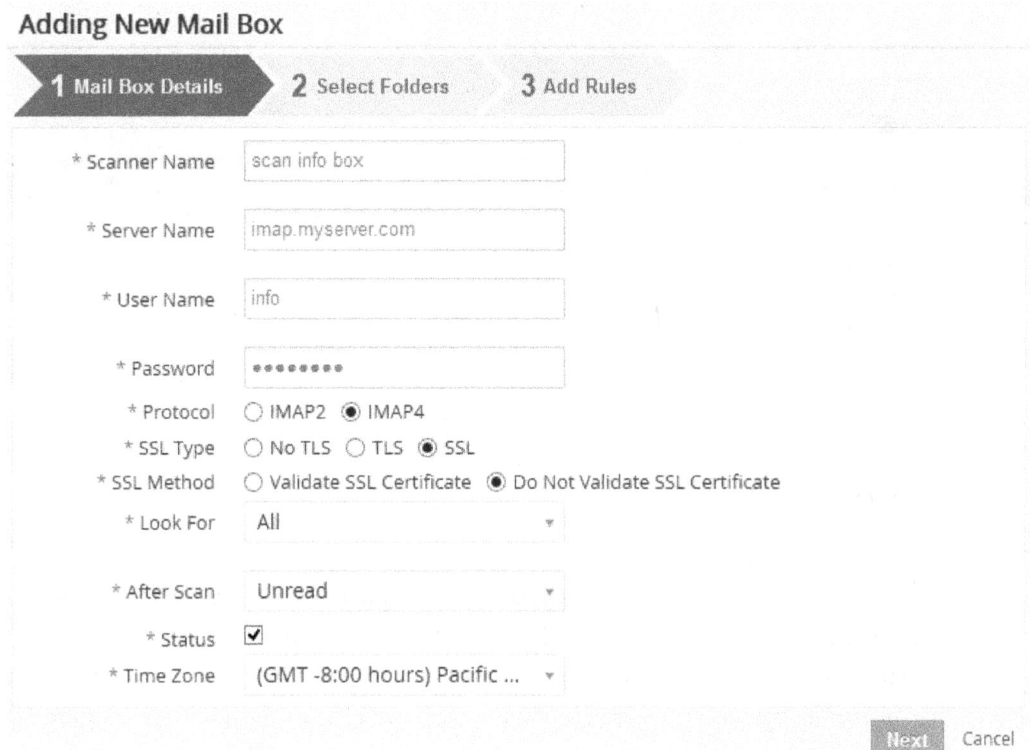

Figure 5-32: Mail Converter Create View

Enter your email box access data. The mail scanner is disabled by default. Make sure that you enable the status before saving.

When you click on the **[Next]** button, the CRM tries to connect to your mail box in order to verify proper operation. If you receive the error message "Connecting to mailbox failed!" the mail box access information is not saved. Should this happen, please check your mail box settings and then try again. If the CRM is able to communicate with your incoming mail box, further configuration options will be made available as shown in Figure 5-33.

This menu presents the mail boxes available on your email server. You can select up to two mail boxes for scanning. If you unable to see certain mail boxes, please contact your mail box service provider and ask what mail boxes are available for the IMAP protocol. This is not a CRM issue.

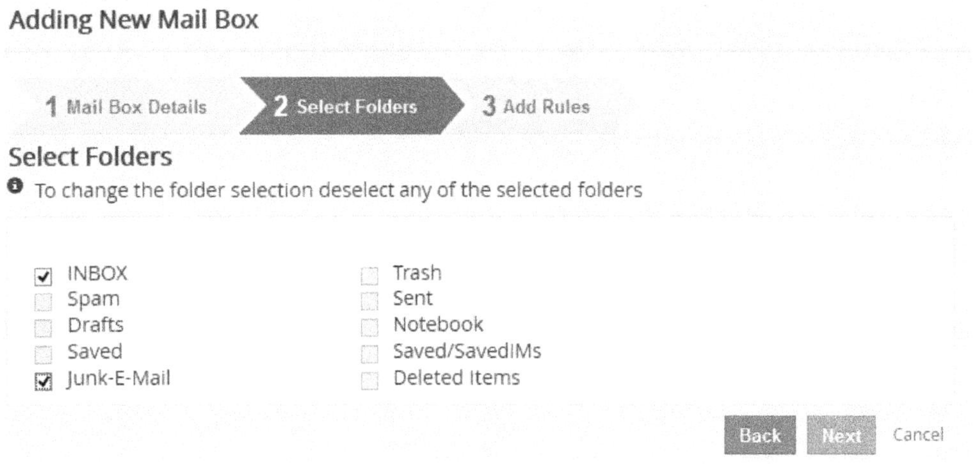

Figure 5-33: Mail Converter Folder Selection

By clicking on the **[Next]** button, the CRM will allow you to set-up one or multiple rules for your incoming emails. The Figure 5-34 depicts possible settings. In this example a CRM ticket with the email content is generated automatically if the subject of the email contains the text **'service request'** and the email body has the term **'ticket id'** included in it. If you want that all emails from a certain mail box create an action, do not include any conditions.

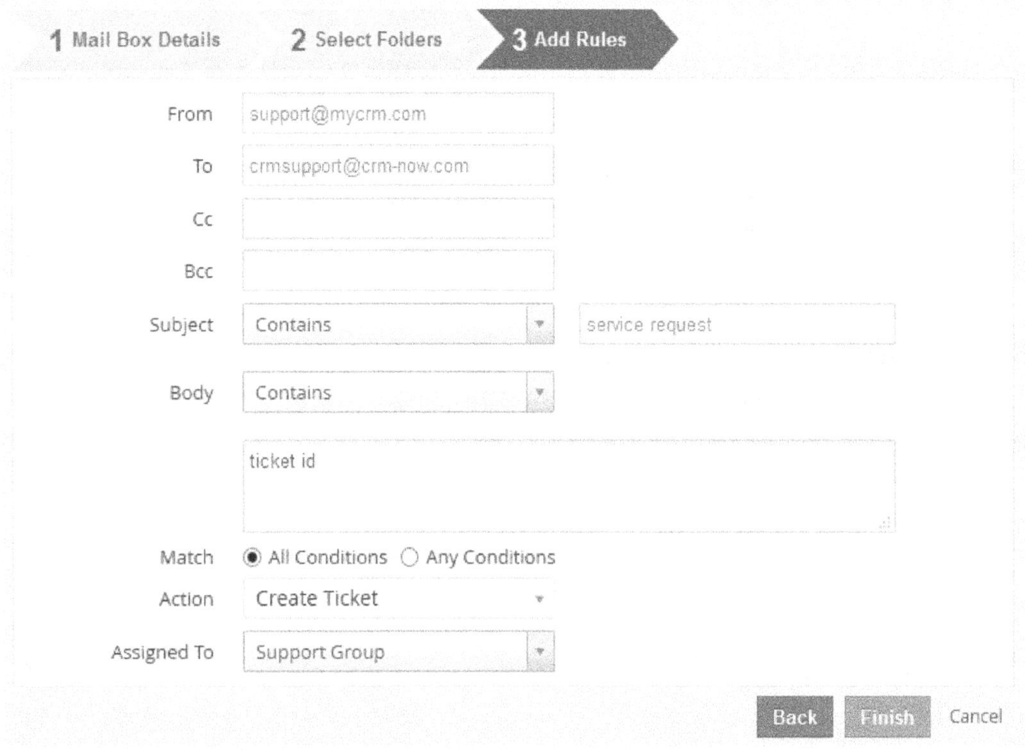

Figure 5-34: Mail Converter Rules Setup

The condition can be just words or in case of a **Subject** also **Regular Expressions**, selectable as **Regex**. **Regular Expressions** are used for identifying strings of text, such as particular characters, words, or patterns of characters.

Regular Expressions are powerful but not simple. You cannot learn to use **Regular Expressions** from a brief overview and these are therefore not subject matter in this manual. For instance, the **Regular Expression /\bweb\b/i** would find the word **web** in the subject of an email.

For a complete introduction to **Regular Expressions,** you can refer to the Wiki at http://en.wikipedia.org/wiki/Regular_expression, a Web Site like http://www.regular-expressions.info/, or other sources.

Click on **[Finish]** in order to transfer the rule to the CRM system. You can set-up one or multiple rules. If you have multiple rules it is sometimes necessary that you are able to set the order of a scan execution. This is done by changing the list order as illustrated in Figure: **Mail Converter Priorities**.

When this has been completed, the CRM is ready to scan your mail box every time you click on the **Scan Now** button in the **[Mail Converter]** menu. Your first scan can take a little bit of time depending on the content of your mail box and the access speed.

It is also possible to have an automatic scan of your mail box. This must be configured during the CRM system installation and cannot be accessed by a CRM user or administrator.

The example in Figure 5-35 illustrates how you could setup mail scanning conditions in order to create and to update tickets. This would be a proper mail scanner setup under the assumption that you have set-up an email box for scanning and every incoming mail should either create a new ticket or update an existing ticket in CRM.

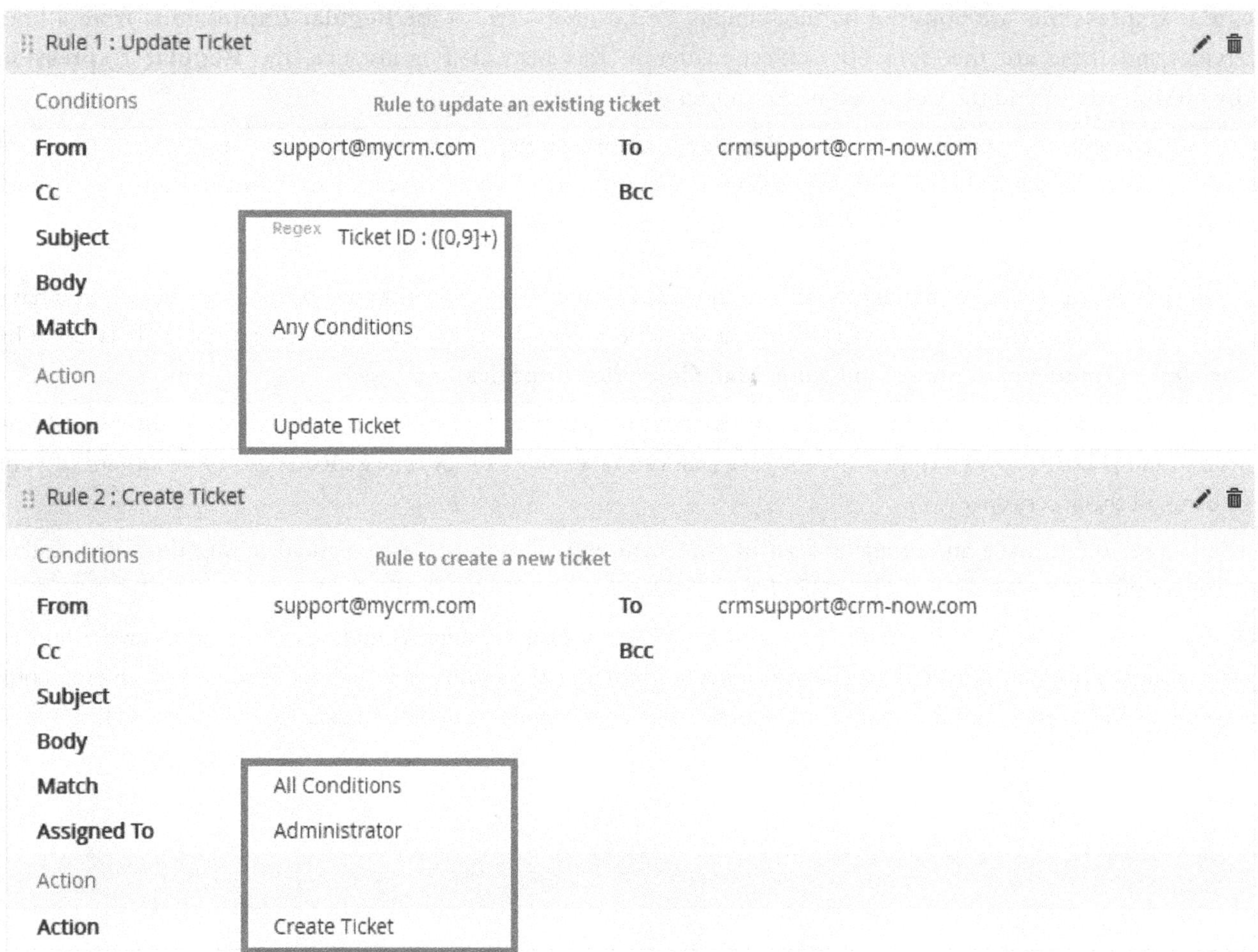

Figure 5-35: Mail Converter Priorities

In order to create new tickets for all incoming emails you need to create a mail scanner rule as displayed in the lower part of this figure. All condition fields are left blank, only the **Match** and the **Action** conditions are set. Whenever a mail is received, a new ticket will be created.

Each ticket in the CRM has a ticket number. This number should be part of the subject in reply message in order to match the email to the particular ticket.

The procedure is illustrated at the left part in Figure 5-36.

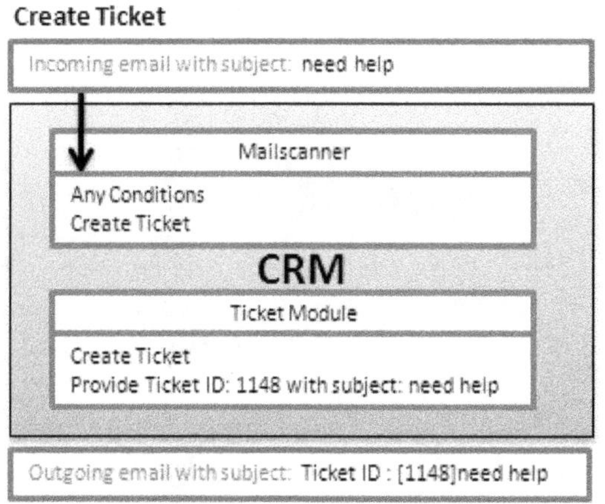

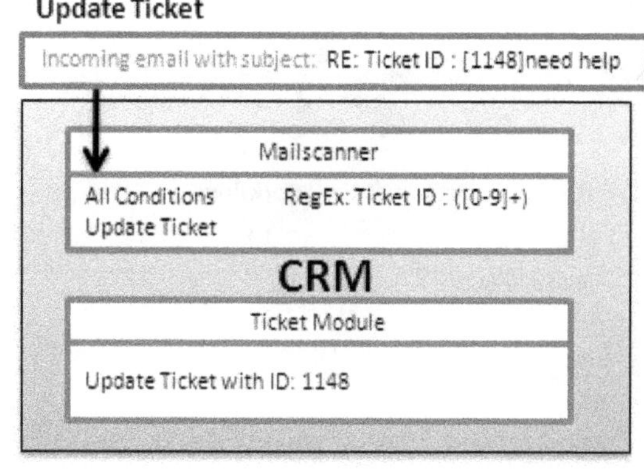

Figure 5-36: Mail Scan Workflow for Tickets

In order to update an existing ticket, you must set different conditions as illustrated in the upper part of Figure 5-36. You need to define a **RegEx** condition in order to scan for a ticket number and set the **Match** and the **Action** conditions as illustrated. The workflow is illustrated on the right-hand side of the figure.

As a last step, make sure that the order of rules is set properly. Your scanner must first check whether an existing ticket can be updated. If there is no ticket to update the second rule applies and a new ticket will be created.

5.5.8 Workflows

A workflow is a depiction of a sequence of operations, declared as work for the CRM system. You can setup such workflows in order to have the CRM carry out a number of actions automatically. The execution of workflows considers the conditions set by you and are triggered

- On the first saving a CRM record only.
- When the first time the conditions are met.
- Every time a record gets modified.
- Every time a record is saved.
- On schedule.

You can use the standard workflows provided, set them up to your specific needs or create new workflows.

In the following, the setup of a workflow is described for the Contacts module for example purposes. You can use the same procedure to create workflows for other CRM modules.

Creating a workflow requires three steps.

Step 1: Schedule Workflow

In order to create a new workflow, please click on **[New Workflow]** in the **List View**. In the **Create View**, as shown in Figure 5-37, select the module for which you want to create the workflow and give it a unique name.

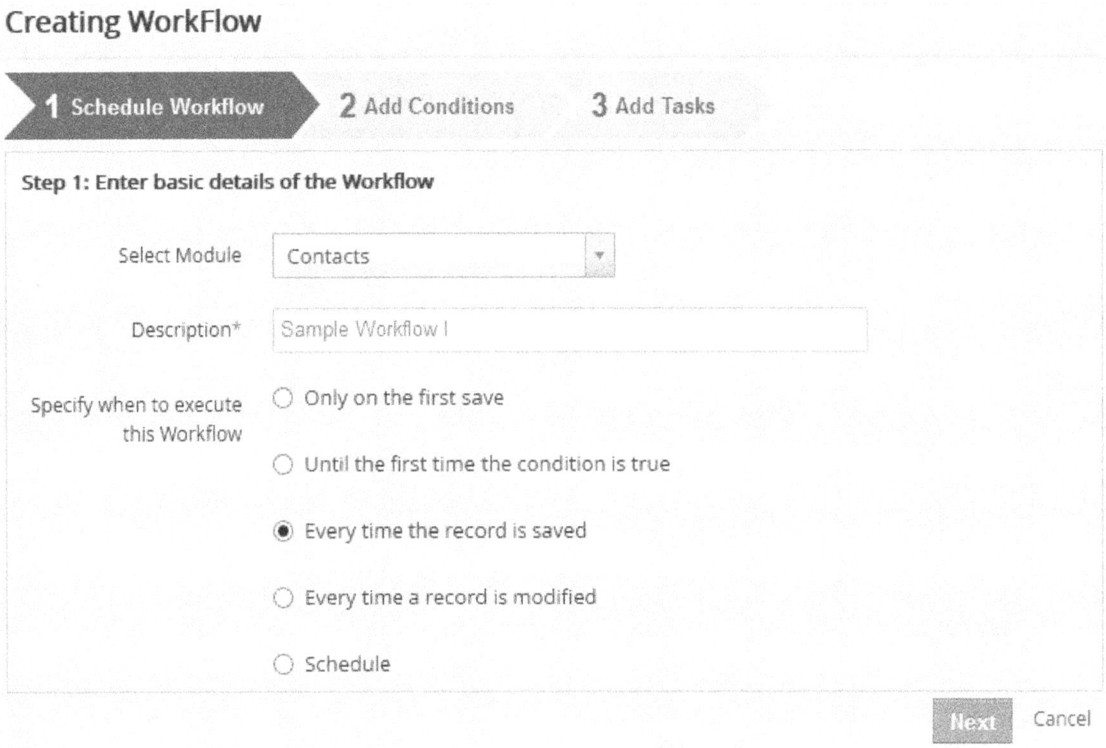

Creating WorkFlow

1 Schedule Workflow 2 Add Conditions 3 Add Tasks

Step 1: Enter basic details of the Workflow

Select Module Contacts

Description* Sample Workflow I

Specify when to execute this Workflow

- Only on the first save
- Until the first time the condition is true
- Every time the record is saved
- Every time a record is modified
- Schedule

Next Cancel

Figure 5-37: Schedule Workflow

In addition, you must determine when the workflow is executed. Click on **[Next]** in order to get to the condition menu.

Step 2: Add Conditions

After the workflow scheduling has been completed, you need to set a single or multiple conditions for the execution of the workflow. In principle, these conditions are filters in the sense of the definition of the user defined **List Views**. In addition to that, you can also define not only comparing conditions like *is* or *contains* to field contents, but you can

- compare the content of a field with content of another field, or
- compare the content of a field with the result of a calculation that was carried out with other fields.

In order to create a condition, please click on **[Add Condition]** as shown in the following Figure 5-38.

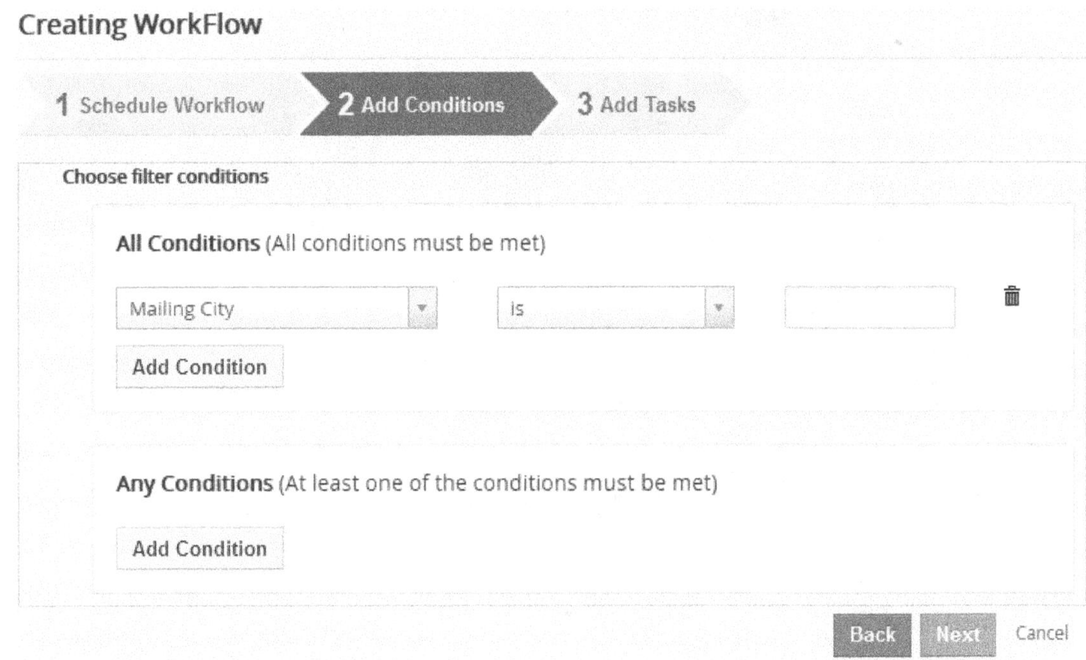

Figure 5-38: Add Condition to Workflow

As known from user defined lists, you can find a list of the master data from the corresponding module in the filter conditions block in the first columns. Make your selection and add your filter condition in the second column.

If you click on the field in the third column a new menu opens as illustrated in Figure 5-39. The content on this popup menu depends on the field you have selected in the first column and the comparative condition in the second column.

The following Table 5-13 explains the types which are available for a comparison in the third column.

Table 5-13: Comparing Types for Workflow

Type	Description
Raw Text:	This is the simplest form of a filter value. You can enter any text. This can lead you to a condition filter like 'Mailing City' *equals* 'Berlin'. For certain entry field types, like a checkbox for instance, the menu will provide the substitute values.
Field:	You can set-up a value that references to another field. The menu offers you a substitute field as it used by the CRM internally. You could setup a filter like 'Mailing City' *equals* 'othercity'.
Expression:	This type allows you to combine a filter with a formula. Select the filed first and the menu will then display the possible formula operations. You can always use standard logical operations combined with special field types related operations as explained in the following Table 5-14.

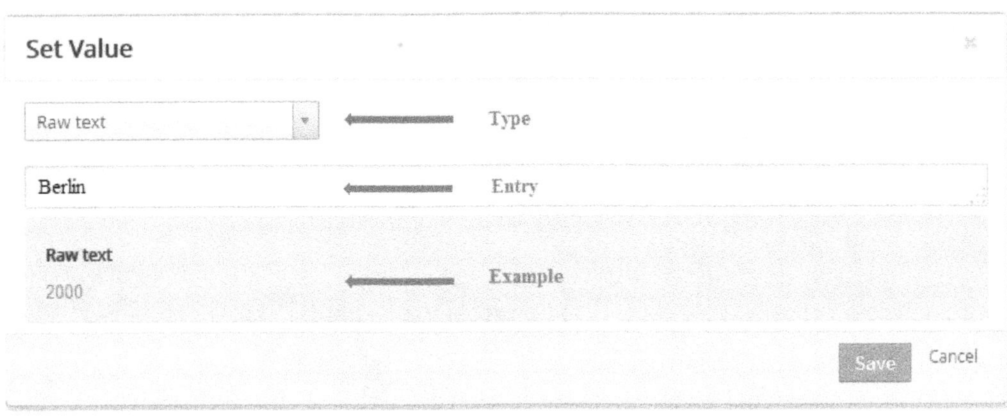

Figure 5-39: Workflow Value menu

Make sure that the spelling of your conditions is correct, especially with respect to small and capital letters.

Table 5-14: Workflow Operations

Formula	Explanation
Arithmetic operations:	You can use the following operations: / : Division * : Multiplication + : Addition - : Subtraction
Conditional Operation:	You can use If and Else instructions. The following format is required: *if <Condition> then <Function> else <Function> end*
concat:	Concat is the short form of Concatenate. Concat is a string operation with which to combine text or field contents to one string. For instance, concat(*firstname,*' ',*lastname*) combines the content of the fields First and Last Name to one string. The concat function is a direct data base operation and will return Null if one of the values is not defined. For more detailed information please refer to a data base manual, available for instance at http://dev.mysql.com/doc/refman/5.0/en/string-functions.html.
time_diffdays:	This formula function is only available for fields of the type date. It allows you to calculate the day difference between two date fields. You can use one or two date fields. For instance, *time_diffdays (support_end_date, support_start_date)* calculates the number of days between the Support start and end date. *time_diffdays (birthday)* calculates the number of days between the birthday and the current day.

Formula	Explanation
time_diff:	This formula function is only available for fields of the type date and works in the same way as the *time_diffdays* function. However, the result is a time difference in seconds.
add_days:	This formula function is only available for fields of the type date. You can use it for example as *add_days (startdate, 2)*. This adds the number of days as provided as second parameter to the date field selected as first parameter. *add_days (2)* generates a date, which adds to the current date the number of days as given in the parameter.
sub_days:	This formula function is only available for fields of the type date and works like the *add_days* function. However, the result is based on the subtraction of values.
today, tomorrow or yesterday	This formula function is only available for fields of the type date. It includes a function like *get_date('today')* and provides the related date.
add_time	This formula function is only available for fields of the type time. You can use it to add a certain amount of minutes to an existing time entry. For instance, the instruction *add_time(cf_989, 60)* adds 30 minutes to the content of the custom field cf_989.
sub_time	This formula function is only available for fields of the type time and works like *add_time* but does a subtraction.

The following illustrates how you can set-up such a concat equation for a opportunity field:

If mailingcounty = "USA" then **concat** lastname "," ,firstname else **concat** lastname " ",firstname

This is an example for a mathematical operation:

amount / probability

Click on **[Next]** in order to transfer your condition setup to the CRM.

Step 3: Add Tasks

The last step in setting up a workflow is the definition of a task which shall be executed when a workflow runs. The CRM supports the following types:

- **Send Email**: an email will be send automatically from the CRM if all conditions are met.
- **Create ToDo**: a task will be created and stored in the CRM automatically.
- **Create Event**: an event (call, meeting or a self-defined event) will be created and stored in the CRM
- **Update Fields**: the content of a field gets a new value

- **Create Entity**: a new CRM entry gets created
- **Invoke Custom Functions**: custom functions for workflows are complex functions designed to provide special tasks. The original CRM comes with only one custom function called **SendPortalLoginDetails** which is designed to send out an email with **Customer Portal** access data. You cannot create additional custom functions with the CRM GUI and should check with your CRM administrator whether further custom functions are available.

Click on **[Add To Do]** and select the task type. As an example, Figure 5-40 illustrates a menu for an **Event** task. You have to give this task a title and a name, select the status and the type and you can add additional time conditions and content as shown in this figure.

Add Task for Workflow -> Create Event

Task Title* make calendar entry Status Active Inactive

Execute Task

Event Name* follow up

Description get address

Status Planned

Type Call

Assigned to Select an Option

Start Time 16:00

Start Date 0 days after Created Time

End Time 17:00

End Date 0 days after Created Time

Enable Repeat

Save Cancel

Figure 5-40: Workflow Task Sample

Please note that each of the task types differs in the menu. Please refer to the corresponding sections in this manual for further information about the entry fields for a specific menu.

Click on **[Save]** in order to transfer your task settings to the CRM and to get back to an overview menu that displays all the workflow conditions you have set.

5.5.9 Configuration Editor

The CRM has some basic settings stored in a **config.inc** file. The **Configuration Editor** menu, as shown in Figure 5-41, allows you to change the content of this file. Any modification becomes valid for all CRM users, in some cases only after logging-in once again.

Please note that your server's capacities have limits and that you should not try to push these limits by means of inappropriate settings. For instance, your maximum upload size depends on your server's PHP settings.

Figure 5-41: Configuration Editor Menu

The following table explains the settings.

Table 5-15: Configuration Editor Fields

Field	Description
Helpdesk Support Email-Id:	Senders Email address for automatic CRM messages.
Helpdesk Support Name:	Senders Email name for automatic CRM messages.
Upload Size:	This is the maximum size for a file that is uploaded to the CRM. This sets the limit for instance for Documents or Attachments.
Default Module:	This defines the CRM start page after Login for all CRM users. Since Home can get modified by individual users in most cases this will be the appropriate start page.
Maximum text length:	This number limits the number of characters displayed in a list view for all fields.
Maximum entries per page:	This number is the limit for the number of rows displayed in a list view.

5.5.10 Scheduler

Provided that the so called cron jobs were installed together with your CRM system, the **Scheduler** menu, as shown in Figure 5-42, allows you to activate or to deactivate certain automatic CRM actions.

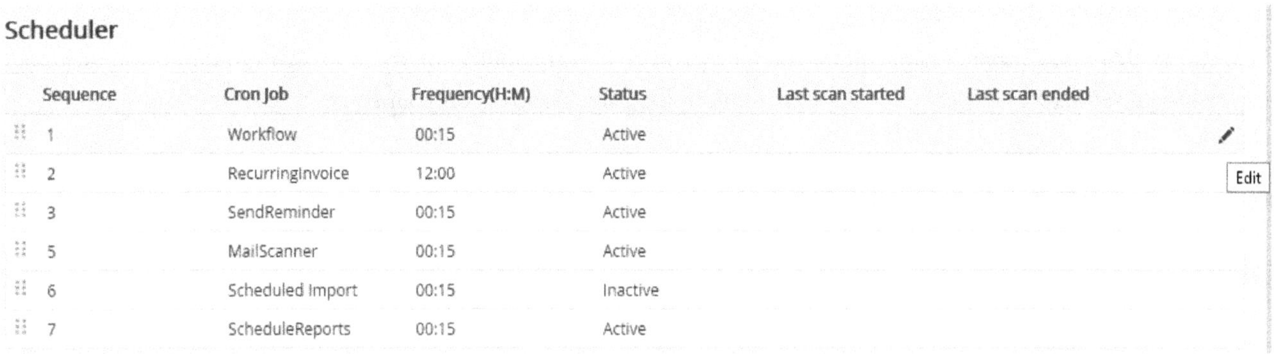

Scheduler

Sequence	Cron Job	Frequency(H:M)	Status	Last scan started	Last scan ended
1	Workflow	00:15	Active		
2	RecurringInvoice	12:00	Active		
3	SendReminder	00:15	Active		
5	MailScanner	00:15	Active		
6	Scheduled Import	00:15	Inactive		
7	ScheduleReports	00:15	Active		

Edit

Figure 5-42: Scheduler menu

The entries in this list refer to the settings from other CRM modules. For instance, the settings in the workflow module define the actions which are executed by the workflow cron job.

Move you mouse to the entry you want to change, in order to call the mouse over **Edit** function by the icon.

You can add additional scheduled actions by clicking on the + icon.

5.5.11 Customer Portal

This menu is only available if you have installed the appropriate optional CRM package. With this the CRM system provides a feature that offers customers limited access to your CRM system in order to communicate with your company directly and to have access to customer related information. That includes but is not limited to:

- The access to CRM system FAQ's by means of a **Knowledge Base**. You can use this to provide release information or to answer common questions on the goods or services your company offers. Please note that only information with the status **Published** will be displayed at the **Customer Portal**.
- The possibility to create and to track tickets.
- The possibility to access further information stored in the CRM such as **Quotes, Invoices, Contact** and **Account** information as well as **Product** listings.

You can decide which information will be provided to the **Customer Portal** as illustrated in Figure 5-43.

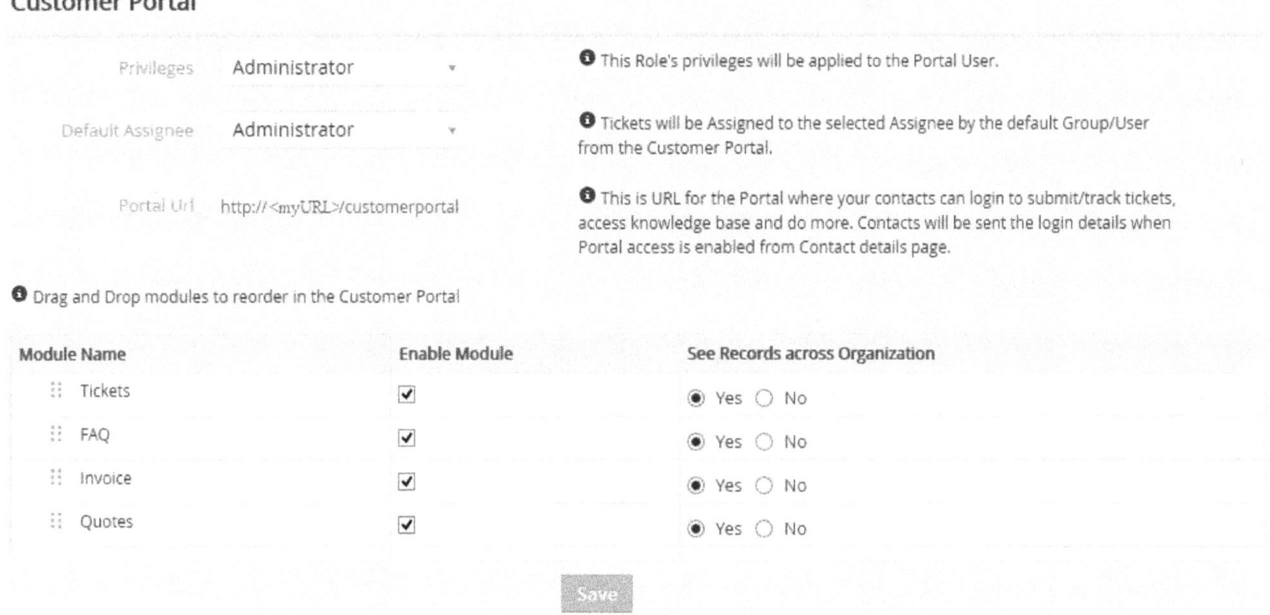

Figure 5-43: Customer Portal Settings

In order to carry out a proper set-up, it is recommended that you create special CRM user who relates to a special customer portal role and profile. This can be used in order to define the fields to be displayed in the **Customer Portal** and is assigned to the **Portal** by the **Privileges** field selection.

You can define who can access the **Customer Portal** by means of a special login procedure and a special URL. Ask your CRM administrator for this URL.

5.5.12 Webform

Webforms are HTML templates which can get placed on a web site to transfer data to the CRM. This can provide the following procedure:

- A web site designer places a **Webform** on the company's web site as a contact form.
- A web site visitor fills out the contact form.
- The visitor's data get saved as a **Lead** in the CRM. The **Lead** gets assigned to a specific CRM user.

Webforms are based on a special CRM interface called **Webservices** which has been designed to exchange information with other applications. The **[Webform]** menu helps you to create the code to get placed on your web site but requires some HTML and web site designer knowledge.

In order to create a new **Webform** click on **[Add Record]** in the **[Webform]** menu. The menu which opens, see Figure 5-44, allows you to enter your basic settings.

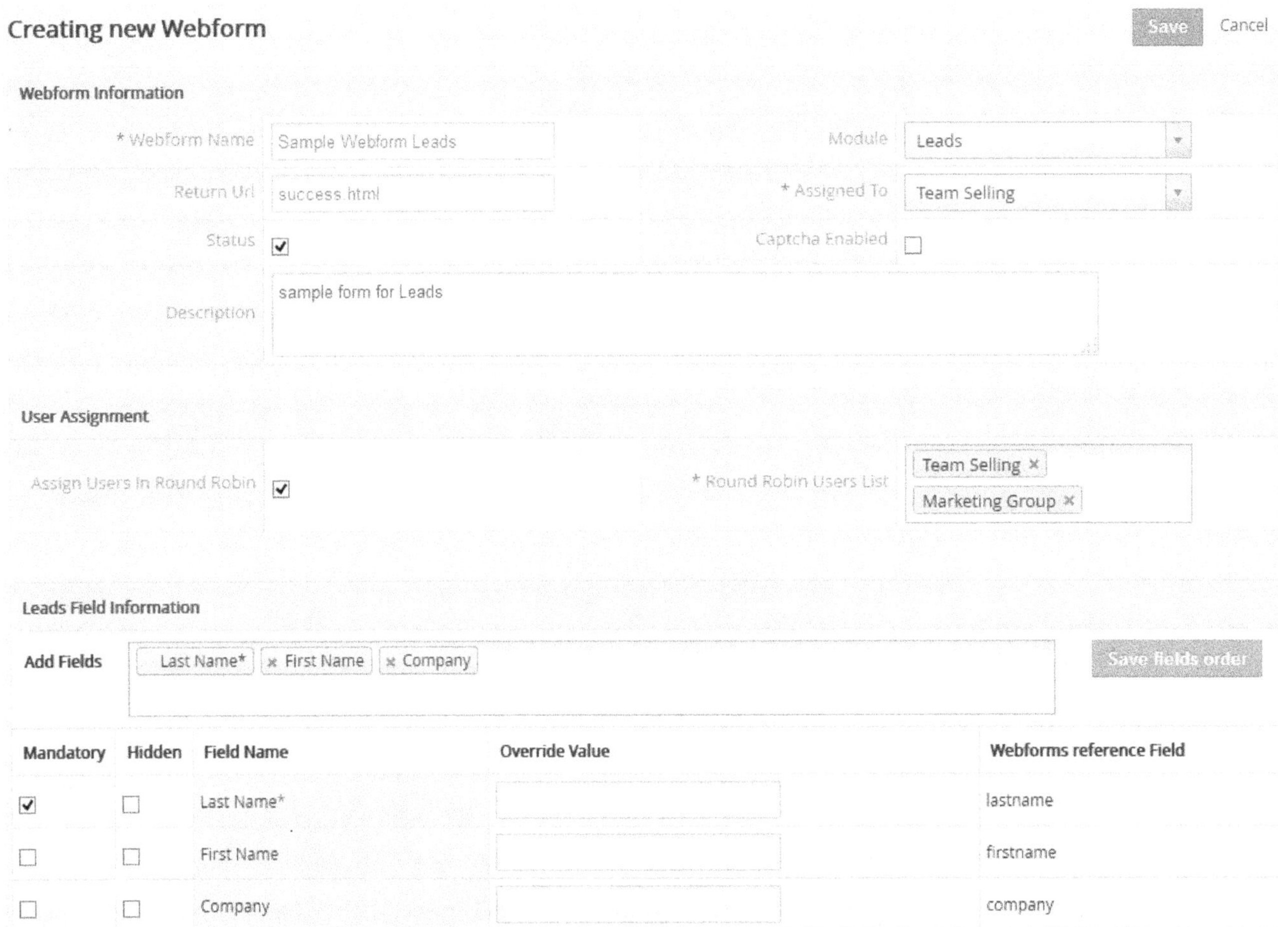

Figure 5-44: Webforms - Create View

The following table explains the fields of the upper menu part.

Table 5-16: Webform Fields I

Field	Description
Webform Name	Provide a unique name for this form.

Field	Description
Module:	Select the CRM module for which you want to create this form.
Return URL:	This field contains a web site address which is the target URL after the webform data are transmitted to the CRM.
Captcha Enabled:	Adds a Captcha to your webform.
Assigned To:	CRM owner of the newly created data set.
Status:	Sets a form to active or inactive.
Description:	For your use.

The entry fields of the **User Assignment** block are used if you want to select more than one user or user group as the owner of a created CRM entry. If you enable **Round Robin**, new records are assigned consecutively to the user or user groups from the **Round Robin Users List**. If the last user of your list got an entry the round starts again.

In the **Field Information** block, you can enter the field you want to display in the form. The next table explains the column contents.

Table 5-17: Webforms Fields II

Column	Description
Mandatory:	These fields will become mandatory fields and the form cannot get submitted as long all mandatory fields are filled. You have to set all fields as mandatory which are mandatory fields in your CRM.
Hidden:	These fields are not shown in the form. You should set an Override Value.
Field Name:	Field names of your CRM menu.
Override Value:	You can set here a default value for your hidden fields.

Click on **[Save]** in order to transfer your form setup to the CRM.

In the **Form Detail View**, as show in Figure 5-45, you can see the two fields **Post URL** and **Public Id**.

▾ **Webform Information**

Webform Name	Sample Webform Leads	Module	Leads
Return Url	success.html	Assigned To	Team Selling
Post Url	https://crm-now.de/modules /Webforms/capture.php	Public Id	705f994f5fdfc45b358c2b7289bd8cbe
Status	Active	Captcha Enabled	No
Description	sample form for Leads		

Figure 5-45: Webform Details

The **Post URL** is the web address for your form which is retrieved when a form is submitted. The **Public Id** is a unique key for your form.

Click on **[Show Form]** in order to open a **Popup** with the HTM code of your form. You can use this code on your website.

5.6 Integration

5.6.1 PBX Manager

The CRM can get connected to an **Asterisk™ Server**. **Asterisk™** is a free **Open Source** communications platform which can get used for handling incoming and outgoing calls with the CRM as a PBX. The PBX itself is not part of the CRM system. For more information about this platform, please see

http://www.asterisk.org

If you have already an **Asterisk™ Server** operating, you can use the **[PBX Manager]** menu to enter the access data.

For a description of the installation procedure, please follow the instructions provided at:

https://wiki.vtiger.com/vtiger6/

5.7 Extension Store

vtiger operates a special website which provides additional CRM extensions and modules for free or a license fee. You can get to this page by the following URL:

https://marketplace.vtiger.com

This **Market Place** content is also available by the **[Extension Store]** menu as illustrated in Figure 5-46.

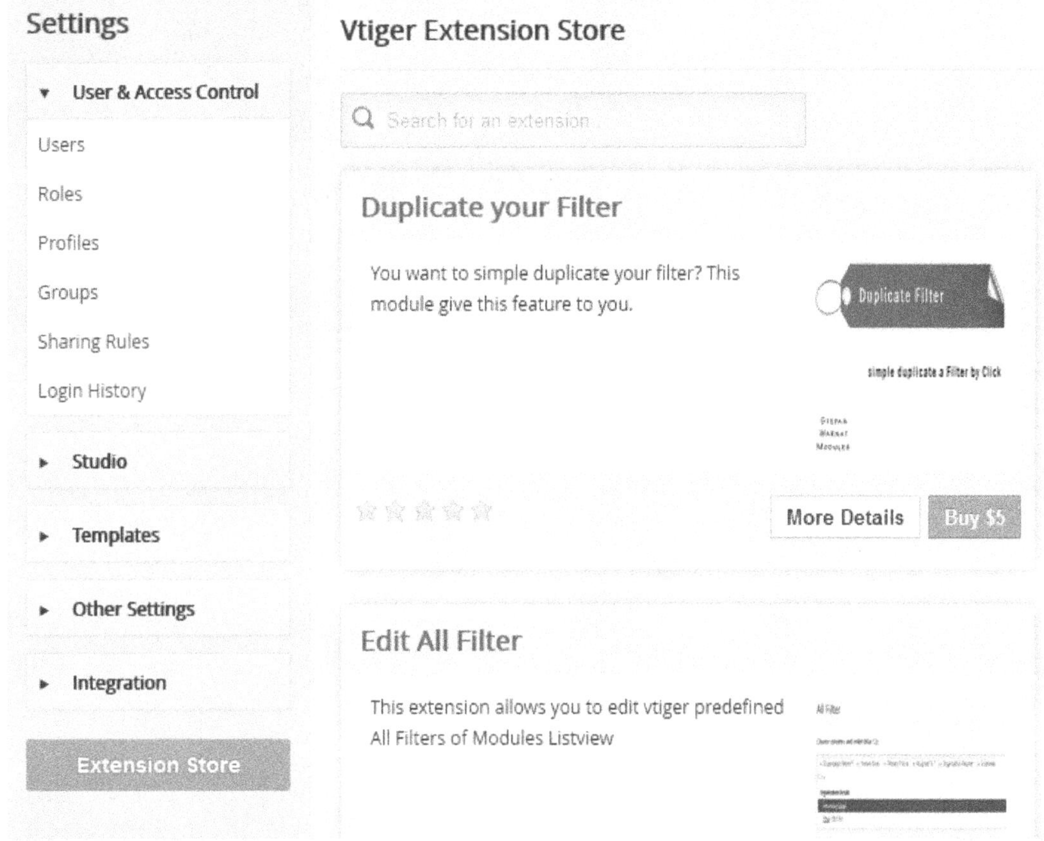

Figure 5-46: Extension Store Menu

The menu displays all extensions which fit to your CRM version. For a description of the installation procedure, please follow the instructions provided at:

https://wiki.vtiger.com/vtiger6/

Appendix A Other Sources

The quantity of information about vtiger CRM is growing on a daily basis. This appendix strives to provide both a complete bibliography of the references mentioned explicitly in this book, as well as a sampling of resources for additional information on vtiger CRM and on CRM in general. Although not all of these resources are focused on vtiger CRM specifically, they still provide helpful information for vtiger CRM users.

The latest version of this manual can be obtained from the document download page at:

http://www.vt-help.de

Easily the largest and most up-to-date list of other vtiger CRM resources can be found on the vtiger webpage:

http://www.vtiger.com.

vtiger extensions to be used with the **Module Manager** can be found at the vtiger's **Market Place**:

https://marketplace.vtiger.com

vtiger hosts a community page that provides installation and operational descriptions about the CRM and its extensions. This includes additional manuals for installation, CRM extensions and documentations for developer:

https://wiki.vtiger.com

vtiger hosts a community page that answers users' questions:

https://discussions.vtiger.com

International vtiger Community

There is a large international community that contributes to the vtiger CRM system. You can check out the vtiger's market place or the discussion pages for other contributions.

UTF-8 Coding

The CRM system uses the UTF-8 format to store data. The following links can help you to understand this format and to use it when you import or export data.

- The online Wikipedia explains everything what you need to know about UTF-8:
  http://en.wikipedia.org/wiki/UTF-8
- Notepad++ is a generic editor you can use to convert data from and to UTF-8
  http://sourceforge.net/projects/notepad-plus/
- vtiger tool for UTF-8 conversion:
  http://www.vtiger.com/index.php?option=com_content&task=view&id=163&Itemid=183

- A collection of other converting tools for UTF-8:
  http://dataconv.org/apps_unicode_utf8.html

vCard coding

You can import data in the so called **vCard Format**. Here you will find further information:

http://en.wikipedia.org/wiki/VCard

You can also look up the **vCard** related information provided with your office applications, like Outlook™.

Appendix B Role-Based Security Basics

For the CRM system to reach its full potential as a means for commercial CRM, access control mechanisms must be in place which can regulate user access to information in a way that serves the best interests of your business.

Role-based security has been implemented to control who is allowed to browse, delete or update information stored in the CRM. This section explains the role-based security concept as it is provided by the CRM system. It's an overview of all types of considerations an administrator should go through before starting to set-up the CRM system for multiple users.

The CRM system operates on the basis of state-of-the-art security management which utilizes the concepts of roles, similar to the implementation of security in many current computer operating systems. Role-based security (also called role-based access control) specifies and enforces enterprise-specific security policies in a way that maps naturally to an organization's structure. It has become the predominant model for advanced access control because it reduces the complexity and cost of security administration and is built on the premise that users are authenticated, which is the process of identifying the user. Once identified, roles and permissions are assigned to a particular user.

Role-based security allows for the specification and enforcement of a variety of protection policies which can be tailored on a company-to-company basis. One of the greatest advantages of role-based security is the administrative capabilities it supports. User membership in roles can be assigned and revoked easily, and new memberships established as job assignments dictate. With role-based security, users are not granted permission to perform operations on an individual basis, the operations are instead associated with roles. Role association with new operations can be established as well as old operations deleted, as organizational functions change and evolve. This basic concept has the advantage of simplifying the understanding and management of privileges. Roles can be updated without having to directly update the privileges for every user on an individual basis.

Furthermore, individual users (e.g. John, Mary) might be assigned to one or more roles, where the roles are based on the user's job responsibilities and competencies in the organization. Users should be assigned to multiple roles to reflect the fact that some users connect to the system in different functions depending on the tasks. For example, user John might be assigned the role **Head-Sales**, because John is the head of sales at your company, as well as the role in admin, because John is also CRM system administrator. If John wants to work as an administrator, he logs in as an admin, if John wants to work as head-of-sales, he logs in as **Head-Sales**. It is possible to let John connect to the system with the same password, regardless of whether he acts as administrator or head-of-sales.

While role-based security can be overkill in trivial settings (e.g. small businesses with a couple of users who are all allowed to browse, delete or update all data), it is an extremely powerful tool for managing complex environments. This includes typical company settings where various sales teams or customer service teams need to browse, delete or update customer-related data while at the same time permissions on such data can vary depending on the function or task of an employee within the company. This concept is especially suited for companies:

- That want to have a larger number of people to be able to work with the CRM simultaneously,
- Who want to have restricted browse, delete or update capabilities for individual users, and
- Who want to have a hierarchical privilege order implemented.

Although role-based security does not promote any one protection policy, it has been shown to support several well-known security principles and policies that are important to commercial and governmental businesses which process unclassified but sensitive information.

These policies can be enforced when profiles are authorized for a role, when users are authorized as members of a role, at the time of role activation (e.g., when a role is established as part of a user's active session), or when a user attempts to perform an operation on data.

Appendix B.1 Definition of CRM Users

There are two types of users for the CRM software:

- Standard user
- Administrator user

Standard users have limited access to the CRM system in order to perform CRUD (Create, Retrieve, Update, and Delete) and limited user-specific customization operations. Administrator users have unlimited privileges for the CRM. Administrator users are capable of managing the complete software including:

- Managing users and groups and their access privileges,
- Customizing the CRM user interface,
- Configuring all organization-wide settings,
- Changing passwords, deactivating users, and viewing the login history and
- Exercise CRUD operations for all data.

Each user must get assigned to a role.

Appendix B.2 Definition of Roles

At the core of role-based security stands the concept of collecting permissions in roles, which can be granted to users. Practice roles are usually structured like a company's organization chart. A role identifies the position of CRM users in the hierarchy and determines the operations that can be executed by persons in particular jobs.

You can set up mutually exclusive roles as well as roles with overlapping responsibilities and privileges.

Each role is based on one or more profiles. It is a user's membership in roles that determines the privileges the user is permitted to perform.

Users in any given role can always view, edit and delete all data owned by users below in the hierarchy.

Appendix B.3 Definition of Profiles

Profiles are used to define privileges for executing CRM system operations. From a functional perspective, the central notion of role-based security is that of profiles representing actions associated with roles and users that are appropriately made members of roles.

The relationships between users, roles, and profiles are depicted in the next figure as many-to-many relationship. For example, a single standard user can be associated with one or more roles by means of different user names, and a single role can have one or more user members. Roles can be created for various job positions in an organization. For example, a role can include sales representatives or assistants in a company.

The profiles which are associated with roles, constrain members of the role to a specified set of actions. For example, within a sales organization the role of the sales representative can include operations to create, edit, and delete their own accounts; the role of an assistant can be limited to browse existing information of a particular sales rep, and the role of the head of sales can be to review all sales data.

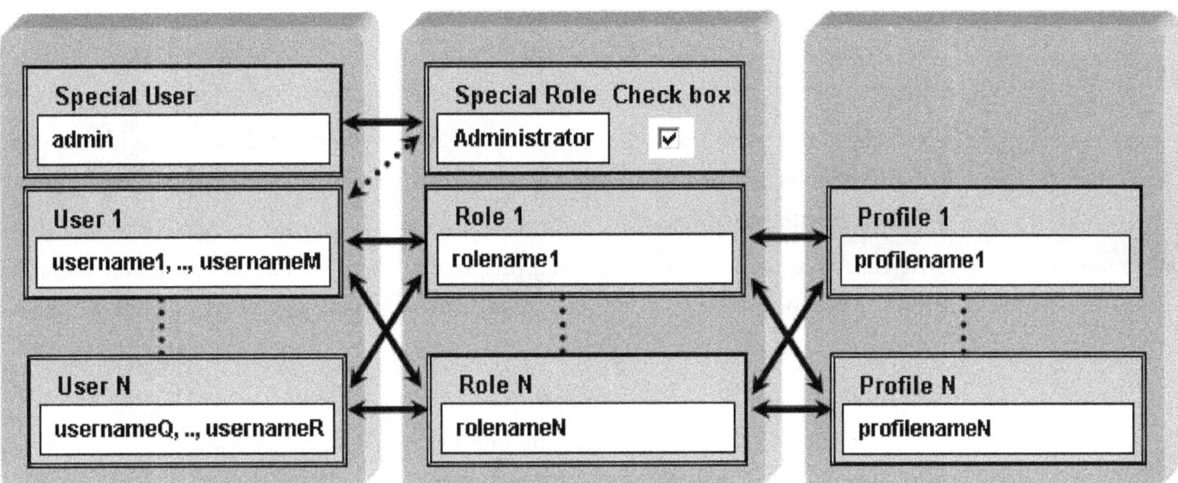

Figure 5-47: Users, Roles and Profiles Relations

The association of profiles with roles within an enterprise can be in compliance with rules that are self-imposed. Profiles can be specified in a manner that can be used in the demonstration and enforcement of regulations. For example, an assistant can be constrained to adding a new entry to a customer's history rather than being generally allowed to modify sales records.

Access privileges based on profiles are set by the CRM system administrator. The administrator has to set these privileges when configuring the CRM system. Therefore, the following privilege types are available:

- the permission to use certain CRM modules
- the permission to view data in certain CRM modules
- the permission to edit or to change data in certain CRM modules
- the permission to delete data in certain CRM modules
- the permission to export data from certain CRM modules
- the permission to import data to certain CRM modules

The CRM system makes sure that a user can only exercise certain operations if the user has proper privileges assigned.

Please note the following **General Security Rules**:

- Special privileges are always superior to common privileges.
- Revoked privileges always override granted privileges.
- Users in any given role can always view, edit and delete all data owned by users below in the hierarchy.
- In addition, the CRM system maintains special rules in the following marked as **Important**.

Table 5-18: Privilege Types

Privilege	Description
Global Privileges:	If you create a profile, the global privileges allow you to decide whether the common privilege to view or to edit all information / modules of the CRM system is given: • **View all**: A user with a role based on a profile that allows all data to be viewed, may view all data from the entire organization. You should not grant this privilege if you want to implement restricted access rules. • **Edit all**: A user with a role based on a profile that allows editing all data, can edit all data in the entire organization. You should not grant this privilege if you want to implement restricted access rules. **Important:** Global privileges in profiles override the permissions defined by **Tab, Standard, Field** and **Utility Privileges** as they are explained below.
Tab Privileges:	The option to set tab privileges allows you to decide which tabs or modules should be shown. For this purpose, the CRM displays all available modules. You can remove a menu tab by disabling all modules of a particular tab.
Field Privileges:	The option to set field privileges allows you to decide whether create, edit, delete, and view privileges are provided for particular fields of a CRM module. For this purpose, the profile menu displays all the available fields, including custom fields.
Utilities	Numerous CRM modules come with utility functions such as import, export, merge and convert lead. The option to set utility privileges allows you to decide whether these functions will be available for roles that are based on a specific profile

Important

Privileges defined by profiles override the **Default Organization Sharing Rules** and the **User Defined Sharing Rules**. For example, let us assume that the **organization sharing rule** allows a user to view the opportunities of others. However, if the profile does not allow access to the opportunity module, these access privileges are then revoked.

Appendix B.4 Definition of Groups

For better manageability, the CRM system allows the collection to users, roles, roles with subordinates, and user groups in groups. It is important to understand that groups are not a tool for defining security settings. Rather user groups are used to manage the data access.

Important

Group settings override the profile settings. Group privileges can become restricted by custom organization sharing privileges.

Group of Users

The CRM system provides functions to define groups of users, sometimes called teams. You can give these groups their own name and assign an unlimited number of users to one group. As an example, a group called **Team A** is shown in the following figure.

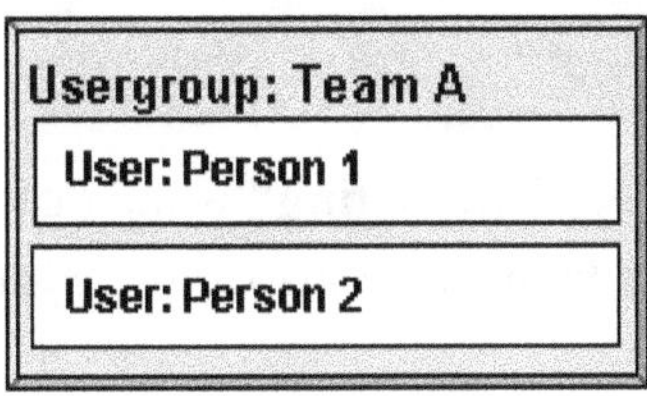

Figure 5-48: Group of Users - Example

Group of Roles

You can also build groups which are based on roles. This might be a helpful function if you do not know the individual users and their particular tasks within the company. An example is shown in the next figure.

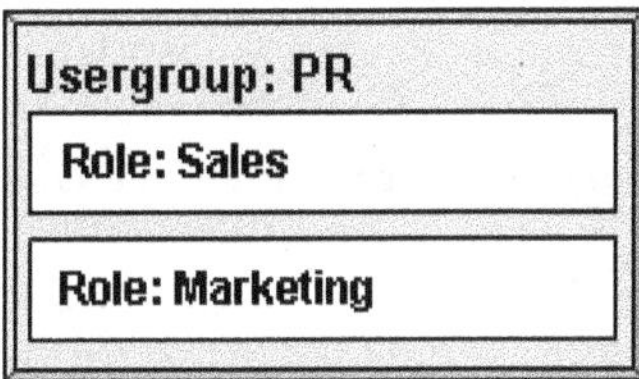

Figure 5-49: Group of Roles - Example

In this group, all users that have the role **Sales** or **Marketing** are members of this group. If you assign a data entry in the CRM system to this group, all members become owners of this entry.

Group of Roles with Subordinates

In addition to simple role-based groups, you can also build groups which include subordinates. This means the users who are assigned to roles which are below a selected role will be included. The following figures illustrate this. Let's assume that your company has set up a hierarchical order as shown in the next figure.

Roles

Organization
CEO
Vice President
Sales
Sales Assistant
Marketing
Marketing Assistant

Figure 5-50: Roles - Hierarchy Example

In this figure the role **"Sales"** has a subordinated role **"Sales Assistant"** and the role **"Marketing"** is the master to the role **"Marketing Assistant."** If you create a user group as shown in the next figure, all users with sales and marketing-related roles, including the assistants will become members of this group.

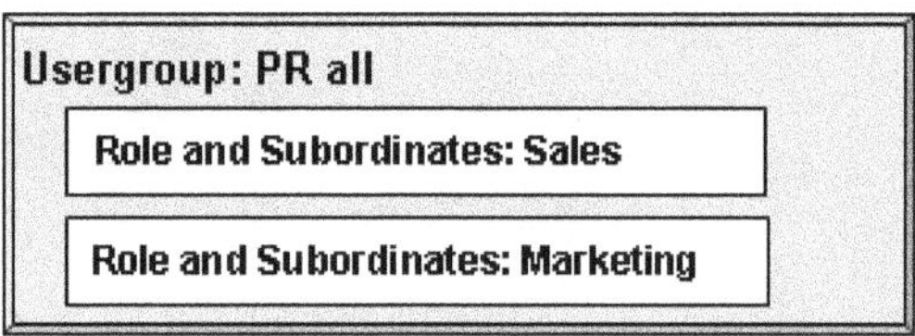

Figure 5-51: Group of Roles with Subordinates - Example

Group of Groups

You can build groups where the members are also groups. That means that all users who are a member of a selected group will also become members of the new group.

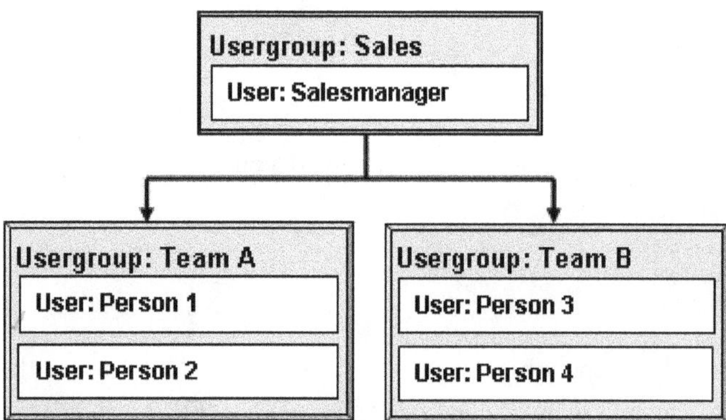

Figure 5-52: Sample Hierarchy for Groups

Let's assume you want to build a hierarchy as shown in Figure 5-52. Based on this structure you can create a user group Sales where the groups **Team A** and **Team B** are members. At this example the **Team A** and **Team B** groups are built with users as members.

If you assign a CRM data entry to the group **Sales**, the **Persons 1 to 4** will all become the owners of this entry with all associated privileges.

Appendix C Examples for Security Settings

This appendix discusses the security setup of, for example, organizations and explains what individual users are allowed to do on the CRM system under certain conditions. These examples do not include all possibilities for configuring the CRM system based on a company's needs. However, the principal functions of the security features are covered so that an administrator might quickly become capable of creating his or her own setup.

a. Example I: Organizing a very small organization

The following configuration examples are based on a sales team as illustrated in the next figure.

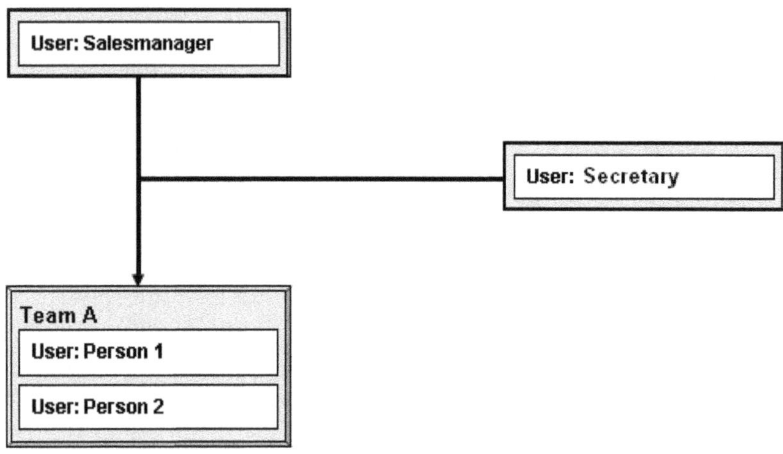

Figure 5-53: Example Sales Team

Appendix C.1 Example I

For the first example settings, we want to have the following rules implemented for **Leads**:

- **Person 1** and **Person 2** have the permission to create **Leads** that are owned by **Person 1** or **Person 2**.
- **Person1** will have no access privileges to **Leads** from **Person 2** and vice versa.
- The **Sales Manager** has all access privileges to all **Leads**.
- The secretary has no privileges to access **Leads**.

The following settings are necessary:

Create one common profile for Person 1, Person 2 and the Sales manager:

We need one profile, called **Sales**, which should include all **CRUD Privileges** for **Leads**. Make sure that the **Global Privileges** are disabled.

Create one profile for the Secretary:

Based on the **Sales** profile create a new profile, called **Secretaryprofile** where the access to the **Leads Module** is disabled.

Create three roles:

We need one role for the sales manager, called **Sales Manager**, and one subordinated role for **Person 1** and **2**, called **Sales Men**. All roles are based on the **Sales** profile.
In addition, we also need another subordinated role for the secretary, called **Secretary Sales** based on the **Secretaryprofile,** who reports to the Sales Manager.

Set the sharing access:

At the **Organization-level Sharing Rules** menu set the rules for **Leads** to **Private**.
Since the role of the sales manager is superior to the role of **Person 1, 2,** the **Sales Manager** has all **CRUD Privileges** to the data of **Person 1** and **Person 2**. If **Person 1** or **Person 2** creates a **Lead**, the **Owner** is assigned. If **Person 1** is assigned as **Owner** of a **Lead, Person 1** and the **Sales Manager** can access and modify this **Lead**. If the ownership is changed to any one member of the team (**Person 1** or **Person 2**), then only this **Person** and the **Sales Manager** may access the **Lead**. The **Secretary** does not see any **Lead Data**.

Appendix C.1.1 Example I: Settings with groups

As another example of settings, we want to have the following rules implemented for **Leads**:

- Person 1 and Person 2 have the permission to create Leads that are owned by Person 1 or Person 2 or by the team.
- If a Lead is owned by a single Person the other team member will have no access privileges to this Lead.
- The Sales manager has all access privileges to all Leads.
- The Secretary has all access privileges to Leads owned by the team.

In order to implement these rules you have several options. These options are based on the following common settings:

Create one common profile for Person 1 and 2 and the Sales manager:

We need only one profile, called **Sales** which should include all CRUD privileges for Leads. Make sure that the **Global Privileges** are disabled.

Create two roles:

We need one role for the Sales manager, called **Sales Manager**, and one subordinated role for Person 1, 2 and the secretary, called **Sales Men**. Both roles are based on the **Sales** profile. Since the role of the Sales manager is superior to the role of the other users the Sales manager has all CRUD privileges.

Create one group:

Option 1:

Create a group of users, called **Team A**. Include the Person 1 and Person 2 and the secretary user. We have to include the Sales Manager because groups of users are independent to the role-based hierarchy and we will need access to the Leads assigned to Team A.

Option 2:

Create a group of role & subordinates, called **Team A**. Include the role of the Sales Manager.

Option 3:

Create a group of roles, called **Team A**. Include the role **Sales Manager**, the role **Sales Men**.

Set the sharing access:

At the **Organization-level Sharing Rules** menu set the rules for Leads to **private**.

If **Person 1** or **Person 2** creates a **Lead**, the **Owner** gets assigned. If **Team A** is assigned as **Owner** of the **Lead**, **Person 1, Person 2,** the **Sales Manager** as well as the **Secretary** can access the **Lead**. If the ownership is changed to any one member of the group (**Person 1** or **Person 2**), then only this **Person** and the **Sales Manager** may access the **Lead**.

Appendix C.1.2 Example I: Settings with sharing access

As another example, we want to have the following rules implemented for **Leads**:

- **Person 1** and **Person 2** have the permission to create **Leads** that are owned by **Person 1** or **Person 2**.
- If a **Lead** is owned by a single **Person**, another team member will have read only access privileges to this **Lead**.
- The **Sales Manager** has all access privileges to all **Leads**.
- The **Secretary** has view only privileges in order to access **Leads**.

In order to implement these rules, I have to implement the following settings:

Create one common profile for Person 1 and 2 and the Sales Manager:

We need one profile, called **Sales** that should include all **CRUD Privileges** for **Leads**. Make sure that the **Edit All** check box under **Global Privileges** is disabled.

Create one profile for the Secretary:

Based on the **Sales** profile, create a new profile called **Secretaryprofile** where the access to **Leads** is set to **View Only**.

Create three roles:

We need one role for the **Sales Manager**, called **Sales Manager**, and one subordinated role for **Person 1** and **2**, called **Sales Men**. All roles are based on the **Sales** profile.

In addition, we also need another subordinated role for the **Secretary**, called **Secretary Sales** based on the **Secretaryprofile** who reports to the **Sales Manager**.

Global Access Privileges:

We need to set the global privileges for **Leads** to **Public Read Only**.

Since the role of the **Sales Manager** is superior to the role of **Person 1, 2** the **Sales Manager** has all **CRUD Privileges** to the data of **Person 1** and **Person2**. If **Person 1** or **Person 2** creates a **Lead,** the **Owner** gets assigned. If **Person1** is assigned as **Owner** of a **Lead, Person 1** and the **Sales Manager** can access and modify this **Lead**.

If the ownership is changed to any one member of the team (**Person 1** or **Person 2**), then only this **Person** and the **Sales Manager** can access the **Lead**. The **Secretary** has read only privileges to all **Lead Data**.

Appendix C.2 Example II

This example demonstrates how the access to certain data can be controlled by a combination of groups with sharing rules.

Let us assume that we have a sales team as displayed as an organization chart in the next figure. The **Sales Manager** is the **Supervisor** for **Person 1 to 4**, all organized in **Team A** and **B**, as well as the sales assistant. This **Sales Assistant** supports the **Sales Teams**.

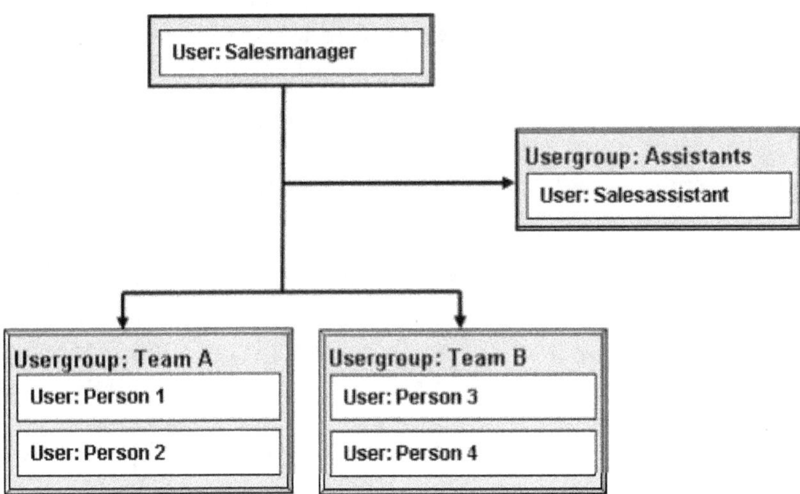

Figure 5-54: Example Sales Team

Appendix C.2.1 Example II: Settings primary based on groups

Let us assume we want to have the following rules for **Leads** implemented.

- **Persons 1-4** have the permission to create **Leads** which are owned by any person or by the **Team A or B**.
- **Persons 1-4** have **Read/Write** privileges to all **Leads** regardless who owns it.
- The **Sales Assistant** has **Read/Write Privileges** to **Leads** of the **Team A** only and cannot access the **Leads** of **Team B**.
- The **Sales Manager** has all access privileges to all **Leads**.

In order to implement these rules, I set the following privileges:

Create two profiles:

We need one profile for **Persons 1-4** and the **Sales Manager**, called **Sales** that should include all **CRUD Privileges**. In addition, we also need a profile for the **Sales Assistant** called **Assistance** which should have the **Edit all** checkbox under **Global Privileges** deactivated. Besides that, the **Delete Permission** for the **Leads Module** must be deactivated, too.

Create three roles:

We need one role for the **Sales Manager** called **Manager**, one subordinated role for the **Sales Assistant** called **Salesassistant** and one subordinated role for all **Persons 1-4** called **SalesAll**.

The roles **Manager** and **SalesAll** are based on the **Sales** profile, whereas the role **Salesassistant** is based on the **Assistance** profile.

Since we have set the **Global Access Privileges** for **Leads** to **Private**, **Rules 4** and **5** are necessary in order to allow that the group members of **Team A** and **B** can see each other's **Leads**.

Create three groups of users:

We create a group called **Team A** with the members **Person 1** and **Person 2** and a group called **Team B** with the members **Person 3** and **Person 4**.

Sharing rules cannot be specified to share data between users. Since we want to use sharing rules for the **Sales Assistant**, we have to create an additional group with only one member. We create a group called **Assistant** with the user **Sales Assistant** as the only member.

At **Default Organization Sharing Access** we set the **Global Access Privileges** for **"Leads"** to **Private**. This will cause that users cannot access other users **Leads**.

Set Custom Sharing Rules for Leads:

1. Leads of Group **Team A** can be accessed by Group **Team B**; we set the access privilege with **Read/ Write Permission**.
2. Leads of Group **Team B** can be accessed by Group **Team A**; we set the access privilege with **Read/ Write Permission**.
3. Leads of Group **Team A** can be accessed by Group **Assistant**; we set the access privilege with **Read/Write Permission**.
4. Leads of Group **Team A** can be accessed by Group **Team A**; we set the access privilege with **Read/ Write Permission**.
5. Leads of Group **Team B** can be accessed by Group **Team B**; we set the access privilege with **Read/ Write Permission**.

Appendix C.2.2 Example II: Settings primary based on roles

As a modification to the example above let us assume we want to have the same rules for **Leads** implemented:

- **Persons 1-4** have the permission to create **Leads** that are owned by any person or team.
- **Persons 1-2** have **Read/Write** privileges to all **Leads** owned by **Person 1-2** and **Team A**. They have **Read Only** permissions to Leads owned by Person 3-4 or Team B.
- **Persons 3-4** have **Read/Write Privileges** to all **Leads** owned by **Person 3-4** and **Team B**. They have **Read Only Permissions** to **Leads** owned by **Person 1-2** or **Team A**.
- The **Sales Assistant** has **Read Privileges** to all **Leads**.
- The **Sales Manager** has all **Access Privileges** to all **Leads**

In order to implement these rules we set the following privileges:

Create one common profile for all Persons, the Sales assistant and the Sales manager:

We only need one profile, called **Sales** that should have the **Edit all** check box under **Global Privileges** deactivated.

Create four roles:

1. We need one role for the **Sales Manager** called **Manager**, based on the **Sales Profile**.
2. We need one subordinated role for the **Sales Assistant** called **Salesassistant**, based on the **Sales Profile**.
3. We need one subordinated role for the **Person1** and **Person2** called **Team A**, based on the **Sales Profile**.
4. We need one subordinated role for the **Person3** and **Person4** called **Team B**, based on the **Sales Profile**.

As a result, the roles **Salesassistant**, **Team A**, and **Team B** are on an equal hierarchical level subordinated to the **Manager** role.

Create three groups of users:

We create a group called **Team A** with the members **Person 1** and **Person 2** and a group called **Team B** with the members **Person 3** and **Person 4**. Please note that the **Sales Manager** has to be included in both groups since groups of users are independent of the role-based hierarchy and he will need access to the **Leads** assigned to **Team A** as well as **Team B**.

Sharing rules cannot be specified to share data between users. Since we want to use sharing rules for the **Sales Assistant**, we have to create an additional group with only one member. We create a group called **Assistant** with the user **Sales Assistant** as the only member.

At Default Organization Sharing Access we set the Global Access Privileges for "Leads" to Private:

This will cause that users cannot access other users **Leads.**

Set Custom Sharing Rules for Leads:

1. **Leads of Role Team A** can be accessed by **Role Team B;** we set the access privilege with **Read Only Permission.**
2. **Leads of Role Team B** can be accessed by **Role Team A;** we set the access privilege with **Read Only Permission.**
3. **Leads of Role Team A** can be accessed by **Role Salesassistant**; we set the access privilege with **Read Only Permission.**
4. **Leads of Role Team B** can be accessed by **Role Salesassistant**; we set the access privilege with **Read Only Permission.**
5. **Leads of Role Manager** can be accessed by **Role Salesassistant**; we set the access privilege with **Read Only Permission.**
6. **Leads of Role Team A** can be accessed by **Role Team A;** we set the access privilege with **Read/Write Permission.**

7 **Leads of Role Team B** can be accessed by **Role Team B**; we set the access privilege with **Read/Write Permission**.

Appendix D Administration FAQ

How to remove not needed modules:

There are two different cases. If a module should not be available any longer within the business, you remove the module using the **Module Manager**.

Should a module be visible for some individual users, but not for all, you adjust the corresponding profiles which are assigned to the role of the individual users.

Users with administrator privileges can always see all the data, so it is not possible for such users to disable modules.

How to delete users, groups, profiles and roles:

If you delete a user, group, profile or role, you will be asked for a new owner of the data. After selection the data will be moved to the new owner and will not be lost.

How to change a user's login name:

You cannot change the login name of a user directly. Instead, create a new user with a new login name and delete the old user. During deletion transfer all data of the old user to the new user.

How to recover the Administrator password:

The **Administrator** password cannot get recovered. The CRM does not store any password. If the administration password is lost it must get reset in the data base.

How to restrict users sharing access:

If you have set everything based on the rules and tips provided and you still not get the desired results please check the following:

- Have you set the default organization sharing access to private?
- Have you disabled **View All** and **Edit All** at the **Global Permissions** for profiles used?
- Have you disabled the admin option for the users?

The CRM system checks the security system in the following order:

The **Global Privileges** are checked first. If the **Global Privileges** are enabled, no other security check will be done. Depending on the settings, any user can view and edit all the data of the CRM System, except the **Settings Module**. At the same time the profile permission overrides the sharing rules, because the CRM system will not include the sharing rules into considerations.

If the **Global Privileges** are disabled, the system will check for the **Tab Privileges at the Profiles**. If the **Tab Privileges** are disabled, a user cannot view a particular module. At the same time the profile permission also overrides the sharing rules. This is because whatever permission you have in the sharing rules, this will not be taken into considerations if you do not have access to a particular module in first place.

If the **Tab Privileges** are available, this means that a current user can view a particular model. Now the CRM system checks for the settings of the **Sharing Rules**.

How to include contacts into a campaign:

Follow these steps if you want to associate a list of contacts to particular campaign:

1. At the Contacts List View:

- If you do have contacts already in your CRM import your contacts (see section: Export and Import of CRM Data).
- Create a custom view for the imported contacts (see section: Customize Lists).

2. At the **Campaign List View**:

- Create a campaign.
- In campaign detail view, scroll down to the contacts related list (or select the **More Information** tab).
- In contacts related list there are three options: **Load List** | **Select Contact** | **Add Contact**
- **Load List**: for associating contacts in bulk from the custom view. Select your required custom view to load your contacts list.
- **Select Contact**: for selecting a few contacts from the available contact list.
- **Add Contact**: for adding new contact on-the-fly.
- Select the contacts you want to include in your campaign.

How to create additional events types:

If you want to add other event types you need to add such a type to the events pick list. As a user with admin privileges go to the **Pick List Editor** and select the **Events Module**. Add your event type to the pick list.

How to connect to a web site or accounting:

If you only want to transfer data from your website to the CRM use the **Webforms**.

But the CRM can do more. It offers a so called **Webservices Interface** which can be used to exchange data between the CRM and any third party application. That means that you can read date from the CRM or write data to the CRM. This can be used to link the CRM for instance with accounting or other ERP systems.

The implementation of **Webservices** requires solid programmer knowledge. An API description and a tutorial are available.

6 Table of Figures

7 Glossary

www.ingramcontent.com/pod-product-compliance
Lightning Source LLC
Chambersburg PA
CBHW080417060326
40689CB00019B/4273

* 9 7 8 1 3 6 5 2 4 7 5 2 1 *